BOOZERS, BALLC

by

Stephen D Smith

With Foreword by Adam Faith

Wharncliffe Publishing Limited

First published in Great Britain in 1996 by

Wharncliffe Publishing Limited
47 Church Street, Barnsley, South Yorkshire S70 2AS

© Stephen D Smith, 1996

A CIP record for this book is available from the British Library

ISBN 1 871647 33 9

Typeset by Yorkshire Web, Barnsley, South Yorkshire
Printed by Redwood Books, Trowbridge, Wiltshire

TO MOTHER
FOR ALL YOU HAVE
HAD TO PUT UP WITH

CONTENTS

THE AUTHOR WISHES TO THANK THE FOLLOWING:

Jack Bennett, Jack Bower, Barbara Bramall, Graham Broom, Lynn and Bob Ego, Adam Faith, Alan Field, Lewis Frame, Christopher Good, Patrick Hargan, The Family of Oscar Hargreaves Deceased, Mattie Hawkins, Michael Jarvis, The Estate of Tim Johnson Deceased, Alison Keys, Peter Large, David 'Bader' Lidster, Sylvia Menzies, Tim Norburn, Sean Page, Karen A. Price, Kate Smith, Rory Leo-Smith and Hydraulic Pumps (UK) Limited (Rotherham), Wilfred Steer Q.C., George Tierney, Alan Twiddle, Derek 'Bill' Townsend, Max Tuouy, Michael Walker, Leslie Walton, Steven F. Wilford, Ronald 'Roni' Wilkinson and Albert . . . . . .

FOREWORD

"Steve Smith is not what you would expect a solicitor to be. However, he is everything you would wish for in a solicitor.

His ability to listen, understand and get on well with people from all walks of life, endear him to so many. His agile mind and powerful wit are his greatest assets in his fight against injustice.

Steve uses the same talents when changing from solicitor to raconteur as he relates his never ending fund of stories and anecdotes to eager listeners on the after-dinner speech circuit.

Boozers, Ballcocks & Bail is the aptly named title of Steve's first collection of memoirs which will allow a much wider audience to enjoy his experiences, told in his own original style.

Where truth makes way for poetic licence, the reader is carried along on a roller coaster ride of laughter and tears, not only wanting more but feeling that he has been an invited guest to the events as they actually happened.

These memories however, are not all happy and amusing, the humour is balanced by the tragedy which exists in real situations. Here, life is portrayed for what it is, a mixture of emotions providing the reader with a *"birds eye view"* into the sometimes secret world of the law.

This book makes you laugh and cry at descriptions of human nature at its best and indeed its worst.

I commend this book as a voyage into the private world of a most colourful and original character."

Adam Faith,
October 1996.

PREFACE

This book is an account of my life within the legal profession as a South Yorkshire solicitor.

This first volume, covers 1981 and 1982 and while all my cases are not chronicled here, I have picked out some of the more interesting ones.

I have not dealt at length with the law's ambiguities and peculiarities, but I have tried to tell the story as simply as possible in the hope that it will entertain.

My memoirs are based on true events, but in some cases the names of the characters have been changed to respect their privacy and avoid writs!

My friends are featured regularly in these pages and I thank them for their participation and the benefit of their memories. I am grateful to them, not only for their assistance, but more particularly their support and friendship over the years. They know they cannot sue me for libel because I could not satisfy a judgement.

I would also like to thank my publishers without whom none of this would be possible and in particular Alan Twiddle for his patience and understanding, help and advice and more particularly the confidence he had given me to write and complete this book.

I entered the legal profession in 1965 by default. I had always wished to be a professional musician and while I waited for that ambition to be realized, I became involved in this job. I began as the office boy's assistant and I recall that my first task was to blow up a rugby ball for the senior partner's son and my second was to collect sandwiches and cakes for the typing pool.

Over the next few years I continued in this 'temporary' job, receiving education in the law on the way. Much to my own surprise I eventually qualified as a solicitor and two years later, formed my own practice. I gave up my musical aspirations to concentrate on working in one of the great professions. This is where my story starts.

STEPHEN D. SMITH.
ROTHERHAM, SOUTH YORKSHIRE, 1996.

COURT
ONE

BLACK
PRINCE
6.8.87.

Chapter One

A LOAD OF BALLCOCKS

It was January 1981 and it began with a simple attempt to test the plumbing. I did not know much about the mechanics of it but as I pulled the chain the ballcock shot out of the cistern and hit me at the side of the head. Water flowed from the top of the cistern carrying with it a mass of cobwebs and a wide variety of livestock, the names of which escape me. As I looked up I could see the sun shining through the hole in the roof and could hear the fluttering of pigeons. Water was getting in my eyes. Turning to look for the stopcock I reached for the door handle which came off in my hand. A startlingly frightening realization came upon me; I could not get out. For one awful moment I believed that the rising waters would cover me and I would be drowned in my own loo. I pictured the headlines for the following day in the local press, "ROTHERHAM SOLICITOR DROWNS IN BOG TRAGEDY".

The water began to surround my black patent shoes and started to creep towards the bottoms of my evening suit trousers. There I was, in bow-tie and dress suit, locked in this antiquated lavatorial prison which was to be part of my future offices.

Although I was in a state of panic, a well aimed kick broke the old lock and I was free. After a great deal of searching, I found the stop tap and turned it off. I sat in the large room downstairs which would be the main office and observed the paper peeling off the walls with the crumbling plaster underneath wondering if I could possibly be doing the right thing.

These were to be the premises of my solicitor's practice, to be known as Wilford Smith and Co., Solicitors of Rotherham, South Yorkshire. We would be the town's tenth firm of solicitors and were due to open around the end of May 1981 with a staff of one.

The premises were dilapidated, antiquated and in the word of one cultured observer they were "crap"; but it was to be home.

I had been employed in the law since 1965, coming to Rotherham in 1971 when my education really began. I had been to night school and qualified as a Fellow of the Institute of Legal Executives which I used as a springboard to qualify as a solicitor of the Supreme Court. I did so in 1979, and became an assistant solicitor with a local firm. In 1981, I set about achieving one of my life long ambitions by opening my own firm.

I joined forces with my friend and colleague, Steven Wilford, who had qualified a year before me. Our relationship went back to the early 60's when we both worked at our first firm in Barnsley. We had teamed up again when Wilford joined my employers in Rotherham in 1973. We were to become partners, with Wilford dealing with conveyancing, probate and matters of a non-contentious nature whilst I would deal with the contentious court proceedings. We were a good match. With me the extrovert and Wilford, the stable one whose other role was to look after the money.

Our plans were already moving forward and by the beginning of January we had rented the premises. This particular night I was on my way to a dinner but the excitement of the enterprise had consumed most of my waking moments, and I could not resist calling in to have another look before I went to the dinner. Despite all the problems and faults, the whole scheme was as exciting as anything I had ever been involved in.

Stumbling down the stairs from the first floor, slipping on the water from the toilet which followed me, lapping down each step as it went, I raced it to the bottom, unlocked the front door and paused as I imagined the brass plate, bearing our names, fixed proudly in the centre. I slammed the door shut and squelched down the quiet street leaving a trail of wet footprints. When I reached my car, I looked back proudly as I heard the water cascading down a drain. A shimmering stream was flowing across the pavement with the moon reflecting in the gentle ripples creating a silvery carpet. It was a good omen. I went to the dinner a happy man paying no heed to my wet feet. The event was the Chartered Accountants Dinner at the Cutlers Hall in Sheffield.

It was a most prestigious affair and Wilford and I were the guests of our great friend Michael Jarvis. He had places for ten of his friends and colleagues and the speech was given by the chairman of British Gas. It was appallingly boring and we opened a book for betting on the length of time he would speak. One of the guests was the Honourable Sean Page, insurance broker and all round good-egg. Page is one of those characters who can brighten any dull proceedings by way of his wit, or more accurately, his lunacy. He was rather unpredictable and anything could happen when he was around as he had devoted his entire life to having a good laugh.

The gathering became more and more restless as the chairman continued to drone on about coal supplies, the state of the pound and British Gas. I lost my bet as my prediction of thirty five minutes came and went. As guests started falling asleep, I began to wonder if we were all suffering from carbon monoxide poisoning but I was told that not even the British Gas chairman's speech was anything more than hot air. He droned on and on, only hesitating briefly when an eruption of muffled laughter from the tables around us stopped him. Sean Page had leaned over to me and whispered "My God Smithy, listening to him is like plaiting shit." In the large dining room Page's words seemed to echo around the walls. I sank deeper into my chair. It was only a few seconds before the Gas chairman resumed and I convinced myself that the whisper was only a whisper.

However, it must have broken the spell because within a minute or two he indicated that he was about to finish his address and a huge sigh of relief went around the room. Before the speaker's bottom could touch the seat, Sean Page, with a mixture of annoyance and relief jumped on to his chair, and to the surprise of everyone, repeatedly shouted the words "Bravo, encore, encore." It was interrupted only by Page losing his balance and falling off the back of the chair. He received a standing ovation and the chairman of British Gas stormed off in disgust. "Laugh" said Page, "I thought my trousers would never dry."

The next day, I felt dreadful. I had two glasses of Andrews liver salts and set off for work, sneezing and remembering my mother telling me never to leave wet socks on.

That evening, I took my family to see the premises for the first time and I knew it was going to be as much of a thrill for me as it would be for them.

My father arrived at about 7.30 pm fresh from his day job and his first task was to mend the ballcock. At first the ballcock was having none of it but after much effort and some swearing the job was done. My father sat back on the toilet seat with a huge grin on his face declaring success. "It shouldn't be a problem now Son" he said pulling the flush to check the system. Before he finished speaking, the ballcock hit him at the back of the head and water shot out of the bowl, completely soaking the seat of his pants. He was livid, but I rocked with laughter and after a few seconds he joined in.

He laughed so much that he could hardly catch his breath and he began to cough. Sweat was running down his temples as he held his sides in an attempt to relieve himself of the pain that laughter can bring. For the rest of the evening, as we cleared up and went about the decorating, I could hear him chuckling in the background, re-living the incident.

I remember that laughter as if it was only yesterday and how I wish I could hear it now.

During the following weeks the whole family joined in, wife, father, mother-in-law and six year old daughter who once accidentally kicked over the bucket of emulsion causing my father even greater hilarity when Wilford slipped in it and decorated his Levi jeans with a magnificent patch of cream around his bottom. They were wonderful days and I lived for the weekends when we could spend all our time in the office.

The intensity of effort was such that within a short time our two rooms had been cleaned and beautifully decorated. We had got hold of some second-hand furniture from a dealer in Sheffield and had bought two brand-new desks, one for reception and one for the room that Wilford and I were to share.

The larger of the two rooms was to be used as the reception area where Anne, our one member of staff, answered the phone, attended to people coming into the office and did her typing. Looking back, I suppose it was a bit of a hovel, but to us it was a dream come true, our own identity, our own office and our own future.

About a week before we were due to open, our brass plate arrived. This bore the name of the firm and the names of the two partners. When it arrived, I rushed to my parents' house to show my father who was delighted and I could tell that he was extremely proud. The following day, my old mate Graham Broom, joiner cum builder cum entrepreneur affectionately nicknamed Bodger because of his exploits in the building trade, kindly agreed to fix the plaque outside our office door.

Having fixed it, Bodger asked me to come outside and check it.

He had mounted it upside down and I pretended that I hadn't noticed. We had a good laugh, he made the neccessary adjustment and the job was done. It looked immaculate.

I later went home, picked up Jennifer and Rebecca and drove to my parents' house. After tea with my mother and father I drove the whole family through to Rotherham to show them the nameplate.

This was one of the most moving moments of my life. My father had always talked about solicitors when I was younger and the only time he had been to see a solicitor, he went in his best suit smelling of moth balls. He was in awe of the legal profession and the fact that his son had achieved his own office gave him immense pleasure.

As he looked at my name on the brass plate he wiped away a tear and to conceal his emotion, he brought out a camera to cover his face and went through the charade of setting up the photograph from a perfect angle. We left him to it and went inside whilst he regained his composure. I later found out that he had forgotten to put a film in the camera so all the effort was for nothing but I will never forget that day.

I was now working the last part of my notice with my old firm. Wilford had taken two weeks' holiday, but I was too excited to take any time off and indeed I was enjoying myself so much more than if I had gone away on holiday.

Only a few days before, we had sorted out the inside of the office and everything looked bright and clean, even though the furniture was a little jaded.

By this time, we had managed to acquire the whole building. We were to rent off the bottom half to a small print shop and the upstairs floors were to be shared between Wilford Smith and Co. and the great Jarvis who needed two rooms to help with the overcrowding in his own offices.

My association with Michael Jarvis began in 1971. At that time I was employed as a legal executive in a Rotherham firm and Jarvis was an articled clerk with a Rotherham accountant. He had been working on the books of my then employers and he and I hit it off immediately and have been friends ever since.

He is about six months older than me, although I have often said that he looks ten years older, but he puts that down to having a hard life! He is a ginger haired, chubby man with an athletic frame as indeed he was a very accomplished table tennis player, playing on a number of occasions for his county.

He has a most pleasant disposition and an agreeable nature and could well and truly be said to be "one of the boys". I think that the nicest compliment I can pay him is that I have never heard anybody say a bad word about him. That is not to say that he cannot be obstinate if he wants, but he is definitely a team player and the sort of man you like to have around.

He is also an extremely able accountant and I would like to make it clear that he never allowed his socializing skills to get in the way of his profession which was always approached in a most competent manner.

Within a short time of our first meeting we had struck up a good friendship and formed our evening dinner club which was the proverbial "rat pack" consisting of Wilford, Michael Jarvis, Sean Page, Tim 'Ten Belly' Norburn, Bodger Broom, the Mad Scotsman Louis Frame and me. They are all characters in their own right, but the combination always led to a most enjoyable, amusing but usually expensive evening.

There are a number of venues on our circuit, including Riley's at Crosspool, Santino's at Ecclesall, and of course Dino's on London Road, all of which are in Sheffield. We also included in our list Jim Lister's place, the Brentwood in Rotherham. We like these restaurants because there is always good food, good service and most of all they are extremely tolerant.

Jarvis moved his VAT department which comprised of one of his old friends, Oscar on to our floor. Oscar was a genius at VAT and the local inspectors held him in high regard because of the extent of his knowledge. He was a great man, but unfortunately suffered from the most dreadful flatulence becoming quite famous in local circles for his ability to break wind almost on demand.

He was also extremely keen on draught Guinness which I am convinced aggravated his problem considerably. He moved in just before we opened our office and had a room of his own and a share of the one toilet which faced the stairs to our part of the building.

Oscar's life was something of a ritual and, he was certainly the most organized person that I have ever met. He had his breakfast at the same time every day, he had a cigarette at the same time every morning, he bought the same paper from the same news vendor and walked the same route to the same office, each and every day. He was truly a most consistent person in everything that he did, not least in his ablutions. Unfortunately there was a down side to this rigid regime and that was Oscar's dreadful problems each morning at not later than 9.45 am. This was the time of his first major visit to the lavatory and as ever he took the *Racing News* with him. Oscar was a keen horse racing enthusiast and he liked to consider the day's form whilst he sat doing his duty. The area had to be avoided like the plague and indeed it was.

The rent was to be shared pro rata to the number of rooms that were taken and we had a gentlemen's agreement with Michael Jarvis concerning this. It would be unusual I suppose for lawyers not to have contracts, but Jarvis is one of my best friends and I trust him implicitly. The same could be said of Wilford and indeed to this very day we do not have a partnership agreement.

In the last few days before we opened we had been extremely busy sorting out all the final arrangements of which there were many. We had to register our practice with the Law Society and the legal aid board as well as informing all the local building societies and banks of our move. The purpose of this was to let people know that we existed in the hope that they might favour us with some work.

Although we had been in Rotherham for about ten years and had built up some business relationships and indeed a clientele so far as the courts were concerned, we were now on our own and had to start bringing in the business for Wilford Smith and Co.

As we got nearer the day all the financial details were put into place. I had borrowed £2,500 from my parents and Wilford the same from his mother. Some of the money had gone to buy office equipment but also funded small deposits for the two cars we had bought. The rest was in the bank as a buffer against wages and day to day expenses. We were indeed working on a shoestring.

Each evening was spent with Wilford in consultation and even though we always covered the same old ground, it seemed to add to the spice of the moment. Our meetings were always held in our new office principally because we liked to be there and after all it was ours.

The date set for the grand opening was to be the 13th May 1981 and in the days leading up to it we received a great deal of help from our friends in the business community.

I would finish work between 5.30 pm and 6.00 pm and most lunchtimes were spent round at the office. One such lunchtime I went to deliver some stationery and as I walked up the stairs I found that Oscar was about to pay his second visit of the day to the loo with the *Racing Times*.

We were aware that he was in there because the toilet adjoined our office and the walls were thin. "How long has he had that trombone?" I asked Wilford.

"All of his life dear boy," he replied.

As we finished our business we left to find that Oscar had finished his. I could have sworn that I heard Oscar cursing but thought nothing of it. As we left our room, out came Oscar rubbing the side of his head. "Good afternoon Oscar, any winners today?"

"Oh hello lads, not today," he said distractedly and disappeared into his office.

"Did you see the lump on the side of Oscar's head?" Wilford said.

"Why don't we get a plumber in?" I asked earnestly and with that we both burst out laughing as we left the building. The ballcock had struck again.

Every working moment was dominated by the thought of that office and it seemed like an eternity as we waited for the opening day.

I left my old job on Friday 8th May with little fuss after spending ten happy years with the firm but I believed that my destiny was to be a self-employed solicitor in Rotherham. The telephone people had been in to put the extensions in place and at the weekend I rang all my friends with the new number. We were to open the office on Wednesday, 13th May.

When the big day came, I had no files, an empty diary, but a lot of hope and I set off for work bright and early, calling at a local shop for the milk. We had decided that the first week would be my turn for the collection rota. (This was just one example of the decisions self-employed business partners have to make.) As I walked to the office, I saw one of the local prosecutors called Philip Chadwick walking towards me on his way to court. Seeing the bottles in each hand, and knowing that I had left my old job he shouted across to me, "That's a rather good idea, until you get established, a little milk round." I laughed at his joke. I knew nothing was going to upset or offend me that day.

I got to the office and saw that someone had stuck a balloon to our front door. It bore the pre-printed words, 'Happy Birthday Margaret'. I couldn't believe Sean Page had been up so early that morning!

I opened up the office and went inside and within a very short time Wilford appeared carrying two bottles of Newcastle Brown Ale. I presumed that they would be part of our lunch, but I was wrong. They were to be part of his lunch. Anne appeared a few minutes later carrying a bottle of Champagne, "What a lovely gesture" I said, until I was told that it was to be her lunch! We opened the bottle there and then.

At 9.00 am the telephone started to ring and we received a number of calls from wellwishers. We even had some post, with one letter confirming that we had been entered onto the legal aid panel, but the others were greetings cards. Page had sent one which bore the legend "A happy Easter to all of you" but I suppose it was the thought that counted.

By 10.00 am all the fuss had died down, the telephone had stopped ringing and all the post had been opened. Wilford and I sat across the desk from each other and suddenly faced the realization that we had nothing to do. Wilford Smith was open for business but had no business.

"I know!" said Wilford. "Pass me the screwdriver. There is one job that I have got to do." He left for the toilet to do battle with the irreverent ballcock.

Before he could leave, the telephone rang and it was a local estate agent who asked if we were interested in dealing with a house transaction for one of his clients. This was Wilford's department and he nervously but enthusiastically took down the details of our very first job.

"I can see them right now if you wish, I'm free at the moment," he said, and within half an hour our first clients came through the door. I suppose we overdid it, for they not only got an interview with Wilford, but an interview with me and our secretary together with copious amounts of coffee from a donated coffee machine that burnt your fingers every time you used it. They went away happily carrying our business cards, a list of our services, our emergency number and a potted history of the firm and its partners. Their transaction was completed in record time and to our considerable delight, only a matter of a few days later they brought in a member of their family who was also buying a house.

We spent the rest of the morning showing a number of visitors, who had come to wish us well, around the premises. At lunchtime we went to the Cross Keys and advertised ourselves to all and sundry for an hour-and-a-quarter.

By 2.15 pm we were back in the office and found a client waiting to see me. Jack, who I had represented before had found out that I had moved. He was a likeable rogue who had a weakness for other people's property but he had never committed a house burglary or robbed an old person. As he put it, he avoided "Joe Public" but scrap yards and commercial properties were fair game for him. Jack also had a flair for driving whilst disqualified and in all the years he had been a driver, I don't think that he was ever insured. He had nine children and when I asked him why he had so many he told me that he had never owned a television. His huge grin completely dominated his face and all his children inherited the same expression. Jack was a loyal client and so were his children. They were well cared for but had all inherited their father's faults. There are certain clients you can't help liking and Jack and his family were welcome members of a small exclusive group. He was due to appear in the Rotherham Magistrates' Court the following day and he wished me to represent him. His small son who was about seven years old had come with him. He was a spotty little urchin with an appealing, almost angelic face which belied his true nature and as I was completing Jack's legal aid application, the little boy picked up a bottle of ink from my desk and spilt it all over my papers. Jack clouted him at the back of the ear and called him a "twat" and told him to be quiet.

Within seconds the lad was checking to see if my plastic telephone was capable of splitting when propelled with great force against the desk. Another clout ensued whereupon the little boy shouted "Gi 'ore."

"Oh, it can speak," I thought to myself as he began to pick his nose.

Throughout the visit, he stared at me, with a kind of a smile upon his face that was quite hard to define. Jack's cup of tea arrived together with a glass of pop for the boy. Significantly, he didn't spill the pop but managed to knock over his father's tea, which crept along my file under the legal aid application which I had just filled in and into my top left hand drawer. I couldn't help thinking that this boy was a disaster area. How I kept my temper, I do not know, but I was placated to some extent by the continual clouts to the back of his head from his father. As our meeting was about to finish, I was aghast to see that the boy was standing on a chair busily trying to capture the koi carp in our fish tank. "Put the bugger back you little bastard," shouted his father with annoyance.

"Yes put the bugger back you little bastard," said I with even greater annoyance.

"Gi' ore," said the little boy, "Gi' ore will tha?" – making it plain that he had an extensive vocabulary. I got up and took the fish's castle from him and put it back into the tank at which point one of the fish bit me.

My immediate reaction was to pull my arm out of the way, splashing water all down the front of my shirt. My immaculately ironed white shirt gave way to streaks of green algae which burrowed into the cotton.

"Anyway, we'll get off now," said Jack.

"OK Jack," I said, "and take that little bugger with you." In as short a time as forty minutes this one little boy had almost destroyed my desk and pillaged my fish tank.

"See you tomorrow," said Jack, "don't forget, I can't be doing any bird just now."

"At least you would be away from that little sod," I said and Jack laughed thinking that I was joking and I laughed knowing that I wasn't.

"Come on son," said Jack to the little moron, "say goodbye to Steve."

"Tarra Steve," said the boy.

"Cheerio you little shit," I thought to myself.

"Shake hands with Steve," said Jack. As he did so, I became aware that my hand had come into contact with something extremely sticky. It was apparent that the little boy had donated his chewing gum to my right hand.

He laughed as he did it and then left with his father who was blissfully unaware of what the little shit had done. "What's your name little man?" I asked earnestly.

"Albert," he replied with a grin as he was dragged out of the room by his father.

"Albert," I thought, "yes, I'll remember you."

Chapter Two

THE DAY THE BANKER CAME TO CALL

We did extremely well in our first month. We had been very lucky and all sorts of work arrived from the most unexpected quarters. Our friends in the business community had also put a considerable amount of work our way.

One morning, Wilford arrived in a very excited and agitated state. He told me that the manager of the Halifax Building Society in Rotherham was calling to see how we were getting on. His name was Jack Bower, an extremely experienced man and being the Manager of one of the largest building societies in the area, he was a very important person.

He was able to provide mortgages and was in a position to put a lot of conveyancing work our way but more importantly, at the stroke of a pen, he could alter the course of our overdraft!

Wilford had met him on a number of occasions and indeed enjoyed an excellent rapport with him. He knew of our practice and had decided to pay us a visit.

Wilford had arranged the appointment for 12 noon the following Friday having confirmed that I would be there too as I had a very light court that day.

We agreed that the office should be in pristine condition and we decided to buy a new coffee maker and half a dozen china cups and saucers. These could be bought from our profits although we had yet to make any, but Oscar had tipped Shergar to win the Derby and we had had a little flutter. Anne was sent out to make the appropriate purchases while Wilford managed the office, answered the phone, made the tea and accepted responsibility for the ballcock which had broken again.

We had three days to prepare for the visit but nature was turning against us. The weather had improved substantially and it was becoming very warm. The flutterings in the roof had increased as the pigeons had been breeding at an incredible rate. We also found, that we were plagued with a small beetle-like creature that was everywhere, in the drawers, on the ceiling, on the floors and on the desks. In the areas which were not carpeted they were in vast numbers and crunched when you stood on them. There was an infestation somewhere, but we didn't know where and time was running out.

The problem became so marked that even Oscar commented that his room was besieged by these yellow coloured creatures.

Action had to be taken when late one afternoon Wilf had found one floating in his glass of whisky. This was the kiss of death for our little friends and we agreed to contact Rentokil.

On Wednesday afternoon, Wilford was interviewing a client who was sitting on a chair placed directly underneath the light. As Wilford discussed the client's proposed house purchase, he noticed that the wire from the ceiling to the bulb appeared to be moving. He fixed his attention on the wire, putting on his driving glasses to see better. A family of beetles were marching defiantly down the wire to the lowest point of the bulb from where lemming-like they leapt from the bulb down to the floor.

Unfortunately, directly between the light and the floor was Mr Granville Entwhistle who was discussing the purchase of his council house.

Wilford watched in agony as the first of this family unit landed on Granville's shoulder. The mother was next, followed by what he believed to be the eldest son and then the other siblings. Granville was soon covered in beetles and Wilford began to feel hot under the collar. He was in a quandary as to what to say. Should he say "Please move Granville, you are infested with beetles from our roof" or usher him out and hope that he would think that he had acquired his infestation somewhere else.

Wilford was a man of honour, and had every care and concern for his clients, and so he made the decision to usher him out in the hope that he would believe that the infestation had come from somewhere else.

Before he could do so, the beetle family began their march to the front of their new home. At this point, Wilford realized that it was only a matter of time before Granville would face the stark realization that he had been invaded by foreign bodies.

As the interview drew to a close, Granville's shoulders were home to the hordes and as one moved onto his neck he scratched violently. Wilford ushered him to the door breathing a huge sigh of relief as Granville walked down the stairs onto the street.

Wilford, watching from the window, saw him disappear scratching his head and neck in a frantic fashion.

On the Thursday, Rentokil came to call and identified the insects as golden spider beetles, that fed upon the waste matter of pigeons. I realized immediately where they must be from and indeed within minutes the source was found. The pigeons had made their home in the rafters, which had also been their burial ground and this is where the infestation had started.

We watched in silence as plastic sack after sack was taken away. I still shudder to think of it.

The entire roof and floor were sprayed with an anti-golden spider beetle deterrent and we vowed to get the roof area repaired before the pigeons returned.

On the Friday, we were busily preparing for Mr Bower's visit. If he was sufficiently impressed he would see to it that we were given what was known as 'Solicitor free work.' Jack had the power to help us, so we treated his visit as one of the utmost importance.

At a few seconds before 12 noon, Jack walked into the office, his timing immaculate as always.

We welcomed him enthusiastically and poured him a cup of his favourite Darjeeling tea into a brand new bone china teacup. We ushered him into the reception area and then into our interview room. Bearing in mind that he had a staff of over eighty, with offices with all the mod cons, he must really have wondered what he had got himself into when he saw our little enterprise. However, he seemed genuinely pleased for us and it was clear that he was impressed with our attempt to "give it a go."

The interview lasted about twenty minutes, ending with his promise of support for the future. He had no fears about our quality of work, because whatever our faults, Wilford was a brilliant conveyancer and Jack knew it. He could therefore entrust some work to us with confidence.

As he left the waiting room we chatted at the top of the stairs, when out of the corner of my eye, I saw Oscar appearing for his midday visit. "Excuse me," said Oscar as Jack moved out of the way and the toilet door opened. I looked at Wilford.

It would not do to go into graphic details, suffice to say that Oscar was on form and the somewhat echoed acoustics from within added to the agony of the moment. "It's the VAT Inspector," I said to Jack, for the want of something better to say.

"He's got a real problem that chap," said Jack as he walked down the stairs. We both nodded in agreement.

The following Wednesday morning I set off for the office with the sky almost black, illuminated by streaks of lightning. It was pouring down and by the time I had got from the house to the car my coat was saturated. I had my briefcase and files for the morning, together with my football kit which should have included two boots, but realized I had brought only one. I cursed to myself as I opened the car door.

I rushed back to the house and found the boot in the passageway. Once back in the car, having been soaked again, found that I had only one football sock. I decided to borrow one from Lidster and set off for work.

My interest in football had begun many years before at school and had continued into adulthood. I was nearly thirty two and it was unlikely in the extreme that Sheffield United would sign me up to play in their attack, but I had always wanted to play alongside the great Tony Currie who was a footballing idol of mine. I always remembered the time when Alan Ball, the former world cup player, came to Bramall Lane with Arsenal. Some weeks earlier the Blades had played at Highbury and with contempt for Sheffield United, (who had only just been promoted from the then second division) Ball actually sat on the ball in the middle of the pitch, much to the delight of the Arsenal fans. Tony did not play in that match, but when the Gunners came to Sheffield, he was in the line up. The Sheffield fans were much aggrieved about Alan Ball's attitude and they gave him an awful lot of stick during the match. During the second half, Tony had been weaving his magic and had himself sat on the ball much to the delight of the Sheffield faithful. Tony Currie was idolized at the Lane and I believe was just unfortunate that he never got the chance to play alongside me!

Wednesday evenings were taken up with football matches on the all weather pitch at the Herringthorpe Leisure Centre in Rotherham. It was a 6.00 pm kick off and our team consisted of some very good footballers. They were not all from the legal profession, because we had to bring in outsiders to bolster the numbers and one of them was a lad called David Lidster or "Bader," as he became affectionately known. "Bader" who became captain, was not only a very good player but he was the main supplier of kit when I had forgotten mine.

It was to be an eventful day, because my best client Jack was before the court that morning to be sentenced for theft of lead and driving whilst disqualified.

I parked the car and ran to the office, getting drenched for a third time in the process. When I got inside and to my desk, I started to go through my letters when I felt water dripping onto the top of my head from the area of the light bulb above me. I rushed to turn off the lights for fear that I would be electrocuted and went upstairs to investigate. Our roof problem was never more apparent as I saw two areas where water was dripping in. We used all the buckets and pans that we had, one of which was perched rather precariously on my desk.

Wilford came in soaking wet, cursing the weather and as he walked into the room, he saw me placing my head into the bucket to check the contents. Not realizing that we had a leak, Wilford announced "You must have had a good night."

"It's for a leak you chuff," I said to him in annoyance.

"Why don't you leak in the toilet like everybody else?" he said. I granted him a smile and he sat in his chair opposite, gazing at the water dripping from the ceiling. He had been sitting down only a matter of seconds when he realized that water had been dripping onto his chair and that too was saturated. "Bloody marvellous," he said "look at this," pointing to a rather wet patch around his backside.

"Must have been a good night last night then," I said.

"Oh bugger off," said Wilford. "What are we going to do about this?" As I had got four cases that morning and had to be at court early, Wilford suggested that we would get Bodger Broom in to see if he could effect some speedy repairs.

After we had been through the post, Wilf set about trying to persuade Bodger to get out of bed and answer the phone. He let the phone ring and ring and ring.

"Who the bloody hell is that?" I could hear Bodger shout down the phone.

Wilf couldn't resist it and shouted "Wrong number" and put the phone down. I then rang Bodger and pretended to be the registrar at the local crematorium.

17

"Who's booked me in then?" said Broomy with great annoyance. "I can assure you that I am not dead," shouted Broomy with the air of a man who was about to die from a stroke. I put the telephone down and Wilford then rang him again. By this time, Broomy must have been frothing at the mouth he was so angry.

He asked Wilford if we had been messing about, but Wilford denied all knowledge of the other calls and told him about our roof problem. Broomy said that he would call at lunchtime and would bring his hammer. He arrived at noon with a hammer and nothing else. I realized that the hammer was probably being saved for Wilford, but as I wouldn't be in I didn't really care.

I set off for court and got soaked again. In the little WRVS tearoom was a rather wet and lonely figure. It was Jack and for the first time in many meetings the big wide grin was missing. I realized that something was wrong and as I ordered two teas, Jack handed me a pink charge sheet. This is a document which the police give you when you have done something wrong and explains what the charge is. I read it and realized that Jack had been driving whilst disqualified again. "Oh Jack," I said to him almost in disbelief. "How on earth could you get another charge, particularly at this time and even worse while you are on bail? You know what this means," I said to him. Jack shrugged his shoulders and nodded his head with a grim acceptance of the fate that was to befall him. "What were you doing?" I asked him.

"About ninety five miles an hour," he said, attempting to revitalize the grin.

"I had only gone to the chip shop, when PC Cawley clocked me." PC Cawley had 'clocked' him many times before and on each occasion Jack had been charged with an offence. "He must have seen me go into the chip shop and then the cheating bastard hid from me, watched me get into the car and then pulled me up at the bottom of our road. What a snidey git he is."

I found it very difficult to sympathize with Jack as the policeman was only doing his job and Jack had been warned not to do anything illegal while on bail.

I was distraught because imprisonment was the likely sentence and all the good work that we had done in the preparation of his case was lost. How could the court have sympathy with somebody who had gone out and committed the same crime yet again?

"I thought that you had got rid of that car," I remarked sympathetically.

"I had, but this was another one," he said.

"What was it?" I asked him,

"It was a Rolls Canardley," said Jack.

"I know," I said, "rolls down hills" and Jack and I, in unison said, "can hardly get up them."

The huge grin had returned to Jack's face. The old ones were the best! It seems that he was more concerned about what I thought than the fact that he was going to be sent to prison.

"I am sorry that I have let you down," said Jack.

"You haven't let me down Jack," I replied, "it's just that I don't want you to be sent to prison."

"Don't worry Steve," he said, "you will do your best and if I have got to go to prison, so be it, I have been before. I should think I will get my old job back in the prison bakery, but I am a bit worried about Madge and the kids."

I told Jack that I didn't want him to go into court with a defeatist attitude, but Jack was an absolute delight to act for because he was realistic, undemanding and, above all, in a funny kind of way he was something of a gentleman. This is a quality sadly lacking in some of the young people appearing before court today. There is certainly a degree of bitterness and jealousy from the 'have nots' towards the 'haves'. Some have no soul and I think that I can say that the old saying 'Honour amongst thieves' no longer exists, if indeed it ever did.

I was thinking about this as the emphysemic usher came into the tea-room and called us in. I was glad to get out of the place because it was very much like being in the grand bazaar in Istanbul with the smell of cigarette smoke and unwashed bodies.

I walked into court number 1, where I found the magistrates waiting for me. I also had some other cases and so called on two adjournments to allow me to gather my thoughts. However, there were no other solicitors waiting for their cases to be called so I was left with no option but to present Jack's case. The Chairman of the Bench was Mr Norcliffe, a very experienced magistrate who had been sitting for many years. He was hard and certainly not given to bouts of sympathy when he believed a defendant had been mocking the system. This was really the worst Bench that I could have got for Jack's case.

One of the interesting things about the courts is that you are always dealing with different personalities and one Bench may take a more serious view of a certain case than another. Some magistrates and judges have a particular abhorrence to cases of violence, some of sex cases and some of any criminal act. Mr Norcliffe had always been extremely courteous to me, but he was not afraid to send people down. Depending upon which side of the fence you stood, he was actually a very good magistrate. He was not, however, a favourite choice of defence advocates and I was cursing my luck when Jack was called into court.

"What is your full name?" asked Mr Cook, the Clerk to the Justices, in a very serious and forceful tone.

"Jack Heptenstall, Sir," said Jack in as much of a respectful manner as he could muster,

"And your address and date of birth?" added Mr Cook.

Jack answered the questions using the word 'Sir' at regular intervals. I looked at Jack and thought how serious he looked and how smart in the rather splendid dark blue suit, green shirt, red tie and pink pocket handkerchief. I reflected upon how only a few days before I had asked him to attend court dressed up! Dressed up is a Yorkshire expression meaning to wear your best clothes. I realized that Jack was dressed up all right but what as! The tie was so bright you needed dark glasses to protect your eyes from the glare. It had an insignia of an anchor on the tie and being an old navy man, Mr Norcliffe asked me which naval squadron it represented.

I said that I wasn't sure but I knew Jack had never been in the navy. The closest he ever got was the Army Stores so I feigned ignorance but Mr Norcliffe looked to his colleagues and with a reassuring nod confided to them "Yes navy man."

Mr Cook put the charges one by one and as he did so Mat Norcliffe's eyebrows reached high into his forehead. As I looked at Jack, I saw Mat staring at him with a piercing glare. I then looked at Jack to see if I could work out the object of concentration. It was then that I realized that Jack's trouser fly was undone.

"That's a good start," I thought and I could see Mat Norcliffe thinking of ways to tackle the problem. He stopped the proceedings and had a whispered conversation with his clerk. Mr Cook then lent forward, beckoned me towards him and whispered in my ear "... flies undone." I missed the reference to Jack and thought that he was referring to me. I was immediately embarrassed as I looked down at my trousers to find that mine were in order, I then looked round and saw Jack who was blissfully unaware of the situation.

I had been ordered by the clerk to tell him and so I thought the best way to deal with this problem was to simply ask the court's leave to take further instructions from my client. I leaned across and whispered in Jack's ear,

"Your flies are undone." Of course I would get Jack's deaf ear and he embarrassed me by asking me to repeat what I had said. I then stood slightly to his side to conceal him from the Bench whilst he rectified the situation. I sat down and smiled at the Bench and thanked them, only to have my attention taken away by a much embarrassed Jack who reported to me that the zip had broken. Trying to think of a way to deal with it, I suggested that he take his jacket off and hold it in a suitable position in front of him. He didn't seem to favour the idea, but I insisted and the general aura of the court seemed to force Jack to my will. As he took his jacket off, I looked in horror as I saw that he had only one sleeve on his shirt. He looked at me, shrugged his shoulders and said "It got tore tha knows, dog pulled it off line ..... when I pulled it, dog pulled it and sleeve came off,....... it's a big dog tha knows ......strong jaws .... it's a bad bastard really."

With that the court clerk had had enough and asked if we could get on with it. As he read out the charges, Jack pleaded Guilty. I then found that he was in breach of a court order. He had been told that he had to keep out of trouble for at least one year or alternatively he could be dealt with for his new offence as well as the old one.

Jack had forgotten to tell me about that problem. It was the kiss of death as far as Mr Norcliffe was concerned and on hearing an outline to the case, I rose to address him. He greeted me with the words "We consider that prison is the only appropriate sentence Mr Smith, what do you say about that?"

"Please don't send him," I replied for want of something better to say. "He has a wife and three children, one of whom is a complete moron and he has a dog that is a bit of a ....." Before I could use the word 'bastard,' my commonsense told me that while it might seem funny to me, the Bench might not agree. I did my very best but unfortunately, Jack, to use his own words, 'Copped for a twoer', meaning two months imprisonment. However, taking everything into account, I believed it was a fairly good result.

It is a strange job in many ways because as a member of the general public, you would look at a criminal and hope that the full weight of the law will punish him, particularly if it is your house he's burgled or your car he's stolen. but when you represent someone, you find that you become partisan to his cause despite what he has done.

As they took Jack down the steel spiral staircase to the cells, he turned and winked at me and gave me the thumbs up sign, confirming that Jack was the ideal client. He did as he was told and he did not complain. I saw him in the cells afterwards and he thanked me for my efforts and told me that he had expected six months. We worked out his release date, which would only be some four to six weeks away and he said he would look me up on his release and buy me a pint.

"So long as you don't bring that kid Albert," I said. "Neither I nor my fish have recovered from his last visit."

Jack laughed, the huge grin re-appearing on his face and as I left him he was busily talking the warder into making him a cup of tea. Walking back up the spiral staircase I remembered the tie.

"Jack there's something I forgot to ask."

"What's that Steve?" said Jack advancing to the cell gate.

"Let me have a look at your tie."

He came in view and as he approached me I recognized a golden anchor. Mr Norcliffe was right, or was he? On closer scrutiny I could see two words printed around the anchor, it read "Captain Birdseye". Where did you get it Jack?" I asked.

"Tesco," he replied with pride, "Twenty eight vouchers, all right i'nt it?"

"Yes of course it is Jack, by the way were you ever in the Navy?"

"Bollocks," said Jack. I concluded that he was not.

When I got upstairs there were two solicitors in front of me, vying for position.

My last case that day concerned a gipsy who was before the court for stealing electricity. His name was Henry Fordem and he lived in a caravan pulled by a Transit van.

He had been spotted down a dark lane by local policemen who were intrigued to see this caravan amongst a row of street lights which were not working. The caravan itself was incredibly well lit and a stereo was working full blast. The police parked a short distance away and walked up to the caravan and looked inside. Henry was sitting in front of a portable sun tanning machine, in a yoga position. They noticed Henry's three children busily playing on a television computer.

It was clearly not possible to fuel those contraptions with a twelve volt car battery and when the police got round to the side of the caravan they saw a large piece of cable emanating from a hole underneath the caravan leading into the street light.

With a great deal of guile and some considerable expertise, Henry had worked out a system where he could utilize the local street light electrical system to accommodate just about every one of the working parts of the caravan.

The police immediately arrested him.

Henry made a statement in which he said it was the first time he had ever tried it, although it would certainly account for various areas of Sheffield regularly losing their street lights over a fairly lengthy period. The magistrates thought that the case was too serious to deal with straight away and so they adjourned for probation reports to be prepared.

If the magistrates decide that a case is too serious for a fine or a conditional discharge, and they are looking at custody or community service hours, they have to adjourn for a probation report which would give suggestions of ways to deal with the defendant. Henry was adjourned on bail and neither I nor the court have seen him since. I last heard that Nottingham were having a great deal of difficulty with street lights and I wondered if it could be him.

I returned to the office that day with mixed feelings about success in court, and as I got into the office Anne came in to tell me that there was a lady in reception called Madge who had come to see me about someone called Jack. Anne said that she had a little boy with her who was trying to electrocute the fish in our tank. It was Jack's wife and she had been unable to find out which prison he had been sent to and wondered if I could assist.

As I telephoned the Allocation Centre, Albert looked at me, with that ever present grin which I found so disconcerting. We avoided the mention of Jack's name so as not to upset the boy. The Allocation Centre told me that Jack had been sent to Hull Prison. I just used the word Hull to Madge and left it at that. She thanked me but as they left, Albert turned to me and said "Hull Prison eh, that's a piece of cake, tarra for now Steve," and with that the little man was gone. I shook my head, "What is he going to be like?" I thought to myself, and set about my dictation.

Chapter Three

BODGER GOES FOR BUST AND THEN
TRAGEDY COMES TO CALL

Wilford Smith had been in business for four months when Sheila, my secretary from my old firm had joined us and we had also employed a full time receptionist called Tracy. Things were looking up as I had a busy court diary and Wilford was doing well with conveyancing.

In financial terms, I was probably better off then, than at any other time in my career. The balance was right because work was coming in and our overheads were not excessive.

One lunchtime Wilford and I were in the Cross Keys thinking of where we might take a holiday when a friend called Tim Johnson, the manager of a local building society, came in and joined us. We were discussing matters in general, when Tim asked us if we knew a builder who might be able to repair his office's large security door. He needed somebody that afternoon to do a repair job as it was sticking and was certainly a security risk.

"Broomy's your man," said Wilford, "he knows a bit about doors, he's cheap and he will be available." I thought about it for a moment, before agreeing with Wilf's suggestion.

The area manager was calling to inspect the Branch and Tim wanted to ensure that everything would be in order for the inspection.

We gave him Broomy's number and Wilf suggested that he give Bodger a ring. "Bodger?" queried Tim.

"Oh yes," said Wilford, "that's Broomy's nickname."

"That's an unusual nickname," said Tim, warily.

"Yes," said Wilford, "it's something of a joke," realizing that he had created a bit of an alarm.

"Leave it with us Tim," I said seeing concern creep over his face. "We'll get Bodg......Broomy on the job."

We finished lunch and went back to the office from where Wilford rang Bodger telling him there was a very large aluminium security door which needed to be repaired. "Very good" said Bodger, "I'll bring my hammer!"

Within the hour Bodger was there with his tool box ... and his hammer and Wilf introduced Bodger to Tim. "Ar do" said Bodger, "Artha alreight?"

"Certainly," said Tim studying the man in front of him.

Bodger was just under 6' tall and had a strong face with two bright blue eyes that lit up when he laughed. He had a boxer's nose and wing nuts (ears) that could have graced a professional wrestler, but unfortunately one of them did not work properly unless you spoke to him at his right side.

He described himself as a 'tradesman' but I would have described him as a man with a hammer. Bodger and Tim shook hands and Tim winced, such was the strength of Bodger's grip.

Tim explained the problem to Bodger, who became concerned when he realized that the construction was made entirely of aluminium! Bodger stared at the task in hand, perplexed. In fact he hadn't a clue because aluminium was not his forte. "Very difficult stuff to get nails into," said Bodger extolling the virtues of aluminium.

Tim left him and disappeared into the building society but as he was working on the computer, his concentration was disturbed by the sound of hammering from the front door!

Four hours and six Anadins later Tim realized that the hammering had stopped and so had the swearing, which had been coming from the frustrated and perspiring workman.

"Nice job that," said Bodger, when Tim went outside to find that the entire door and front window was propped up in the street outside.

"What the fuck?" said Tim despairingly.

"Don't worry," said Bodger with great confidence. "I'll have it back in a jiff and it will fit perfect."

It was 5.00 pm and the area manager was due at 6.30 pm together with fifty or so visitors, all of whom were going to have the wares of the building society laid before them in the hope of attracting investment. Tim was desperate but Bodger set about his task as only he could. Tim took a last look before setting about the preparation of the buffet but concern was etched across his face as he saw Bodger begin to open a new box of nails! He telephoned Wilf.

"Does he know what he's doing?" asked Tim, with a tremor in his voice.

"Of course he does. He's always building something or other isn't he?" looking at me imploringly.

I shook my head and lifted my tie up into the air as if hanging myself. Wilf made a rude gesture and returned to his re-assurances.

"What time are you coming?" asked Tim.

"6.30 sharp," said Wilf.

"I've got some Gevry Chamberlain '79," said Tim invitingly.

"6.00 then," said Wilf contemplating the Burgundy and with that the call was over.

We set off at 5.45 pm and walked the short distance down the road to Tim's office. As we did so, my attention was drawn to something glinting in the bright early evening sunshine.

It was Bodger's mighty hammer repeatedly connecting with the side of the door. As we drew closer, Bodger was adding the finishing touches. A variety of nails lay at his feet damaged beyond usefulness. I dared to look at the door and window frame and it looked good. In fact it looked surprisingly good.

Bodger opened the door and closed it repeating his action six or seven times to prove that this was a job well done.

"Excellent Bodger," I said approvingly. "Bloody excellent! It works."

"Course it works you daft bugger," said Bodger resenting the implication of incompetency.

Tim was delighted. "Please come in," he said, "and get to the buffet before anybody comes." Bodger took four pieces of pork pie and ate ravenously, Wilf on the other hand concentrated on the wine.

Tim started to read the guest list which began with his worshipful The Mayor, a nice bloke who liked a drink. He was a man in his late fifties with a considerable beer belly which caused the top of his trousers to curl over with the pressure of his midriff. We laughed when we discovered that Shaun Page had been invited. "He's been told to be on his best behaviour" said Tim sternly, "He won't be a problem." I looked at Wilf and Bodger. We knew that Pagey had been playing golf in a charity tournament and the beer had been free.

"It's the kiss of death," I thought to myself. I hope Pagey turns up after the speeches because if not we're in for it!

27

At 6.30 pm the area manager arrived. He was the archetypal area manager down to the C & A suit and brogue shoes. His hair was suspiciously unlike the real thing, with the colour of the top of his head not quite matching the sides.

The back didn't seem to fit, as the neck part hung at least an inch away from the back of his head.

Wilf had also noticed.

"Eighty quid?" I ventured to Wilf.

"No more than that," said Wilf with the air of a man in the know.

The area manager smelt strongly of Aramis aftershave and garlic dip. He surveyed the buffet and the drinks table with the air of a sergeant major. He then inspected his troops, resplendent in their society issue frocks and jackets.

More people arrived, including a chap from one of the local banks, called Victor. He was less than average height with bottle bottom glasses which concealed a squint. He also had the standard issue of pin stripe suit and brogue shoes and I'm sure there was a smell of Aramis aftershave with a hint of garlic dip! I introduced everyone to Bodger and I did the honours with Victor.

"Victor is a banker," I shouted into Bodger's deaf ear,

"He looks all right to me, don't worry Cock, Smithy's rude to everybody," he said to the confused banker.

The area manager one Gerald McAndlish was introduced to Bodger who immediately noticed the toupee. He stared at the man's head while they talked about the guests.

"Do you know many people here?" asked the area manager, making polite conversation.

"One or two," said Bodger. "That's Wilford and that's Smith and there's Fred the Mayor, I used to work with him at the foundry."

"Who's that small chap with the bottle bottom glasses?" asked the area manager.

"Beg your pardon?" asked Bodger, catching him on his deaf side. The area manager repeated his question. "Don't know," said Bodger, "but Smithy says he's a bit of a wanker." Another pint being put on offer, Bodger set off again for a refill, leaving the area manager completely perplexed.

I saw Tim and managed a word with him and he told me how impressed he was with Broomy's workmanship. "I didn't think he would have managed it in time, but he's done very well, there was quite a gap between the door and the door-frame, which must have been at least an inch wide."

As we were discussing it Broomy arrived with another seven pieces of pork pie and four chicken legs. Tim said, "I'm just telling Smithy just how impressed I am with your workmanship. You seem to have cured the fault on the gap between the door and the frame?" queried Tim earnestly.

"Definite," said Bodger confidently, "you couldn't get a gnat's cock in that gap now."

The timing of this unusual comment couldn't have been worse as I was unable to contain a mouthful of Newcastle Brown which went straight down the front of my shirt. As Broomy walked off, wondering what all the fuss was about Tim said, "He's got a way with words hasn't he?"

"Certainly has," I replied, "but he is a brilliant golfer."

The evening went very well until Pagey walked in.

Pagey is quite a commanding character who stands out in a crowd. He is a little over six feet tall with blonde hair, which at that time covered the majority of his head. I say this because he has now nearly lost it all, a condition which he claims, was brought on by worry!

Pagey was wearing golfing shoes, tartan trousers and an Yves St. Laurent shirt with a golfing motif on the chest pocket, together with a Haldini silk cravat. His cream jacket gave him the air of nobility as he puffed on a large Havana cigar which he had swindled from another player on 3 tosses of a coin. He had a round and jolly face which was always smiling with an infectious grin. He was for all the world Dickens' Steerforth from Great Expectations, but with the laughs.

It was quite evident that Lord Page as I called him, had had a good day. While he didn't win the tournament, he had amassed a considerable number of points which meant he had won a prize.

By the time Jarvis had appeared, it was really like the old Firm getting together again. We were all having a laugh about Bodger's handiwork when Page insisted upon showing us his prize which he had secreted in his sports bag. "I brought this one to show you chaps," said Pagey with a twinkle in his eye. He then bent down, opened his bag and pulled out of it an extremely large turkey. It had been part plucked and when Pagey threw the object across at

Jarvis, there were roars of laughter. Pagey then embarked on a trip round the room dropping turkey feathers on people's heads shouting "Christmas is coming" even though it wasn't.

I have to admit that we were all egging him on, when Pagey spied the area manager. "That's torn it," I said to Wilf who, by this time was heading for the beer table. "My God, that's a good one," said Pagey spying the wig. He took the turkey by the legs and marched it across to the area manager. Pushing the turkey up, he dropped its legs onto the area managers shoulder and its head onto the neat cushioned dome. Pagey moved the claws up and down the man's collar, much to the delight of the assembled party. The area manager jumped causing the toupee to move to one side.

"Oh, it had to be you. You are a maniac Pagey," said the angry area manager.

"Hello Godfrey old chap, how are you?" said Pagey who had clearly forgotten Gerald's real name.

"Much better for seeing you Pagey," said Gerald, "and by the way you owe me £20."

I was relieved to see that Gerald knew Pagey, but I must admit that I was horror struck at first when I saw the deceased turkey dance towards his unsuspecting shoulders.

Fortunately, the fact that Gerald had managed to laugh about the incident, quite endeared him to the guests and by the end of the night, he had really entered into the swing of things. He had even tried to match Pagey gin for gin, but having experienced that contest myself, I knew that he had made a very big mistake.

At the end of the evening, Gerald insisted that there be a grand opening of the new door. He ordered the remaining guests, about five or six in all, to stand outside while he declared the door open. Everyone was in good spirits and good spirit was in everyone. The group which included Wilford, Jarvis, Bodger, Pagey and I were assembled outside together with one or two members of staff. Gerald officially declared the door open and slammed it shut with rather more force than I thought was necessary. As he did so, he had to run out of the way as the door quivered and then rolled out of its frame falling to the floor in front of him. The window then followed together with the frame. Just at that moment Pagey had his hand on Gerald's head and was playing around with his toupee. Gerald moved so quickly that he left Pagey's side leaving a rather expensive toupee in Pagey's hands. At that moment Gerald's wife arrived to pick him up and as she got out of the car Gerald failed to see her as he turned and shouted at the top of his voice, "So much for the gnat's cock."

"What's going on?" said Gerald's wife.

Gerald gulped.

"Steady on old man, keep your hair on," said Pagey replacing the limp and disconsolate wig sideways.

I did not stay for the repair job but I am told that it was dealt with extremely quickly, both to the door and to Gerald.

The following morning, I was getting ready to leave for court when Tracy, asked me if I would be prepared to see a lady on a matter of great urgency and delicacy.

The subject intrigued me but I only had five minutes because I didn't want to be late for court.

The lady was called Lorraine and she was in a rather agitated state. She was tall, slim, and very smart in appearance, wearing an extremely smart blue suit that fitted so well it could have been tailored.

I showed her to a seat and sitting down rather nervously she blurted out that she had been threatened and was convinced that he was going to kill her and I had to do something. I had to interject because none of what she said made any sense. It was almost as if she had only a matter of seconds to explain the position to me.

I tried to reassure her and asked her to give me her personal details, which she did. I managed to find out that she had been married for about a year or so and that her marriage had taken place after a whirlwind romance. However after a very short time, she became aware that her husband was extremely jealous and violent when he had been drinking. She told me that she was frightened to go out of the house and his conduct had become so bad that she had decided to leave him. Unfortunately, he had not been prepared to accept the separation and had been a considerable nuisance, threatening her on the telephone and in the street whenever he saw her.

His conduct was so bad that she had given up her job and she explained that she was so distraught that she did not know which way to turn. I was conscious of the pressure of time but also of the woman's plight as she was clearly extremely frightened. I explained

31

that I would be finished with my court list for about 12 noon and if she would be good enough to come back and see me then, I would try to resolve her difficulties.

She agreed but asked if she could stay in the office because she was worried that her husband may be in town looking for her. She had told him that she was going to see a solicitor and he was none too pleased. She said that he might even be aware that she was in my office and would I mind looking out of the window to see if he was there. It reminded me of John Buchan's famous book *The 39 Steps* when Miss Smith as she described herself was seeking the assistance of the book's hero, Richard Hannay. Lorraine gave me a description of her husband but I could see no one like him outside.

I agreed that she could stay in the reception but would have to wait until my return. I left her with Tracy and headed for court.

I was thinking about the woman throughout the morning because she seemed genuinely frightened and although I was dealing with a number of similar cases, this one stood out because I had never had a client who had taken refuge in the office before.

I was as good as my word and returned to the office a little earlier than I had planned at 11.45 am to find Lorraine still waiting.

I arranged some tea and took her into my room where she continued her story. It seemed that she had met her husband about a month before they were married. She knew little about his background other than that he had a very good job with a firm as a salesman. She was working as a supervising cashier and, having just left one broken relationship, John Wilson became a convenient and sympathetic ear.

They had hit it off from the start and within a week were going out together at every available opportunity. He would telephone her in the morning and see her at lunchtime and then he would telephone her in the afternoon and they would meet straight after work.

Within a fortnight she allowed him to stay at her flat where he had remained until the separation.

As she went through her story I watched her intently; confirming that her upset and concern were certainly genuine.

She then explained how he had taken her into Derbyshire for a candle-lit meal at a very expensive restaurant before popping the question.

"I don't know what I was thinking about but I agreed immediately, believing that he was the finest thing that had ever happened in my life. I had a little girl, Louise, by my first marriage and she was only four at the time. John took to Louise straight away, although for some reason which I couldn't understand at the time, she didn't take to him". She told me that her daughter was a beautiful child with platinum blonde curly hair and a magnificent skin.

"It was the happiest time of my life and I was completely blinded by what I thought was my love for him," Lorraine continued.

"We obtained a special licence and we were married. My mother didn't approve but events had moved so quickly I didn't seem to be able to stop them."

"When did it start to go wrong?" I asked sympathetically.

"Everything was absolutely wonderful for about a month and then I was asked to go out with some of the girls from the office for a birthday night out. They were going for a meal and then to a nightclub. I mentioned it to John thinking that there wouldn't be a problem, but he said that he didn't want me to stay out late. I thought that was reasonable so I agreed to return fairly early but I noticed he was somewhat subdued when I set off for the party .

I went and quite enjoyed myself although I realized I had stayed out a little later than I had intended.

I got home a little after 2.00 am bringing with me a bottle of his favourite beer which I'd carried throughout the evening, I thought he would be pleased but when I got inside to surprise him with the present, he was sitting in the chair waiting for me. He just stared at me with an odd sort of expression which made me feel uncomfortable. I showed him the beer and he snatched it off me and threw it against the wall. It shattered and I just looked at him, I didn't know what to do, I was shocked. He then slapped me across the face and seemed to lose control. He punched me, kicked me, and Louise came downstairs and saw it all. It was heartbreaking for me. As he hit me Louise screamed but we were both helpless. When he tired of his attack I managed to get to my feet, pick Louise up and lock ourselves in the bathroom. We stayed there until the house was quiet when we crept into Louise's room where I rocked her to sleep, curled up on her tiny bed.

The following day I heard him get up and leave for work. I immediately rang my mother and told her what had happened. She was extremely annoyed and upset and demanded that I go home.

I decided to go early to avoid a confrontation but before I left John came back to the house. He was entirely different and was carrying a bunch of roses. I didn't want to speak to him at all but he started to cry and told me that he had foolishly imagined all sorts of things which made him lose his temper and his self control. He said that he had just flipped."

"What did you do then?" I asked.

"I stayed with him," said Lorraine attempting to hide her embarrassment, "and things were better for about a month, but then it started to happen again. I got sick and tired of putting up with the constant beatings. But I stayed because he told me that if I ever left him he would hurt Louise and I believed him. For the rest of our time together I lived in fear and misery.

There were times when he tried to be nice but I was living in a daze, I didn't know what to do or how to cope and I was always worried about Louise, and myself. I hid things from my mother because I didn't want to upset her until one day Louise was at her house. She was very upset. My mother has a good relationship with Louise and she managed to get her to explain what was wrong. Louise told her how she had seen one of John's attacks."

"He hit my mummy," said Louise repeatedly, Lorraine recalled.

My mother told me that Louise had shouted "He hit my mummy, he hit my mummy," over and over again.

"Things came to a head one day when I went to school to collect Louise but she wasn't there. It was after an argument we had the night before and I told him that I was going to leave because I couldn't stand it any longer.

"I was frantic when one of the teachers told me that Louise's step-father had collected her early saying that we were going on a family outing.

"I panicked and called the police. It wasn't until 9.00 pm that John wandered in with Louise claiming that they had just been to the fair and apologized for forgetting to tell me about the trip. As he looked at me he had a slight smile on his face which told me that he had done it on purpose. It was a cold callous act and I hated him for it.

When he went to work the following day I packed as many of our belongings as I could and we left and have been staying at a

34

friend's house so as not to disturb my mother."

She was clearly telling the truth and I feared for her safety. I completed all the necessary forms and a legal aid application. I treated the matter as an emergency and I contacted the court for the earliest possible hearing date to be fixed. I had decided to apply to the court for an Injunction, which is a court order restraining a party from interfering with another.

I asked Lorraine if she could telephone me later that afternoon when I would be able to tell her whether I had managed to get her application before the court the following day. I had a copy of the proposed injunction with a power of arrest prepared and gave Lorraine a copy.

She asked me again if I would check to see if it was safe for her to leave.

Looking out of the window into the street, I was astonished to see a man lurking in a doorway looking up at our rooms. From the description that she had given me I realized that it was her husband. He was a small man some five feet five inches tall, with an unremarkable face. He was clean shaven and very smartly dressed, wearing a dark suit and but for his skulking manner, looked for all the world like a businessman. Lorraine came to the window and looked as I held back a corner of the curtain. She drew her breath in panic when she realized that it was him.

Having heard her story I felt tempted to go outside and give him a clout but I hatched a scheme whereby we got Lorraine out through the back door before he was any the wiser.

I managed to fix a court hearing for the very next morning. Lorraine telephoned, telling me she had not gone to her friend's house but had merely sat in the local library out of the way. I told her that it was safe for her to go back to her friend's house as her husband was still outside the office. She agreed to get a taxi to the office the following morning and I arranged to meet her at the office steps and take her to court. She was enthusiastic and hung up having said "Louise and I will be safe now."

A little after 5.30 pm some members of our football team arrived to give me a lift to the match. As we left the office, I noticed that there was no sign of John Wilson.

The next morning I was waiting on the office steps for Lorraine to arrive. Since she had told me her story, I had not been able to get her and Louise out of my mind. She had promised to be at the office for 9.30 am and when at 9.50 she still hadn't arrived I began to worry as the court hearing had been arranged for 10.30 am.

I went back into the office and rang the two telephone numbers that she had given me but there was no answer.

Just after 10 o'clock Tracey told me that there were two police officers in reception waiting to see me. Although it was extremely inconvenient because I would have to rush to court to try to explain why Lorraine was late, I called them into my office. I recognized both officers but they were grim faced. "Not Guilty" I said trying to lighten the proceedings, but it was clear that neither of them were in the mood for merriment.

"What's wrong?" I asked.

The sergeant said, "I understand that you were representing Lorraine Wilson."

"Yes I am," I said, "I'm with her in court this morning, but she's not turned up yet, but what do you mean, were?"

"I'm afraid that she is not going to be turning up," said the sergeant.

"What's happened?" I asked.

"At about 6.00 pm last night, Mrs Wilson was walking to the bus station when her husband approached her and spoke to her. Witnesses say that she refused to speak to him and turned away, but as she did, he took a knife from his pocket and stabbed her a number of times. One of the blows pierced the heart and she died almost immediately."

I sank into my chair in a state of disbelief.

"Where is he," I asked, "have you got him?"

The sergeant went on to explain that after the police had been called Lorraine's husband spoke to a witness and told him that when the police came he would be in the public house across the road waiting for them.

Within minutes the police were on the scene and he was arrested. It seems he sat quite calmly in the public house drinking a glass of whisky. "There's been a straight cough. He told us that he intended to kill her and he is before the magistrates' court this morning on a charge of murder. At least eight people witnessed it, and he never attempted to get away. He was oblivious to the people who watched in horror at the bus stop. He calmly put the knife down on the pavement and walked away. It is one of the most cold blooded murders I have ever been involved with," said the sergeant despondently.

I had a number of questions to ask, but for the moment I just couldn't think of an order in which to ask them.

"How did you know I was acting for her?" I asked.

The sergeant said, "Well she had some sort of a court order in her hand saying that John Wilson had not to molest her. The court order had your firm's name on it and from that we realized you were her solicitor."

I couldn't speak, but the sergeant broke the silence by asking me if I would make a statement just for the record to prove that we had applied for the court order. I asked if I could make the statement that afternoon as I had to be in court at 10.30 am. The sergeant agreed, we made arrangements to meet later, and I set off for court.

When I got to the robing room I was in a daze, I had to put my wing collar and gown on and as I didn't spend much time in the County Court I was not used to fastening the wing collar with the brass studs and I couldn't fasten the damn thing. I was still trying to complete the manoeuvre as my case was called. Dashing into the court room I just managed to fasten the stud as His Honour Judge Walker came into court. The case was called on and rising to my feet I explained to the Learned Judge what had happened.

When I finished, the judge said, "The case will be marked withdrawn." I bowed and as I turned to leave the Clerk of the Court simply called the next case on and that was that. No fuss, no palaver. "What price life?" I thought to myself. "It's all a bloody treadmill, a cattle market." Lorraine Wilson was just another statistic.

I went into the robing room to get the wretched collar off and then set off to my other client in the magistrates' court.

Although I hardly knew her, Lorraine's case had got to me.

When I arrived at court, I was told that I had two clients in custody and I was asked to go down to the cell area to see them. As I waited at the cell gate to be allowed in, the usher appeared at the top of the stairs and shouted the name Wilson. The court was calling the murderer's case on. It was inevitable that our paths would cross and as they were letting me in, they were taking John Wilson in handcuffs to stand before the magistrates. He looked me in the face, his eyes twitching nervously. I stared directly into them and for a second time stood still. The moment was broken by him saying, "I know what you're thinking." I didn't reply but my eyes followed him as he walked up the spiral staircase to the court.

I was still looking at him when he got to the top of the stairs and he turned to face me. There was half a smile on his face, and I thought that he may know what I was thinking.

Six months later Wilson appeared at the Sheffield Crown Court and pleaded not guilty to murder but guilty to manslaughter. I believe the jury also knew what he was thinking because they found him guilty of murder and he was sentenced to life imprisonment. He remains in prison to this day.

A week after the trial had finished, a lady with a little girl came to the office. The little girl who was about four years old had tight curly platinum blonde hair.

"I am Lorraine's mother," said the lady, attempting to keep her composure. "Could you please spare me a few minutes." "Of course I can," I said, "Louise will be all right here with Tracy, come in and see me."

I offered her some tea, which she politely refused and I asked Tracy to give Louise a pen and some paper to pass the time.

I was searching for the correct words, but I couldn't think of anything to say. The silence was broken by Mrs Yardley, telling me that Wilson had written to her demanding to see the child and she wanted to know what she could do. We discussed possible adoption and she told me that Louise's natural father raised no objection, as he had no contact with the child and had not seen her since the separation. Mrs Yardley's main concern was about Wilson and I reassured her that there would be absolutely no prospect of any court acceding to any request that he might have in relation to Louise. She gave me his letter, which was politely written, but he ended with the words, "Louise is the only connection I have left with Lorraine."

I was appalled to read it and I told Mrs Yardley that I would write to Wilson myself and this put her mind at rest.

I dictated the letter in front of her and it merely said,
    "Dear Sir, RE; Louise,
            Your letter has been passed to me. I write to inform you

38

that your request is refused. There will be no replies made to any further communications.

Yours faithfully,"

I didn't think it necessary to say anything else. I asked about Louise and was told that she had settled down well after a very difficult start. She had been asking continually about her mother but during the six months since her murder her questions had become less regular and had now stopped altogether. "Young children soon forget," said Mrs Yardley with a voice of authority. "Fortunately, she has not been scarred!"

After about twenty minutes Mrs Yardley left my room to collect Louise. Louise went straight to her grandmother and took her by her hand. I said, "Bye bye Louise," but she didn't reply. They walked down the stairs and I watched them go as the little girl clung onto her grandmother, pausing only to wave to me as she moved out of sight.

I went back into the waiting room and couldn't help noticing a child's drawing on the coffee table. It was of a woman in a long blue suit and the word 'mummy' was written underneath!

Chapter Four

CORGI 1 - YOBS 0

It was the end of a warm August day when I went into the toilet to change into my football gear. Avoiding the offending ballcock, I put on the blue and white hooped shirt but found I had only one football sock. At least it was the right colour, white, and I knew I could borrow one from Lidster when I got to the match.

I put on my tracksuit top and left the office. As I was locking up, two of my ne'er do-well clients flew past in a car barracking me with wolf whistles. I gave them a V-sign and they drove off laughing.

By the time I got into the car it had started to rain. However, it was still warm and the rain would be refreshing during the match in which we were playing the representatives of a large firm of solicitors from Sheffield. They were a very good team but we were confident because we had three "ringers" in our team, the Lidster brothers, who were all very accomplished footballers. David Lidster called us together for a team talk just before the match to point out that his big toe was going septic and that tonight we should not place too much reliance upon him as he would have to play in defence.

This was a great disappointment to us as he was one of the mainstays of the squad. I played up front as a striker but suffered from a lack of fitness. However, I was an adequate player and providing that I was not expected to run about too much, I could contribute the odd goal when the wind was in the right direction.

As the game got under way, the rain was pouring down but nevertheless within a quarter of an hour, I was sweating profusely. Some of us had left refreshments behind the goal. I had brought a large bottle of Lucozade which was lodged next to a bottle of Newcastle Brown Ale, which belonged to our reserve goalkeeper. He was the team's weakest link that night as only the first choice goalie had the use of both legs.

By half time, we were leading 1 - 0 but it became apparent that we were beginning to tire and the opposition had more reserves of energy to call upon. Unfortunately, Dave Lidster had been injured and although I hadn't seen the incident, I saw him remove his right boot to display the ugliest and most offensive looking big toe I have ever seen. It was twice its normal size and quite clearly septic. I asked Dave what had happened and he said he had hurt it kicking the opposition's centre forward 'up the arse'.

The final scoreline was 4 - 4 with the match ending with Lidster in goal and our one legged reserve keeper just standing to the right of him blocking half the goal area with his considerable bulk.

When we got into the pub after the match, Dave exhibited his foot for all to see and as he pressed it, yellow pus shot out of the top of his nail. The other players around the table, particularly the ones who were eating sandwiches bellowed their displeasure and I told him that his foot was definitely going septic.

"You're going to have some very serious trouble with that foot Dave if you don't have it seen to, it's obvious to me it's going septic".

"It's all reight," he said squeezing the toe with the air of a devoted masochist.

I asked him to stop what he was doing and spare us all.

"I've told you, you want to be very careful, that's how Douglas Bader started and look what happened to him." (I was referring to the Second World War fighter pilot Douglas Bader who lost both his legs after they had turned septic following an air crash.) Dave thought for a minute and then as only he can, he announced to the enthralled audience with his unique brand of home spun philosophy, "But Bader didn't have any legs!"

At least six of the eleven players present spat out their beer as they were overtaken with fits of laughter, Dave amused us even more when sometime later after the laughter had subsided, he asked us what we had been laughing at.

From that evening on Dave Lidster became Bader.

When I arrived at the office the following morning an old lady, accompanied by a small Corgi dog, was waiting to see me.

She appeared to be in her early 70's, wore a still smart green tweed suit, which had obviously done much distinguished service and had a hairdo which must have been done especially for this visit. She sat nervously twirling the dog lead in her fingers. I discovered her name was Mary Daniels and she had called to see me, without an appointment, in the hope that I would give her some urgent advice. She had the air of a lady with a great deal on her mind, but I was extremely surprised when she showed me a criminal summons for assault.

I was very intrigued because I would not have believed her capable of being involved in any criminal case, let alone an assault.

I invited her into the office and asked her if she would have a cup of tea which she politely declined as she wished to talk about her problem without further ado. She handed me a neatly folded bail sheet which gave me the date and time of her court hearing.

There was no doubt that Mrs Daniels was very worried about going to court and she told me that she was seventy three years old and was a widow, her husband having died of cancer some ten years before. She explained how she had nursed him through his debilitating illness before he had passed away a day before his birthday. She had no children or close relatives and lived in a small maisonette on the outskirts of Rotherham, having sold the matrimonial home because it had held too many memories for her. The only company she had apart from her weekly visit to see an old friend in an old persons' home was her Corgi dog with the unusual name of 'Dancer'. It was a name that she had given the dog when he was a pup because when certain music was played on the radio he would get on to his hind legs and dance in tune to the music. She said that, like her, his dancing days were over now as he was quite old but it was obvious that she doted on the animal. However, her eyes narrowed as she began to relate the facts of her case.

For some time a gang of youths had been congregating near to Mrs Daniels' flat and were terrorizing the local pensioners. They made merry by intimidating the old folks, using them as target practice, throwing eggs and old fish and chip containers at them. She spoke of the terror which faced the old people as they tried to go about their daily business.

She had complained to these yobs on occasions when she was out walking her dog but she was always met with abuse. Many people would have looked the other way and avoided a confrontation but Mrs Daniels was of the old school and believed that she should be able to speak to young people without fear.

Unfortunately, the yobs had 'marked her card' and it was to their great delight that they had seen her on the night in question. She

42

had eggs thrown at her and was surrounded by the group who taunted and abused her. Dancer understandably took exception to his owner being threatened in such a way so he barked and pulled at the lead. One of the yobs saw fit to kick the little dog, and as he did so, Dancer yelped in pain. Mrs Daniels saw the blow and fearing for the dog's safety, struck out with another dog lead that she carried in her other hand. She carried it to allow the dog to walk on a longer lead. She hadn't really given much thought to what might happen as a result but the buckle of the lead caught the young man in the eye causing a very serious injury.

After this the old lady scurried away in fear for her own welfare, but the yobs went home conspiring as to the story they would tell. The police were called, a complaint was taken and a CID officer had the unenviable task of calling to arrest Mrs Daniels, and take her to the police station. As the old lady told me her story, I felt considerable anger welling up inside me at the way that this lady had been treated. Here was an innocent old lady who had managed to get to the age of seventy three without a stain on her character and then, in her twilight years, she was being forced into such humiliating circumstances.

At first I was annoyed at the police for charging her, but realized that if someone had made a complaint and suffered a serious injury, the police had to take action.

The system has now changed with the Crown Prosecution Service reviewing all cases, and I would be extremely surprised if she would have been prosecuted today. Soon after the incident the same group of yobs paid Mrs Daniels a visit and to their undying shame broke her windows, terrifying the old lady in the process.

Mrs Daniels explained how in all her seventy plus years, neither she nor her husband, had ever been involved in any form of trouble with anyone and she clearly felt the humiliation of having to appear in Court.

Throughout our conversation, although she was most upset, Mrs Daniel kept her dignity and did not once lapse into tears.

By the end of the interview, I had been so moved by her plight that the question of money never entered my head. She reminded me of it by saying that she had some savings and would be in a position to pay for her representation. She was in receipt of Widows Pension, which at that time was a rather paltry sum.

However, legal aid was just out of her reach because her husband had left her a small amount of money, and as with many of her generation Mrs Daniels was most insistent that she should pay her way and even wanted to pay something on account. I tried to put her mind at rest by saying that we would worry about it later, but in doing so I felt that I perhaps made it worse because of the uncertainty it raised.

Before she left, I again offered her a cup of tea and this time she readily agreed, I asked Anne if she would bring it in the new china cups that we had bought for V.I.P. guests. We only had four left because the handle had come off one during washing and Albert had destroyed the other.

She trembled as she held her tea-cup, the saucer rattling against it in tune with her nerves. I was delighted when she told me that I had put her mind at rest on a number of points and she would look forward to seeing me at court on the first appearance date.

Within seconds of her leaving my office, I rang one of my colleagues at the prosecutions department to give him hell. Unfortunately, he knew nothing of the case, but he was certainly concerned about what I had to tell him. It was set to be heard at the end of that week and on the appointed morning I waited outside the court building to meet my aged client.

The Court House was a dilapidated building with few facilities. There was no air conditioning and the main corridor was an Aladdin's cave of property which was being offered for sale by the criminal fraternity.

In the small ante-rooms which joined the court corridor, there were masses of ne'er do wells in a variety of guises, some large, some small and some intimidating. I was determined not to subject Mrs Daniels to that and so I decided to take her straight into court and let her sit at the back of the room away from prying eyes and the 'Rolex' watch salesmen. After a consultation with a most helpful clerk, I called Mrs Daniels' case on first. She agreed that the case could be dealt with in the magistrates' court and a not guilty plea was entered to the charge. As she stood in the dock giving her plea, one of the other solicitors on the front bench next to me, asked me what she was in for. When I mentioned assault, he looked at me with a look of disbelief and said "Never". I later told him the story and he too was horrified that she had been prosecuted.

The clerk went through the formalities, asking Mrs Daniels her date of birth. She gave it and said, "And I am seventy three years of age." It wasn't a protest, it wasn't a complaint. It was simply an old lady who thought that the court would want to know.

The Chairman of the Magistrates was extremely thoughtful and referred to her in a most pleasant fashion. Mrs Daniels thanked him at the end of his speech which released her on bail and she left the court. As the door opened for her, two youths pushed past us both in their haste to get in court to listen to a case. I complained about their actions and one of them just looked at me with a blank expression and said, "Tha what?"

"Never mind, you wouldn't understand what manners are anyway," I said to him.

"Eh?" came the reply. Here was a splendid example of early Neanderthal Man who I believed was extinct but I was wrong. I decided to telephone the British Museum and say that one such specimen was alive and well and living in Rotherham.

That evening I wrote an extremely long letter to the prosecution suggesting that they should drop the entire proceedings. They replied by telling me that the complainant and his family had been to their local Councillor and MP insisting that the prosecution continue.

The prosecution therefore took the view that it was a matter for the court.

It was clearly in the interests of Justice to have the case heard as soon as possible and at the next hearing I was able to get an early date for the trial and my confrontation with the yobs, which indeed was a confrontation that I was looking forward to.

On the morning of the case Mrs Daniels came early to my office so that we could travel together to the court. So that she would not have to sit in the court corridor with the complainant and his witnesses, I took her into the solicitors' room. She had had her hair done and wore the tweed suit which she always wore on important occasions. She was extremely nervous and suffering from stress induced breathlessness and so when we got to court, I took her to an interview room and bought her a cup of tea from the WRVS kiosk.

Her tea remained untouched as we rehearsed what would happen during the trial.

I explained that the court clerk would check her name, address, and date of birth, although she would not be required to state her age. The prosecutor would then stand up and explain his case and the first witness would be called. I showed her into the courtroom to get her acquainted with the surroundings which she would occupy for the next three or four hours. As we waited for the case to be called, I recognized a member of the local press who had come in. It was obvious that the case had attracted some interest, which worried me, but as it is an open court, you cannot object to their presence. I also noticed a group of some four or five youths sitting towards the end of the corridor who were clearly the prosecution witnesses.

By going into the solicitors' room, I had the excuse of walking towards them to see who I was up against. They were all well dressed, wearing white shirts and smart ties. The complainant's parents had done their bit to ensure that their children were as presentable as possible.

They did not look anything like I had imagined they would, as I expected to see ruffians dressed in tee-shirts and denims. However, I overheard a middle-aged couple, standing with the youths, mention something about compensation and I immediately realized the real reason behind the charade of the court case.

The prosecutor was a pleasant chap who told me that he was unhappy about prosecuting the case, but as the decision had already been made to continue there was nothing that he could do about it. He certainly had a considerable degree of sympathy for my client, especially when he saw her sitting alone at the back of the court. She had no friend or confidante upon whom to rely, and gave the appearance of a sad and lonely old lady.

The clerk of the court called the advocates before him and asked us how long the case was likely to take. I told him that I would be a long time with the prosecution witnesses as I was angry that this case had ever come to trial.

The clerk had done it all before and with no disrespect to him, it was just another day and another case. He was clearly a professional and although detached it was clear that he did have some sympathy for my case. The Bench were called in. There were three magistrates in all, two of whom were elderly, which I thought was an advantage to me. The third one was a lady in her forties and there was a chance that her parents would be in the same age group as Mrs Daniels.

My colleague opened up his papers and produced some colour photographs which showed a nasty injury to the lad's eye. It was not in my interests to have the pictures shown to the court, but there was nothing that I could do to stop it. The clerk called Mrs Daniels forward and she answered her name, address and date of birth, giving her age again. She pleaded not guilty to the charge.

I could see the Bench weighing up the defendant who stood before them, as they had not been given any prior information about this case (which is quite normal). In the crown court, the judges usually have the papers served on them beforehand, so that they are acquainted with the case that they are to deal with. However this is not possible in the magistrates' court because of the number of cases that have to be dealt with.

The prosecutor rose to his feet and outlined his case, which was that on the night in question a group of four lads were on their way home when they met the defendant. One of the group claimed that he had attempted to stroke the dog, but it had snapped at him. As a result of that he had accused the lady of owning a vicious dog. The prosecutor told the court that without justification Mrs Daniels lost her temper and struck out at the lad with the spare dog lead, catching him in the eye and causing serious injury. It was a case, the prosecution contended, of an old lady who was intolerant of young people and consequently lost her temper and acted very badly.

Mrs Daniels was horrified at the prosecution opening but, unlike most defendants, kept her dignity and did not utter a word.

The complainant was then called into the witness box. As he gave evidence, I wondered why he had left out any reference to throwing eggs at the old lady or indeed throwing the chip papers and dancing round her shouting obscenities. Of course he wasn't going to admit that, as it would put him in a bad light. Urged on by his parents from the back of the court, he continued his evidence. There was an air of arrogance about this young man and as he had walked past Mrs Daniels he sneered at her, but the magistrates saw it and I knew we had got off to a good start.

As the prosecutor finished taking him through his story, he asked the youth if he had done anything to cause the lady to act in the

47

way she had. Very much to my surprise he did not answer straight away, but when he did, he used the words 'not really'. Fearing that he might open a can of worms, the prosecutor sat down and as he did so he stared at me, raising his eyebrows. I got to my feet, stared at the youth and waited until he turned away from my gaze.

"What do you mean, not really?" I said forcefully.

The youth hesitated and then said, "I didn't really do anything to cause it".

"What did you do that might have caused it?" I asked him,

"Nothing," came his reply.

"Who threw the egg at her?" I demanded,

"It wasn't me," said the lad, clearly conceding that it had happened,

"So someone did throw an egg?" I continued,

"Well yes," said the lad, realizing his mistake.

I looked at all three magistrates who were clearly becoming uneasy at what they were hearing.

I continued ...."But somebody threw an egg, didn't they?"

The youth bowed his head, realizing he had made a big mistake and was being forced to agree that it was true. "Why didn't you tell us about the egg when you first gave your story to the prosecutor?" I asked.

There was no reply and the youth buried his chin into his chest. I waited a long time, knowing that I would not get an answer, but I hoped the silence would highlight his reluctance to say anything.

By this time, the lad was clearly uncomfortable and there were noises from the back of the court. I looked and saw that his parents were unhappy at the way the case was proceeding. I asked the clerk of the court to caution them about their interruptions. More 'points for the defence' I thought.

I was in full swing by that time, and I pointedly asked the youth, "Why did you all laugh when the egg hit her?" Again no reply.

"I said why did you all laugh when the egg hit her, was it funny?" The youth clearly thought I was party to information about what had taken place. It seemed obvious to me that he was frightened of being shown up to be a liar.

He began to back-pedal, but I pressed on, demanding to know who had thrown the egg and who had laughed. The lad simply remained silent. The magistrates were not impressed. By this time the witness did not know what to say, and then I said, "For the last time, I'm going to ask you, did you laugh?"

I could not believe my luck when he replied that he had. My next question was obvious.

"Did you laugh because it was funny?" He had no option but to answer.

"YES".

"If I came up to your grandmother and threw an egg at her, would you find that funny?"

The lad's head sank even deeper into his chest, as he said, "I don't know". I seized my opportunity and began to throw a barrage of questions at him and eventually got him to agree that all his group had laughed. I asked him who had kicked the dog. "It wasn't me," he answered, clearly accepting that someone had done it.

The complainant was a pathetic witness, and as I put my version to him, his parents interrupted from the back of the court. They did not help their son's case by doing so and the magistrates took note of this.

The next witness came in to give evidence and interestingly enough, gave exactly the same account as the complainant.

I began my cross-examination of this witness in the same way as before, and I asked him who had thrown the egg at the old lady. This youth was a cocky, clever dick, and he completely denied that any egg was thrown and he also denied that the dog had been kicked.

I asked him if his friend, the complainant, was a liar. He said that he wasn't. I asked him if he was the sort of lad who could be believed and he said that he was. I then asked him if it was possible that the egg incident and the kicking of the dog could have occurred without him seeing it. Fortunately the clerk did not stop this unfair question. The witness was adamant it never took place and if it had he would have seen it.

The prosecutor looked at me, as did the clerk, and the Bench. Everyone was waiting for me to tell him what his friend had already admitted, I paused for what may have seemed an eternity before I spoke.

"Your friend has just agreed that an egg was thrown and that the dog was kicked. Therefore I put it to you, young man, that you are telling lies."

49

The witness looked across at his friend who had just given evidence and I spotted it and cautioned him:

"Don't look at your friend for the answer, just try telling me the truth."

"I don't know," came the answer.

"You don't know what?" I said forcefully,

"I'm all confused," said the witness.

"You have committed perjury," I said pointedly.

"I did not see an egg and I did not see the dog kicked."

"But it happened," I said. "Your friend has told us so."

"Well yes, er no, er I don't know," he shouted.

The magistrates began to speak to each other in whispers. They were clearly unhappy at the state of the proceedings. I leaned across to the prosecutor and asked him if he was going to continue. He said he would call another witness and a third youth took the stand. Witnesses can only remain in court after they have given their evidence and consequently, they are not able to hear what the earlier witnesses have said.

The third witness was another cocky youth, who had a permanent sneer on his face, and when called, gave his evidence in exactly the same way as the other two. I therefore decided to follow the same line of attack.

"Who threw the egg?"

"Not me," came the reply.

"So an egg was thrown then?" I asked.

"I didn't see it," came the reply.

"So why did you say it wasn't you?"

"You got me all confused," he said.

"But it was the first question I asked you, how could you be confused about that?" I asked.

There was no reply. This witness then began to exhibit the same symptoms of the bad neck as the original complainant. I then asked him, "Why did everybody laugh at her when the egg was thrown?"

"We didn't," came the reply.

I then took a fairly substantial risk, for Mrs Daniels had told me that this was the one who had kicked the dog. I challenged him with it and asked, "Why did you kick the dog?"

"Because it bit me," he said.

It is fair to say that I got different answers from this lad. And he was clearly telling a different story from his compatriots. To my surprise, he admitted that an egg was thrown, that the dog was kicked and that the whole group of them had laughed.

"The old lady struck out with a lead to frighten you off, didn't she?" I asked.

"I don't think so," he replied.

"Well that's what she told me," I put to him. "I suggest that she was frightened and, fearing for her own safety, and the safety of her dog, she struck out with the lead at a group of five lads who had surrounded her."

"Not true," he replied.

I then asked him, "If you had been surrounded in that fashion, and had an egg thrown at you would you have been frightened?"

"I suppose so," he replied.

"I suggest to you, that it was obvious that this lady was frightened and panicking."

"Yes," he said, "but she had no need to. We were only larking about."

With that I sat down, and asked no further questions. The prosecutor buried his head in his hands. I asked the court to consider a submission of no case. This is a procedure you adopt when the prosecution is so bad that the case should be stopped there and then.

The magistrates retired, and before I had time to explain to Mrs Daniels what was going on, they returned and said that they accepted the submission and the case would be dismissed. There was uproar at the back of the court and the father of the youth swore. He was ordered out of the court room and threatened with proceedings for contempt. I did my best to persuade the court clerk to place him in contempt, but by that time the group had gone and there did not seem any point.

I applied for Mrs Daniels' legal costs to be paid out of central funds, which meant that she would not have to pay her solicitor's fees and thankfully the court agreed. As Mrs Daniels and I left the court to go into the tea-room, one of the yobs shouted, "We'll get you for this you old cow." I felt sorely tempted to go across and belt him around the ear, but fortunately thought better of it.

As he was leaving, the father turned and shouted, "We'll sue you for this." I just looked at him, smiled and turned away, thinking that this would offend him more than if I told him what he could really do with himself. Mrs Daniels, showing emotion for the first time since I had been dealing with the case, began to cry, more with relief that her ordeal was over than out of fear for the threats that were being made.

She shook my hand warmly, but it was some minutes before she was able to pull herself together. As she set off down the road she paused to turn, smile and wave. I shouted, "Corgis 1 Yobs NIL"- and she laughed. This was one occasion when I was convinced that justice had been done.

On my way out of the office the following day I noticed that a parcel had been left for me in the reception area. It was a chocolate cream cake that Mrs Daniels had made for me. There was a card with the cake which had a simple message which read, 'Thank you, I will never forget you'.

I looked forward to eating it on my return from court but by the time I got back there was only a quarter of the cake left, as Jarvis, Shaun Page, Broomey and Wilford had shared my gift.

I was not to see Mrs Daniels again, but I heard from the police officer in the case that a group of yobs had smashed all her windows and the council were busily seeking to re-house her.

I discovered that the only place she could go, was a council flat where tenants were not allowed to keep animals. I desperately wanted to help her, but she did not call me, and I was later told that she had not wanted to trouble me again.

I wrote to her at her flat but the letter was returned, marked 'gone away' and when I checked at the local council offices I was told that she had left the area without a forwarding address.

A year later, on the anniversary of the acquittal, a neat box holding a chocolate cream cake arrived in reception. There was a little card which simply read, 'To Mr Smith with grateful thanks for all you did for me a year ago, I will never forget you, with very best wishes, Mrs Daniels'.

I still had no idea where she was and so was unable to thank her.

For the next three years I received a chocolate cream cake, boxed with a card. It was clear that she would never forget but sadly on the 5th anniversary no cake arrived.

Chapter Five

IRISH JOKES, SICK NOTES AND MEDICALS

It was a beautiful summer in 1981 and Wilford and I were very happy with the way that business was going.

On the litigation side, I was very busy, and I had to work hard to get round all my court appointments, see the clients and keep the flow of paperwork to acceptable levels.

The main problems for solicitors are the clients, without whom the job would be quite enjoyable. The bigger the trouble they are in, the bigger the problem for us. Some clients are incredibly devious and the clever ones are the worst. The modern tendency towards negligence actions protects the vulnerable but gives a forged licence to the dishonest and it never ceases to surprise me just how devious some people can be. However, it is said that necessity is the mother of invention and I have certainly represented some real inventors in my time. This has never been more apparent than when criminals decide they do not want to attend their own trials.

Most defendants dislike attending court and they will use any excuse to put off the 'evil' day. In thirty years in the profession I have seen the full songbook of excuses and stories describing the reasons why they fail to turn up.

Over the years I have received numerous sick notes, but it has always been a source of wonderment to me to understand how defendants manage to get them at all. They obviously have the ability to simulate all manner of illnesses and some defendants even write out their own notes. One had committed a burglary at a doctor's surgery, stealing a book of prescriptions and a pad of sick notes.

He knew that when he finally attended at court he would be sent to prison, so he tried to put it off for as long as he could. Adjournments had been achieved for a variety of reasons including taking instructions, going through the prosecution statements and entering a not guilty plea. His final resort was to try the sick note.

He had obtained one bona fide note claiming that he was suffering from gastro-enteritis. This is a favourite among the criminal fraternity because it is easy to lay claim to such an ailment. Broken arms and legs and matters of that nature can be easily established but gastro-enteritis is very difficult to disprove. I doubt very much whether doctors require proof, other than the patient's word. Certainly, having to show soiled underwear would be met with less than enthusiasm from long suffering doctors. The other difficulty is that some defendants cannot pronounce gastro-enteritis and know it by a different name. I once acted for a client with a cleft pallet who found it very difficult to pronounce 'sh' and gastro-enteritis came out as 'nits'.

On the day that this particular client was due to attend court, his girlfriend turned up with a sick note which appeared to be signed by a doctor giving the cause of illness as 'piles'. I was suspicious because I am sure that doctors can spell haemorrhoids.

My perennial client Jack once turned up at court with a sick note describing his condition as 'tired and listless'. This sick note was not met with great enthusiasm by the court who issued a warrant for his arrest.

The list is endless but my favourite involves another client who sent a sick note with the ailment described as 'rash to feet (both)'. The magistrates didn't accept that either.

However for ineptitude, you couldn't beat my Irish client, Shamus, who had been caught in a department store in Sheffield city centre.

On the day in question, he had visited one of the large stores in Sheffield and had decided to purchase a number of items. He used the store's own credit card which is supplied to valued customers. The limit on the card was £400 and so Shamus decided that he would buy a number of items to almost that value. He picked out a toaster and a mini hi-fi. It was obvious that he could not come from anywhere other than Ireland. He had red curly hair and as pale a skin as it was possible to have. He handed over his credit card and the girl looked at it and immediately suggested that she might parcel the items together with string so that it would be easier for him to carry. Shamus thanked her and said he would look around the store for five minutes whilst she carried out this task.

However, unknown to Shamus, the shop assistant went straight to the telephone and called the police.

Within ten minutes, just as Shamus was getting ready to pick up his ill gotten gains, he felt a hand on his shoulder and the words "You're under arrest for handling a stolen credit card," rang in his ears.

Shamus was aghast and simply couldn't understand how the store could have come into receipt of that knowledge so quickly. He questioned the burly police sergeant as to how they had got him.

The sergeant, in a rather monotonous tone, simply pointed out that the shop assistant was suspicious when she looked at the card.

"Why?" asked Shamus in total confusion.

"The card bears the name Tariq Mahmood Hussain. You do not look like a Tariq Mahmood Hussain to me," said the sergeant.

Shamus looked at the credit card, read it and held out his arms in a gesture of defeat.

Unfortunately this was not the first time that Shamus had been involved in dishonesty, as only a matter of five months before he had been made the subject of a suspended sentence for deception. He knew therefore that prison was inevitable and he simply couldn't face it.

I appeared at the Sheffield magistrates' court one morning to represent him and of course he failed to show and a sick note was handed to the magistrates which had a word scribbled out and underneath written in red biro were the words 'very ill'.

Unfortunately it was the signature on the sick note which did for my Irish friend because he had signed it using his own name, S. Monoghan, and obviously hadn't realized what he had done. He was eventually arrested, brought before the court and sentenced to nine months' imprisonment. The last I heard of him was that he had gone back to Ireland to work on a farm. He was not suited to city life!

Doctors are often the brunt of jokes because of their handwriting but I don't believe that they are any better or any worse than anyone else. I accept, however, that some of them are none too clear in their written submissions and I have always admired chemists for the way that they are able to decipher some of the prescriptions. I remember one sick note which was none too clear. I handed it to the chairman of the magistrates to see if he could read it and he announced quite boldly to the court that it appeared to read 'brown shorts'.

I looked at the certificate myself and ventured to say that it was the likely consequence of the ailment but we never did find out exactly what that problem was.

I remember handing a court clerk a certificate which bore the word 'scabies'. This is a highly contagious condition involving a mite which burrows under the skin and spreads like wildfire. It causes skin eruptions and dreadful irritations and you can usually tell a sufferer by the way that he persistently scratches himself. This particular clerk of the court was in a particularly bad mood and he advised the magistrates that he thought that such a condition would not preclude anyone from attending court and invited the court to issue a warrant for the defendant's arrest. In view of the rather unpleasant way that he dealt with me I decided to tell the court that the condition was highly contagious and could easily be passed on from items which had been in the defendants possession. The clerk dropped the sick note in horror onto his desk and for the rest of the morning he scratched himself endlessly, much to the amusement of the other solicitors who were in on the joke.

Apart from the question of sick notes I have always had a considerable interest in the question of health and alternative medicine.

I remember meeting one of Jarvis's friends at a charity cricket match. He had snow white hair and a heavily lined face and had the misfortune to have to walk with two sticks.

We were discussing the question of longevity and I announced that I took a considerable amount of vitamins. Our elderly colleague announced that he smoked sixty cigarettes and consumed at least a bottle of whisky a day. He had been married three times, had nine children and an extremely stressful job, but took no vitamins or medication of any sort. I had to ask him what his secret was and he simply said that his life was ruled by consistency. It wasn't until later that Jarvis told me that his friend had reached the grand old age of fifty-two.

It was clear to me that my job was extremely stressful with rushed meals and indeed missed meals. Too much work and not enough rest were both recipes for disaster. It is also called burning the candle at both ends. Tearing about the place without a minute's respite from punishing schedules can lead to health problems and so I was resolved to try and do something about it.

The Great Jarvis is a fairly healthy person apart from his liver, but as we were both approaching our forties, we decided to have one of the comprehensive medical checks to establish that we were still alive. In my case it was to satisfy me that I didn't have cancer but Jarvis on the other hand worried about little if anything. However he is such an agreeable sort of chap that he thought we might be able to make it a day out. We discussed the visit over one of our monthly soirées which involve a massive meal with unlimited supplies of wine and liquors and a most dreadful hangover the following day. This was just the sort of preparation that we needed prior to a full medical.

We chose a well known private hospital in Leeds where we obtained the particulars to see what to expect.

I had had medicals before, but this was supposed to be an in-depth examination and from what I could gather the checks were very extensive. We were told to set a full morning aside and we decided to enjoy a large meal with plenty of grog to either celebrate our complete fitness and a clean bill of health or to commiserate if we found that there was anything wrong.

Jarvis had had a nasty scare about a year or so before, when his liver fell out with him.

He had found something of a rash on his shin. It was purely an irritation, but, as it persisted, Jarvis became a little concerned and so he decided to visit his GP.

When he got to the surgery, he mentioned briefly that he had a rash on his shin. The doctor examined his hands feeling between his fingers; as this, apparently, is one of the Harley Street tricks which tells you whether a person's liver is healthy or not. It was clearly not and he insisted that Jarvis give urine and blood samples.

Once the results were known Jarvis was told that he had damage to his liver, the medical term being cirrhosis. The non medical description of this is when you have drunk too much alcohol over too long a period of time. Your liver cannot handle it and accordingly loses its temper and starts to shrivel up.

Jarvis was told that he should abstain from taking alcohol for six months and was placed on a special diet. He was distraught, not so much by the fact that he was ill, but because he couldn't have anything to drink. Jarvis described himself as a social drinker but I found out that socializing included sitting on his own at home reading the paper, sitting at home watching the sport on television and having a drink before his lunch. It was quite obvious that he was the most social person you could ever meet.

Poor old Jarvis suffered from a torrent of sarcastic remarks and quips from his many friends, who taunted him with great relish. It was not malicious and indeed Jarvis took it on the chin, but was to get his own back.

As he left the doctor's surgery with the word cirrhosis ringing in his ears, he recalled the original reason for the visit.

On the realization that both he and the doctor appeared to have forgotten, he turned before leaving and asked the doctor, "What about this rash on my shin?"

The doctor replied with all seriousness, "Oh, I think that's some form of rash, put a bit of cream on it and it might go away!"

Jarvis' shoulders dropped and he left the doctor's surgery to begin his six months of abstinence.

I went out with him on numerous occasions during that six months and once when he ordered yet another bitter lemon, I ventured to say that it was a very healthy form of endeavour and with brilliantly quick wit and amazing speed of repartee, Jarvis looked at me and said "Fuck Off". Amazingly quick I thought and left it at that.

When we arrived at the hospital for our checkup, we were greeted by a very pleasant and self-assured middle-aged lady who escorted us to our lockers and supplied us both with dressing gowns which we were to wear throughout the morning. She went about her work very politely and, being a good judge of character, Jarvis assumed that she had been connected with the medical profession for many years. Jarvis asked her how long she had been associated with the hospital and she said "seven weeks".

"Really?" said Jarvis, "Which hospital were you at before that?"

"Asda," she replied. There was a pregnant pause and then she said, "At Otley, just outside Leeds if you know it," another pregnant pause and then she said,

"I was a supervising cashier". Gentlemanly as ever, Jarvis said,

"Very nice", and picked up the booklet that we had been given explaining what was going to happen to us.

We were not allowed any tea or biscuits and indeed had been

told not to eat or drink anything from tea-time the previous day. I understood that the reason for this was to ensure that our systems were clear, so that when samples of blood and urine were taken they would be easier to analyse.

'Asda Price' explained that there was a male and a female doctor. The man was senior in years and as she put it, "He's been around a bit, but he is all right apart from being deaf." The lady doctor was in her early 30's. I must confess that this worried me because part of the examination was to test for hernias and matters of that description which meant the old hands down the shorts and engage in a coughing fit while your tackle was being squeezed. However, a very smart man appeared with horn rimmed spectacles and wearing the traditional white coat. I guessed he was about sixty years of age, and he had Stewart Grainger style hair which was brilliantly groomed. He was wearing an expensive silk, Italian tie and tailored shirt. He looked extremely fit and healthy. The tests began and passed without incident until we got to the stage of the dreaded rubber glove. When you hear the doctor pulling the glove over his hands and saying the magic words, "Lie on your side and lift up your knees," you know that you are in for the dreaded internal.

I politely declined this test saying that I felt perfectly well in that area, but I pointed out that my friend, Mr Jarvis, had been worried about difficulties there and was too nervous, shy and indeed worried about it to ask for the test. My doctor said that he would pass on the information to the person who was doing Jarvis's medical.

From this I realized that Jarvis had got the female doctor. As I left the examination room, I found Jarvis in his ill-fitting dressing gown. He asked me if everything was in order and I had just told him that there was nothing to fear from this part of the examination when his doctor appeared. She was 30 years old, very attractive and looked more like a fashion model than a doctor. Jarvis gulped as he had told me earlier that he was embarrassed by female doctors. I had to smile knowing that he was going to get the rubber glove treatment whether he liked it or not.

By this time, all my blood and urine tests had been taken so I was given a cup of tea and biscuits. After about fifteen minutes, Jarvis re-appeared with a red face which matched his nose which was permanently in that condition. There was a look of horror across his face.

"Do you know what she has just done to me?" asked Jarvis.

I could not contain my laughter any longer hearing only the words 'rubber glove' and 'my arse' from the tangled rhetoric.

To conclude the tests, we were given an ECG and much to my surprise, apart from me being told that I was overweight, I was given a clean bill of health. However, Jarvis was called back to the doctor's office from where I could just hear him being asked to confirm his drinking habits and I heard Jarvis say that he had just the occasional drink. "Yes, occasionally in the morning, the afternoon, the early evening and at night, lying bastard," I thought to myself, as Jarvis appeared from the doctor's room with a relatively clean bill of health and some cream for the rubber burns.

"Did you get the rubber glove?" asked Jarvis.

"No," I said faking shock and surprise.

"Well I can't understand why she did it to me then," said Jarvis.

"Perhaps she just likes to do the rubber glove treatment," said I.

"Bollocks," said Jarvis, and we left for the pub.

We went to a local Leeds restaurant and enjoyed a fine lunch during which I tried to get Jarvis to see the funny side of what had happened.

"I suppose you will be telling the lads about this?" asked Jarvis.

"Who me?" I replied.

"Well at least we have got a clean bill of health," said Jarvis.

"Yes," I said, "I am pleased to hear that your bowels are all right."

He looked at me with a critical stare, beginning to realize that he had been had.

Chapter Six

AN OAP GETS RIPPED OFF: SO THEY TRY TO TAKE HIS HOUSE

The best advice I can ever give to any 'would-be' litigant is to say, "Don't do it."

It is a risky business and should be avoided at all costs, but of course there will be occasions when, for a variety of reasons, people will have no alternative but to seek the protection and the remedies the courts can provide and it is my firm belief that judges do their very best to be fair and produce the right result.

It is not possible to achieve this all the time and inevitably people will sometimes leave the courts with feelings of disappointment.

Someone once said that 'You can suit some of the people some of the time, but you cannot suit all of the people all of the time.' The law is a classic example of this, but I have always held the belief that if you do your best, at least your client will not be disappointed with you and that way you will always live to fight another day.

So often in my career I have seen solicitors and barristers who are so intransigent that they will fight anything, sometimes leaving their client with a massive costs bill or, indeed in criminal work, a term of imprisonment when it might have been possible to avoid it. It is a balancing act, but a very difficult one.

One of my friends in the law is Les Walton, who, in the early 80's was a solicitor and partner of a most prestigious firm in Yeovil. He has since moved to Southampton where he flourishes. I met him in the early 60's when we both started work at the same firm in Barnsley. Leslie was a Grammar School boy with a high intellect which he has subsequently put to good use in his profession.

We were junior office boys and as I said in the preface, my first job was to blow up a rugby ball for the senior partner's son and my second, to collect some cream buns for the typing pool.

Walton, or Walt as I refer to him is certainly a character; a dying breed within the legal profession as it now stands. The constraints placed upon lawyers by the general decay of the legal aid system calls for a stereotyping of personality and ideas and this will undoubtedly lead to a reduction in the quality of the intake into the profession. There are those who will say that the death knell had already been sounded for the legal aid practitioner but I hope they are wrong.

Walton's membership of this breed was earned through years of study and sacrifice in a profession which now begins to desert us. We trained together until I left Barnsley and Walton moved south to pursue his career.

Fortunately for me, he would make guest appearances in our football team on his visits to the north as his father still lived in Barnsley and after visiting him he would come to play football and then drink far more than was good for any of us.

In the latter part of 1981, he made one of his flying visits to kill a number of birds with one stone. Firstly to see his father and some other relatives, secondly to see my office for the first time, thirdly to play football for our team in a fairly important match and finally to wake up the following morning wondering why he had bothered.

The match was arranged for 6 pm and typically Walton arrived five minutes before kick-off, giving him insufficient time to change. He actually set about the difficult manoeuvre of putting on his football kit while being involved in the match itself. I remember receiving one magnificently floated pass from mid-field from a man in a pair of blue shorts, one boot and wearing a white shirt and tie.

After the match we changed and set off for my office which I showed to him with great pride.

As he was looking around the office Les suddenly excused himself to pay a call of nature. I was pouring out drinks before I suddenly realized that I had not warned him about "the ballcock". I dashed out of the room but it was too late.

"You want to get that fixed," said Walton minutes later, handing me the ballcock and rubbing his head.

"I certainly will," I said, scraping another notch on the ball which we had named 'Mountie'. Why? Because the Mountie always gets his man.

As we were enjoying a drink, and Walton was drying out, our attention was drawn to the window, through which we could see an old man in the street, busily sorting some papers and putting them into an envelope.

"It looks as though he's got something for you," said Walton.

The old man shuffled to our front door. We heard the papers fall to the floor with a thud and the man shuffled off down the street.

"I wonder what that was about," I said as curiosity got the better of me.

Before I could get downstairs we heard the blast of a car horn from the taxi I had ordered to take us to Jim Lidster's restaurant and hotel called the Brentwood in Rotherham.

We walked downstairs, and I saw a large envelope on the floor, "Shall I?" I asked Walt.

"Go on," said Walt. "It might be a cheque."

I picked it up and in the taxi opened it to find a letter written by a man called Eric Sharpe.

He was asking for help because he had obtained a mortgage with a loan company and it seemed had been unable to pay the instalments which resulted in an application to the court for an order for possession. This meant that the loan company was seeking to kick him out of his home, take possession and sell it, using the proceeds to pay off their debt and interest.

The summons was fairly straightforward and showed that he had borrowed the sum of £13,000 repayable by fairly substantial instalments at an astonishingly high rate of interest. I was intrigued, particularly when I saw that the certificate to say that the terms of the loan were accepted and understood was signed by Mr Sharpe himself.

I showed Walton the papers and between us we decided it was a case that needed investigation.

By this time we had arrived at the Brentwood and were greeted by James and his wife Angie who were busy in the restaurant. As James is a connoisseur of wines and Angie an expert in the kitchen, all we had to do was to sit there and consume it, something at which Walton and I are experts.

The evening went extremely well, and as we left the hotel after midnight, I felt wonderful.

I don't know what it is about good food, good wine and good company, but they seem to lose a lot of their attraction the following day, when, I had to face an extremely long court list.

However, the next morning I dictated a letter to a Mr. Sharpe offering him an appointment, before setting off for court feeling a little less than my best – something which appeared to have communicated itself to two of my clients who were waiting for me at the top of the court steps.

"Tha looks crap," said John Surtees standing with his minder who looked almost human.

"Thank you Mr. Surtees," I said sarcastically, "your good wishes are most appreciated, what can I do for you?"

"Tha's got to sort out these twats from the Consumer Protection," and he handed me a large pile of summonses.

The 'twats' in this case were the Investigating Officers of Her Majesty's Consumer Protection Office who, in carrying out their lawful duties, aim to prosecute wrong doers who pray upon an innocent public by selling them bangers (poor quality cars).

John Surtees was not so much an entrepreneur, but more a gangster who had progressed from thuggery to the noble art of milo - meter clocking. He had been charged under the Trades Descriptions Act for selling vehicles which had had the mileage clock interfered with.

The allegations were that he had taken second-hand vehicles and wound the mileage back from, for example, 150,000 miles to 80,000 miles with a view to selling the vehicle for a much greater profit than would have originally been the case.

Surtees had obtained a sales pitch just outside the town centre, where he relied upon his dubious charm to sell cars and his considerable physical presence to collect the payments. His minder was a man whom I know as Crip, which was a shortened form of his nickname, Crippler.

He was a body-builder who was a mass of tattoos; one in particular on his left arm had a skull and crossbones with the words, 'Fuck it' tattooed underneath. Crip was a minder in the traditional sense, meaning that if anybody came to complain about any of the cars that Surtees had sold, Crip would try to deal with the situation. Surtees had informed me that Crip was perfectly 'Legit' and he was on the books as 'Head of Complaints', although he only let him out after dark!

I advised this version of Morecambe and Wise to order some tea from the WRVS kiosk while I sorted out a court list and checked where my cases were to be held.

I took the first of my clients to the interview room while I sorted out the charges. "They have set me up and fixed me good and proper and I am not happy."

"He's not 'appy," said the Neanderthal Crip, proving that he was just capable of speech.

I disregarded the ogre as Surtees continued.

"We never touched these cars. They were all good quality motors and when they left our garage they were in first class nick," Surtees tried to assure me.

"First class nick," replied Crip from the echo chamber. I looked at him with a rather surprised expression which meant to say,

"You're not really adding anything to this conversation, you ugly bugger so why don't you keep quiet". I thought better of actually putting this into words and fixed my attention on Surtees again who continued, "If they are saying that these cars have been clocked, it weren't me and they must have been clocked before I got em."

"Before he got 'em," came the echo. Both Surtees and I looked at him in wonderment and returned to our conversation.

I noticed that some of the summonses appeared to be duplicated because they referred to the same car registration number, but I then realized that the charge was slightly different. There were six charges under Section 1 (1)a and six charges under Section 1 (1)b. The a's were alternative to the b's and the basic difference was that under Section (a) the suggestion was that the defendant had clocked the cars himself, where under Section 1 (1)b, it was less serious because the allegation was that the vehicle was sold on in a 'clocked' state.

"We need an adjournment to sort this out," said Surtees.

"Sort it out," said Crip.

I decided to go into Court to apply for an adjournment.

The courtroom had recently had an extractor fan fitted, no doubt to improve the air circulation in what had been a very stuffy room. However, it had been installed close to the magistrates Bench and some found it noisy and distracting.

As I joined other solicitors on the Court Bench, it was clear that members of the bench had been discussing the merits of the fan. The chairperson, a rather old spinster, on hearing the extractor, announced to the whole courtroom, "I want to have it off".

One wag in the public gallery shouted, "Tha's no chance."

The gallery burst into laughter and my colleague and I had difficulty keeping our faces straight.

"Silence in court," shouted the clerk. "This is a court room not a music hall," and with that the same wag started to sing. He was ordered out of the court room.

The wag did not like being verbally chastised and as he was leaving he shouted back at the clerk, "I hope thee arse falls off".

With that, the clerk quite properly and quite rightly, ordered that the man be arrested for contempt of court.

My case was called on and Surtees answered his name beautifully, giving his date of birth and address. Crip sat at the back of the court in the public gallery where the local wags had no hesitation in moving out of his way to let him sit down. They listened with great curiosity to Crip's echo. The magistrates queried whether an adjournment was necessary, but after I had explained that the charges were alternative ones and the matter could be resolved next time, my adjournment was granted and Surtees left the court followed by an eager Crip who had put out his hand to help himself up. He missed the back of the seat and put it on another defendant's head who was waiting his turn. He pressed himself up, injuring the other defendant's neck in the process,

"Bastard," shouted the unknown defendant,

"Ah tha talking to me?" said Crip.

"No," said the unknown defendant, and being satisfied, Crip left the Court.

The prosecutor was kind enough to show me his file of evidence from which it was quite clear that while the prosecution could not prove that Surtees had actually wound the milometers back himself, they had enough evidence to prove that he had sold the cars after the vehicles had been clocked.

The main problem Surtees had to face was that the prosecution could prove that when the cars left their previous owners, they had considerably more miles on them, than when they were sold by him. My advice was that he should plead not guilty to actually clocking the cars, but guilty to selling them on afterwards. He decided to consider my advice during the adjourned period,

"What will I get if I plead guilty?" said Surtees.

"Yeh, what will he get?" asked Crip,

"A break from you," I said.

"Tha what?" said Crip, missing the point completely.

"The problem is," I continued, "that there are six different instances and the magistrates are likely to think that you made a business of selling clocked cars."

"Is there any bird in it?" asked Surtees. As he finished speaking, I immediately looked at Crip but the echo wasn't there.

"I think it could be a heavy fine, but of course I cannot rule out entirely the prospect of a short prison sentence."

"Fuck me," said Surtees.

"Fuck me," added Crip.

"Fuck the both of you," I thought but again didn't say it.

Surtees went away to think about it, saying that he would telephone me the following day to give me his decision. Crip said the same, so I expected a call from both of them.

I finished court at about 12.30 pm but had to be in the Huddersfield Magistrates' Court at 2.00 pm so I took the short cut out of the court by going through the cells where I saw the prisoners eating bangers, beans and mash. I didn't have time to collect a sandwich, but I realized that I had a Mars bar somewhere in the car so that would have to do. As I was leaving the cell area, one of the defendants shouted a request for more bread. The jailer had served 30 years in the force and he had seen and heard it all. He shouted his reply as I was leaving, "Certainly Sir, would that be white, brown, wholemeal or pikelet?".

"Fucking bread is what I asked for, fucking bread is what I want."

"Would you like a glass of Château Neuf du Pape as well, or perhaps a glass of Chambertin, or would a simple Chianti Classico do," said the jailer sarcastically.

"I want some fucking bread," said the angry inmate.

The jailer looked round to see who was about before giving the occupant of the cell short shrift.

"You can't have any fucking bread, there is no fucking bread left in this fucking cell area for fucking you or any fucking one else. You can have a fucking biscuit if you want, otherwise fuck off."

The lad in the cell could not deal with the jailer's sparkling repartee so he just kicked the door. As the jailer let me out and was locking the door behind me, I heard him say, "He's off the pudding list."

It was certainly an education to see the old cell area of Rotherham, where there was definitely no place for manners and tact. As I wandered off to the car park, I couldn't help wondering why I had spent so many years learning the trade. I had taken difficult examinations and worked as an articled clerk for next to nothing to be able to qualify as a solicitor. Perhaps it was the charming after-dinner banter in the cell area that I found so attractive.

When I got to the car, I found that I had already eaten the Mars bar. The only thing left was half of a ham and tomato sandwich from the day before, which I had left sitting unhappily in a torn sandwich bag on the back seat. The warm sun had permeated through the windscreen and toasted the bread until it resembled a Baghdad carpet salesman's slipper.

I still tackled a bit of the bread and all of the ham, but the tomatoes were definitely past their best.

I arrived at Huddersfield at 1.45 pm with sufficient time to pick up and eat a Mars bar en route to the court. I was representing a schoolmaster who had been caught misbehaving in the boys toilets. It was a particularly unpleasant case, but no more so than for the teacher himself who faced ruin if he was convicted. He had denied the offence and had suggested that boys had got together and told a false story because they hated him for having rebuked them, on many occasions, for bad behaviour.

He had chosen to remain in the magistrates' court as opposed to elect trial before a jury, because of the expense that a jury trial would incur.

The difference between a summary trial in the magistrates' and a trial at the crown court is that in the magistrates' court you are tried by three lay magistrates or one qualified stipendiary magistrate. In the crown court it is a jury of twelve ordinary people who decide guilt or innocence and it is often said that you have a better chance at the crown court if you are pleading not guilty.

The general feeling against the magistrates' court is that they have heard the same old story so many times that they would be more inclined to find someone guilty than to acquit him. Generally speaking, I would say that magistrates get it right. Juries on the other hand are more likely to convict the more serious the offence.

My teacher client decided to stay before the magistrates and the case was adjourned to a date three months later for the court to decide upon his guilt or innocence. As I look back on the matter now, that three months' period before his case was heard, must have been the most difficult and arduous time of his life.

When I got back to Rotherham, I found that I had two appointments. One was a lady who had not paid some fines and was frightened about going to prison and the other, the old gentleman who had delivered his papers to me the day before. He had made an appointment before I had chance to send my letter to him.

The papers he had pushed through my door the night before told me that Eric Sharpe was 79 years old and had been self-employed as a market trader until he was 75, when he had suffered a slight stroke which left him partly paralysed down his right side.

He had no immediate family and his wife had died of cancer 20 years before.

After his stroke he had become acquainted with Linda Sharpe, who was no relation. She used to visit the patient in the next bed to Eric while he was in hospital and over a three month period they became friends.

Unfortunately, Eric had suffered some impairment mentally and although he was fully able to speak, his mind did not function as well as it did prior to his stroke.

He shuffled into my room, his head slightly bowed which rather highlighted his health problems. He wore an old but smart suit, slightly frayed at the cuffs and a dark kipper type tie, which he had clearly owned for many years. He wore expensive shoes, which were rather worn, but he had all the hallmarks of a man who had known wealth.

Eric's face was heavily lined and his eyes looked tired and bloodshot. His hair was snowy white and generally unkempt and he lowered himself into the leather armchair with a groan.

We spoke for a short time exchanging pleasantries and then he began his story.

"Where shall I start?" he said with an air of depression, "because it's a long story and none too pleasant at that."

"Try the very beginning," I said to reassure him.

"I don't want to waste any of your time Mr Smith," he said, "But if you are prepared to listen, then I will tell you."

"Carry on," I said, "and take your time."

"I believed that Linda was a good girl and I had no reason to doubt it. When she turned up at my house one day after I was released from hospital saying that she had just called to see me as she was in the area. I was glad to see her as I don't get too many visitors and, because I don't go out much, I get quite lonely. She promised that she would visit me at the weekend and so I invited her for tea. I managed a trip to the local supermarket and I prepared a nice meal for us. After that Linda visited me every week, usually on a Sunday, and we would have tea together. One Sunday she broke down in tears but said that she didn't want to talk about it. I insisted, thinking that I might be able to help. She then told me how she had had an affair with a man and they had gone into business together. She had put all her money into the business, but unfortunately it had failed and he ran off leaving her in debt. She told me that she was suicidal but I told her that it was silly to talk that way and found myself telling her that I would help as best I could. She told me that the man had not been paying the rent and consequently she had been evicted.

"Before I realized it, I had told her that she could stay with me while she sorted something out.

"The very next day she moved her belongings in and took over the spare bedroom. She said that she was not in a position to pay any rent because she had no money and she could not claim any benefits, because she had not got sufficient stamps on her card.

"After a month or two I agreed to let her act as my housekeeper, with free bed and board. She agreed but on the understanding that it would only be for a short time. This continued for about six to eight months, during which time she was always courteous, my meals were always ready on time and she was generally excellent company.

"She was out most days looking for work but I looked forward to seeing her come home. I had not been too well and I realized that I was becoming totally dependent upon her, so much so that I was worried that if she was to leave I would not be able to cope on my own and might end up in a home. I didn't want that because I had always enjoyed my privacy and independence."

"Did she ever give you any cause for concern?" I asked earnestly.

"No, not at all, she was the model tenant. She was clean and tidy and indeed she gave the house a considerable facelift. I was quite happy because on the one hand she had security and on the other so did I. It seemed a wonderful arrangement."

"What happened to spoil it?" I asked.

"I had to go back into hospital and when I went home again after about three weeks I was in a rather poor state so I decided that I would ask Linda if she would stay on a permanent basis.

"However she was concerned about her own security because she said that if anything should happen to me she would be out on her ear. I have a daughter, who I see very rarely, who would inherit the house but when I offered to put Linda into my will, she told me that my daughter might challenge it and she would still end up homeless."

"That's not strictly true Mr Sharpe, because your daughter could only challenge such a will if she was financially dependent upon you at the time of your death. Was there any such dependency?" I asked.

"No," said Mr Sharpe. "She has her own business and she has a far better income than me."

"Well in that case, I suspect that Linda was not telling you the truth."

"I realize that now," said Mr Sharpe. "But at the time what could I do?"

"Please go on," I said.

"I came up with the idea that I would put her name on the deeds, so if anything happened to me she would get the house and this would exclude my daughter from it. I realize now that that was silly.

"She told me that there was no need to do that, because she wanted to stand on her own two feet and so she suggested that I help her with a business venture. If I could put some money into the business, she would let me be her silent partner and that way she could maintain her own dignity and look after me at the same time. When she spurned the offer of a half share in the house, I believed she was a woman of integrity who did not want to live on charity. Unfortunately, I have very little money in the bank and so I had nothing to give her as my only asset was my bungalow. She told me not to worry about it and we put the matter to rest for about a week. I trusted her implicitly."

As the old man continued his story I became aware that he was heartbroken. He began to gather his composure as he had become quite upset.

After he had finished a cup of tea, his eyes hardened as he continued his story.

"One day she came in to say that she had the chance of buying a car fitted with hairdressing equipment which would allow her to become a mobile hairdresser. I thought it was an excellent idea as she was already spending a lot of time away from the house on hairdressing appointments.

"She would need £13,000 to buy the van and all the equipment but she had worked out something of a business plan, showing what her earnings would be each week.

"It looked to me like a good idea. She told me that she would arrange a loan and we would both be responsible for it. She insisted that she would make all the repayments out of her profits and I would merely act as guarantor. It meant that I would not have to pay anything out at all, but simply give her this start and the payments would be made and within a fairly short time, the loan would be paid off."

"Did you realize what you were getting into?" I asked sympathetically.

"Not really. I wasn't too well at the time and Linda appeared to know what she was doing when one day a man from a loan company came to the house. He said he wouldn't stay long because he was aware that I was unwell. He produced a large number of papers which Linda said she had seen and checked. I thought that we ought to get the advice of a solicitor, but Linda told me she had seen one who had said that all the papers were in order.

"I remember the day fairly well because I was in an awful lot of pain and I really wanted to go to sleep. I was in bed at the time and I was somewhat embarrassed at having this man, who I had never met before, in my room. I signed the documents."

"What documents were they?"

"I can't remember, but I signed about five times."

"Did you ever receive anything through the post by way of acknowledgement?"

"Well if I did, Linda dealt with it."

"What happened then?" I asked.

"It was Friday and Linda said that she was going to visit a friend over the weekend. She had purchased the van by this time which was a nice vehicle which she took me out to the shops in. I had a bit of difficulty getting in, because it was a large transit van, but she seemed thrilled with it. I should have known that there was something wrong when I asked her where her hairdressing equipment was but she said that she had left it at a client's house. I remember at the time thinking that that was odd.

"She told me that she had paid £6,000 for the van and the other £7,000 was going to be used to pay for the equipment and the remainder would be put towards some premises which she had arranged. We even drove past the shop on one occasion, although we didn't go inside. I now realize that she had never any intention of renting the shop.

"The following week she left to stay with a friend and said that she would be back after a day or so. She never returned and I never received a letter or a telephone call.

"By this time I was quite desperate because I didn't know what had happened to her. Then one morning I was woken by the postman who told me that I had a letter but it required a signature. The postman said that it was a recorded delivery so I signed for the letter and took it inside. It was from the loan company who told me that only one payment had been received and that there were arrears. It was a final demand.

"I was horrified because I had never owed anyone anything and I simply did not know what to do. Then, one night Linda telephoned. She told me that her friend had been taken ill and that she had been looking after her. I immediately told her about the letter but she told me not to worry, saying that she would sort the company out the following week when she returned. I don't know why I believed her, but I did and I simply threw the letter onto the fire as she had told me to.

"The next thing was a bombshell. I received all these court papers. They talked about arrears and failing to pay and lots of court costs saying I had to pay £20,000 by a certain date or else.

"I have not heard from Linda since her call and a lady at the Age Concern place gave me your name and told me that you might be able to help.

"I am so worried, I do not know what to do. Will they take my house off me Mr Smith?"

I felt truly sorry for this man. Life had been extremely hard for him. He had been robbed of his health and his money and now he faced losing his home.

I did not have the heart to tell the old man that I thought that this girl had hatched a rather ingenious plan to rob him but I gave him what assurances I could and told him that I would speak to the courts and adjourn the case if at all possible so that we could apply for legal aid and try to save his home.

The difficulty was that he had signed all the papers and I found one document in particular which he appeared to have signed, confirming that he knew and understood the transaction and if there was any default in payments, the loan company could sue for possession.

As I looked at the documentation, I could see that his writing had got systematically worse. It was the handwriting of an old and feeble man, except for one signature.

This signature was very similar to his own, but it did not have the usual broken flow of print. Because he trembled, and could not keep his hand still, it had the effect of making his signature look as though it had been written in a moving vehicle.

On the photostat copy of the satisfaction note, the signature was in the same style but with the tremble clearly missing.

"Whose is this signature?" I asked.

"It's mine," said Mr Sharpe, "I've signed them all."

"Do you remember signing all the documents?"

"Well I remember signing a lot."

"How many times did you sign?" I asked.

"Four or five," said Mr Sharpe, "but I can't remember exactly."

I handed him the dubious signature and asked him if he recognized whose it was.

"It's mine," he said, "it's my writing."

He clearly had been unable to see the difference in the signatures but when I pointed it out, he took a magnifying glass from his pocket to look at it.

"How long have you used that?" I asked him.

"Ever since I lost my glasses," he said. " I never bothered to replace them."

"When did you lose them?" I asked.

"I can't remember," he said, "but it was some time ago."

As we finished our meeting, I couldn't help thinking that Mr Sharpe was the victim of a very cleverly thought out scam by an evil calculating woman. Old people can sometimes fall easy prey to the wicked and despite a lifetime's experience they can be naïve and gullible. Courts try to protect these people, particularly in criminal law when such offences are usually met with long sentences of imprisonment.

The problem in this case was being able to prove that Linda Sharpe had been dishonest and/or acted in a criminal fashion.

I anticipated that she would say that she acted with Mr Sharpe's full agreement and consequently she had not done anything criminally wrong. Nevertheless, it was my opinion that any civil court would have sympathy with this man and I was resolved to have her brought into the proceedings as a second defendant. The trouble was finding her.

The hearing was only a week away and I had no hesitation in telephoning the local police station to report what had happened in the unlikely event of her admitting her wrongdoing.

In the meantime I wrote a long and detailed letter to the loan company, suggesting in no uncertain terms that Mr Sharpe had been duped. I asked for an explanation to persuade me against the view that their representative had been involved. I also asked what commission had been handed over to the person who had "clinched the deal" for them.

On the morning of the hearing, I travelled to the county court, but fortunately the matter was before a Registrar in Chambers. This means that you appear in an office with the Registrar sitting at a table. It is fairly informal and consequently you are not required to wear robes. If you are in open court in the county, court robes have to be worn.

The loan company's representative had demanded an order for possession, but we had prepared an affidavit for Mr Sharpe stating our case and the Registrar was quite justifiably perturbed. Consequently he adjourned the matter to enable us to apply for legal aid and file a full defence.

Throughout the hearing, Mr Sharpe did not utter a word, but sat with his head slightly bowed. It would be fair to say that the experience terrified him.

He was an old man who had never been into a court before, and the thought of losing his house only increased his torment.

Over the next three weeks we applied successfully for legal aid, sought the advice of Counsel and filed a full defence in the court, alleging misrepresentation and also joining Linda Sharpe into the proceedings.

The press got wind of the story and one morning shortly after the hearing, I was confronted by newspaper and television representatives asking for information. Apparently they had been to see Mr Sharpe and he had given them an interview.

He was mentioned in a local news programme and many people who watched it had an enormous amount of sympathy for him.

On the following day I received a telephone call from an unnamed person who had seen the programme and knew where Linda Sharpe was living. The caller was more than delighted to give me the information and I was able to have the court papers served. The next day I received a very irate phone call from a woman giving her name as Linda Sharpe. She had taken great exception to the television programme because it had "blackened her name".

"I think you're a twat," she said confidently.

"Many people do, but I have to live with it," I replied and promptly put the telephone down.

"Peculiar woman," I thought to myself. "I will remember this conversation when we meet again but it will be on my territory and not yours."

Chapter Seven

I DRESS UP AND THE OAP GETS
HIS OWN BACK

The barrister thought that we had something of a case and so I had all the papers typed and the next morning they were filed before the court.

I telephoned Eric to give him the news and he told me that Linda Sharpe had rung saying that she wished to meet him. I advised him against it because I believed that this woman was up to no good and not only that, she had already had the audacity to question my parentage. I finished my day at 5.40 pm and changed for the 6 pm football match.

Wilford was waiting for his lift and offered me a glass of Canadian Club which I declined on the basis that sportsmen did not drink before a match. Wilford pointed out that I was not a sportsman and agreeing with him I took the drink and we set off for the game.

It was a nasty affair against a team of lads from the local abattoir. They were certainly used to butchery, but that night we had Lidster in our ranks and we were more than a match for them. The game ended in a draw and after showers everyone went through to the bar. I was very lucky to be given the Man of the Match award, which was an egg dripping bread cake and a pint of draught Guinness. I had just about consumed both when Jarvis arrived wearing his best suit and accompanied by a distinguished looking stranger. I was dressed rather casually and because I had forgotten a change of shoes I was wearing the football boots that I had played in. Therefore I was not the height of sartorial elegance.

I was introduced to Jarvis's acquaintance, whose name I can no longer recall, except to say that it rhymed with dip stick which I thought at the time was most unfortunate. It is always said that first impressions do count and they certainly did on this occasion. As Jarvis introduced us, I was holding my pint of Guinness and carrying one for Lidster with the remnants of a sandwich in my mouth. Jarvis took one of the pints while I shook hands with the newcomer. He surveyed me from head to toe as clients often do on the first meeting to see what sort of person they are going to entrust their case.

I could see from his eyes that he was not impressed and when Jarvis explained to me that Mr Dip Stick was a Methodist lay preacher, I could understand his concern.

When we arrived at James Lidster's place, Jarvis ordered the drinks explaining to me in a rather forceful tone that Mr Dip Stick did not drink. I told him later that I wished he had mentioned it before I had asked for a pint of Guinness and a gin and tonic. Nevertheless, I was resolved to watch my 'P's and 'Q's as far as alcohol was concerned.

One of the problems of playing football when you are not incredibly fit is that a ninety minute match can really take it out of you. The worst thing to do straight after a match is drink beer as the alcohol tends to get into the system a little more quickly then would normally be the case and of course on this occasion my resistance was extremely low. By the time we started our meal, I had managed four pints of Guinness and a gin and tonic and had already begun to feel the effects. I knew that a pint of orange or lemonade straight after the match would have been much better for me.

The potential client's problem was one of a boundary dispute where his Chapel grounds joined those of a local Mosque. The argument was about the position of the boundary fence.

Boundary disputes are not really my forte as Wilford was the expert in that field. However, I did not wish to embarrass Jarvis who had been kind enough to recommend us to deal with the work and so I did the best I could before suggesting a full meeting with Wilf. Our Methodist friend was a very personable and reasonable chap apart from being abstemious but by the time we got to the main course, I had thrown all caution to the wind and, as Jarvis was paying, ordered another bottle of wine.

Jarvis and I were having a whale of a time, very much to the amusement of Mr Dip Stick who was becoming rather unsettled at entrusting the only civil action he would ever be involved in to a badly dressed, dehydrated solicitor wearing football boots.

When we got to the cheese and biscuits, Jarvis and I were exchanging Catholic jokes and I am ashamed to say that my speech was slurred and I kept referring to my new client as Mr Dip Stick.

At about 11.30 pm he excused himself and left agreeing that we would have a meeting with Wilf the following morning.

The next day I felt slightly under the weather and when I got to the office I rang Jarvis to check whether my behaviour had been acceptable as I thought I might have offended the client and lost the work.

When I spoke to Jarvis, his first words were,

"Oh dear, oh dear."

"Oh no," I thought to myself "What have I done."

Jarvis, in his customary way was simply winding me up and frightening me unnecessarily. It seemed that our guest had thoroughly enjoyed his evening and had stored up all the Catholic jokes to tell at one of his committee meetings. In the event, the advice which I had given to him proved not only to be sensible, but avoided a very expensive court case.

Within a fortnight, the problem was resolved by correspondence on a most amicable basis and Mr Dip Stick was delighted with us; so much so that the following week a gift appeared on our reception desk. It was a bottle beautifully wrapped with a blue bow. I thought it was an extremely nice gesture and I love to receive bottled gifts.

However, I was not as impressed when I opened it finding that I had acquired a bottle of Dip Stick's home-made lime cordial. To this very day the bottle gathers dust at the bottom of one of my filing cabinets.

We had been soldiering on with Eric Sharpe's case for some months with exchanges of court papers and correspondence with the loan company's solicitors. Linda Sharpe had instructed her own solicitor and my correspondence file had become three inches thick. As the hearing date drew nearer, we had briefed counsel to attend and represent our interests. I was going to attend as well, but counsel was to do the speaking part as I am never too confident appearing in the County Court. Also I always have difficulty with the detachable wing collars and inevitably when I am in a rush I can never fasten them properly and I lose my temper and end up with a pile of torn collars in the wastepaper basket.

The hearing had been fixed for the following month, but we were not sure which day the case was to be heard. This is something of a lottery, because you cannot guarantee that your barrister will be available at the drop of a hat to deal with the case. Cases can be fixed for weeks in advance and these are called "Fixtures". I had tried to arrange Eric's case as a fixture but it had not proved possible. The night before the case was heard, the barrister's clerk rang me to say that my counsel was not available to deal with the case the following morning and unfortunately no other counsel was available in the area to deal with it. This couldn't have been worse news. He suggested that we try to adjourn the case for a few days, but unfortunately this was not possible since the court would not consider our convenience and so I was left with two choices. The first was to commit suicide and the alternative was to deal with the case myself. The first option did not appeal to me for I was only thirty two and had a wife and a child to support, but the second seemed only a little better.

I telephoned Eric to tell him that the barrister would not be available and that I would have to do the case but he gave me great confidence by saying that he preferred me to do it anyway.

I told Wilford that I had to appear in the County Court and he simply laughed, banged on the toilet door and asked Oscar for the best bet for the 2.30 pm at Beverley.

I do not wish to give the impression that all Wilford did was drink, play the space invader and back horses, because that would not be true or fair. He drank, played the space invader, backed horses and dealt with the probate and conveyancing.

I was already beginning to spend the majority of my time fighting criminal cases but the County Court was a different thing altogether. I began to feel that dull ache in the pit of my stomach that tells you that all is not well. I read the papers over and over again and when it got to 3.00 am I thought it was time to turn in but unfortunately, I couldn't sleep because I couldn't stop worrying about the case.

As I watched day break, I thought it was time to get up and read the papers again.

By the time I left home I knew the script, word for word. However, when I arrived at the court building I suffered a sharp intake of breath when I saw that the television cameras were already there.

Eric had arrived with a large number of wellwishers from the locality so I realized that the courtroom would be absolutely packed. This also increased the pressure upon me.

I took Eric into an interview room and asked him how he was.

"I've got butterflies in my stomach," he said pathetically.

"I've got giant bats in mine," I said even more pathetically.

"Ey but you come 'ere every day. You're only kidding me," said Eric.

"Of course I am Eric, don't worry you're in safe hands." Saying this, I reached for my papers which were difficult to collect because all my fingers were crossed.

There was a knock on the interview room door and a rather large Barrister appeared in the doorway. I had not met this chap before but I had been told that he had travelled from London to deal with the case. He was a senior barrister which was obvious from the state of his robe and the colour of his wig. My eyes nearly popped out of my head when I saw that he was carrying about nine law books. He asked to speak to me about the case, so we went into a side room.

"You have absolutely no chance at all with this defence I hope you know that" said the Rumpolian character.

His general attitude offended me and I was in no mood to be bullied.

"If I thought that, I wouldn't be here would I?" I replied.

Rumpole continued, "If you chuck your hand in now we will not ask for costs".

"I am legally aided," I said, "That's the least of my concerns."

"Are you calling any witnesses?" said Rumpole.

"Only the Defendant," I said.

The barrister laughed smugly and went about his business.

"See you in court," I thought to myself. You have to have confidence in cases like this, so why didn't I have any? I looked at Eric and could see that he was relying upon me completely and so I took a deep breath and marched into court. The press were occupying a full row and the public gallery was almost packed. Rumpole came in and sat on the Advocate Bench, opposite me. He looked across and I smiled, I noticed that his gown was well worn and bore all the hallmarks of being owned by a man who knew his business. I looked down at my gown which was pristine and had all the hallmarks of an owner who had never worn it.

The judge came into court. He was known for being a stickler for everything and that did not make me feel any better.

The first case was called on and this involved two solicitors. The judge announced that he had read the papers and found a number of faults, listing them in numerical order. I lost count after number 11. The solicitor to whom he had referred trembled with fear. His gown looked as new as mine and I couldn't help but have a great deal of sympathy for him.

The way that standards are kept up in court, is for advocates to know that if they have done something wrong or they fall below the standard required they will be brought to book. I have no real objection to that but it can be daunting at times.

My colleague was being subjected to a grade three bollocking. I could see the pain etched across his face, almost as if emblazoned with a neon sign saying, "Why me," and another on his back saying, "I have just found a complete cure for constipation."

He had my very considerable sympathy, as I watched beads of sweat trickle down his temples onto the wing collar of his shirt.

At the end of his case, he hobbled out of court for his blood transfusion and I sat upright as I heard the clerk shout the case of Sharpe and Sharpe. I took a deep breath and attempted to look learned.

Rumpole rose to his feet and gave a brief summary of the case and the Judge peered at him over the top of his horn-rimmed spectacles and asked, "Is this matter agreed?"

"I'm afraid not your Honour," said Rumpole, turning his head to stare at me as though it was my fault.

"How long is this case going to last?" said the judge.

Rumpole rose to his feet again, "Four hours your Honour," he said confidently.

"Four hours," shouted the Judge, "Have you seen the state of this list?"

He then looked at me for my input. I coughed to clear my throat but before I could say "Your Honour" the judge, fumbling in his papers to find my name, was saying,

"Mr er, Mr er...."

"Smith your Honour," I replied.

"It's what?" said the judge.

"My name is Smith your Honour, I act on behalf of Mr Eric Sharpe."

"I know that," said the judge, "I was asking you how long the case was going to last."

Seizing my opportunity to score points I said,

"I believe this matter could be dealt with in two hours your Honour".

This appeared to please the learned judge and he nodded and said, "Quite so, quite so, proceed to call the evidence."

I turned round to look at Eric as if to say, "round one to us," but he was looking out of the window and appeared to have missed it.

The evidence was called and the representative of the loan company came into court to explain his part in the case.

He gave his evidence very clearly and concisely with the air of a man who had given evidence many times before. It was all too exact for my liking.

He explained how he had been approached by Mr. Sharpe and asked for a loan. He went on to confirm that he had been to the house and interviewed him and that Mr Sharpe had signed all the documentation and fully understood the implications thereof. He mentioned that Linda Sharpe was also present although he was quite satisfied that the transaction involved only Eric.

Eric tapped me on the shoulder and I turned to see what he wanted. He just whispered the words,

"It's looking pretty bad isn't it?" to which I simply replied,

"We have not had our turn yet."

The judge said "Yes Mr. Smith?" and I got up to cross-examine.

"Did you have any contact with Linda Sharpe at all?" I asked.

"No" came the reply,

"But she was present when you made your visit to the house,"

"Yes" he replied.

"Are you telling me that she didn't have any part in the conversation at all?"

The witness paused for a short time before answering and he was clearly working out what to say. The judge noted the delay and watched the witness as he chose his words carefully.

"She may well have said something but I do not remember it."

I then checked my papers and found the signature E. Sharpe on the document to which I wanted to refer.

"Will you look at this document and tell me what the signature says?"

"Something Sharpe" he replied.

"No, it's not something. It is an E. Isn't this the note that Linda

Sharpe signed at the house saying that she understood what the loan was?"

"I don't recall that" he replied.

"You don't recall that but that's what I have to suggest."

"I dealt with Mr. Eric Sharpe," said the man.

"What was the loan for?" I asked.

"I've no idea," said the witness.

"You mean to tell me that you arranged a loan for £13,000 but you don't know what it was for?"

"No, it was not our business to enquire."

"I've never worked for a loan company but I would have thought that even if it was not relevant you would have at least expressed some interest."

"No," came the reply quite firmly.

"Let me see if I can remind you, it was for Miss Sharpe to buy a motor vehicle and set herself up in business wasn't it?"

"Mr Sharpe signed the contract so as far as I was concerned the loan was for him, what he did with the money was his affair."

"What was Mr. Sharpe's condition on the day that he signed the documents?" I asked.

"He was very well, quite chirpy in fact. He was talking about going on holiday to the coast somewhere," he said confidently.

"How is it that you can remember that in such detail and you can't remember any conversation with Linda Sharpe?"

"It was just one of those things," he said with a swagger. "You can remember some things and not others."

He was rather sarcastic in his remarks and I decided to let him continue because I believed that he was not impressing the Judge with his off-hand manner.

"Did Mr. Sharpe appear to be ill?" I asked,

"No I don't think so," said the man. "It is not my habit to deal with important business matters with people who are ill and not able to understand what is going on."

With that the judge interjected, "Would you just answer the question please and keep your comments and opinions to yourself."

I decided to continue the 'softly, softly' approach because as far as I was concerned the witness was damaging his own case.

"Did you know that shortly before this transaction Mr. Sharpe had had a stroke which left him dependent upon medication?"

"No I didn't but then that's nothing to do with me."

"No it's nothing to do with you. I suppose so long as you get your signature you wouldn't be bothered about the state of your client would you?"

The man didn't answer so I continued, "Did you know that Mr. Sharpe had to take very strong medication which has the effect of making him drowsy and slow to comprehend things going on around him?"

"No," said the man.

"So you didn't find that he exhibited any of these problems?"

"No certainly not," said the man.

"Would you have been bothered?" I said.

"Well, not really. It's not a matter for me. He seemed to be all right."

"Can you explain to me why you went back the following day?" I asked.

"I don't recall that I went back," said the man.

"Well let me see if I can remind you," I said. "You went back the following day because Mr. Sharpe had not signed the Satisfaction Note. He was in bed and ill and couldn't sign, that's when you asked Linda Sharpe to sign the form on his behalf isn't it?"

"No," replied the man.

"How long had you been doing the job at that time?"

"Six weeks," said the man.

"So wouldn't it be possible that you didn't fully understand all the systems yourself?"

"I understand them perfectly."

"Did you deliver the cheque yourself?"

"Yes," said the man.

"What sort of reception did you get?" I asked,

"He was absolutely delighted," he replied.

"Are you sure about that," I queried.

"Definitely he was like a kid with a new toy."

"And yet you do not know what the money was for?"

"Not really," said the man.

"What date was it when you delivered the cheque?"

"The 9th August," said the man.

"Are you absolutely certain about that?"

"Yes of course I have it here in my work log."

"And you gave the cheque to Mr. Sharpe?"

"Yes certainly."

"I put it to you that Mr. Sharpe was not present and you gave the cheque to Linda Sharpe."

There was another pause as the witness began to gather his thoughts. I could see he was wondering what I was getting at. It would have been the easiest thing in the world to admit it because the cheque was in Eric's name but the witness suspected that there would have been something wrong in that and so he continued to deny it.

"And there would be absolutely no doubt that you gave that cheque to Eric Sharpe in person?"

"Yes," said the man.

I handed the witness a letter from the Rotherham hospital which explained that not only on the 9th August but for two days prior and days afterwards, Eric was an in-patient at the Rotherham District General Hospital.

Sweat started to appear on the witness's brow and he asked for a glass of water. The judge interjected again, "Well what do you say about that?"

The witness remained silent and the Judge took over the reins,

"Pass me that log that you have been referring to" said the Judge. I handed over the log and the judge looked at it.

"You have got that date in this book and it appears that you obtained a receipt is that right?"

"I don't know" said the man.

"Well," said the judge "you have actually got a signature in this book as accepting the cheque."

The judge passed me the book to look at and I compared the signatures with another signature on the documents. I recalled that there was one signature in the documents which was written without the 'tremble'.

It was interesting that the receipt for the cheque was the same style of handwriting as the signature without the tremble.

I looked back in the book and found an earlier signature following the representatives first visit to Eric's house and that signature displayed the tremble.

"What point are you making in relation to the signature Mr.

Smith?" asked the judge. I explained about the style of the handwriting and while it looked the same, there was a distinctive difference by virtue of the said 'tremble'.

"Please continue," said the judge.

"Eric Sharpe didn't sign these two papers did he?" I asked.

By this time the witness realized that he had been rumbled, but instead of sticking to his guns and referring only to the loan documents and the satisfaction note, he tried to argue his way out of it.

"You must have been at Mr. Sharpe's home on that date, otherwise how could you have got the signature? You got the signature from Linda Sharpe," I said.

"I'm no expert, but if you look at the signature 'E. Sharpe' which I say she made and the signature 'E. Sharpe' which I say he made, you will see the difference."

The judge was unhappy at going into areas of styles of handwriting because he thought that was a matter for an expert, but he seized upon the differences in Eric's signatures and asked a number of pointed questions of the witness before asking me to continue.

"Eric Sharpe did not sign the Satisfaction Note which said that he understood what was involved in signing the loan and I also submit to you that Eric Sharpe did not know when he signed the other documents that if there was default in payments, his house would be repossessed. That's true isn't it and by the way would you please remember that you are on oath."

I noticed that throughout my cross-examination Rumpole had not interfered and indeed if he had, I think that the judge would have stopped him, but I think he too realized that there was something amiss.

The judge decided to retire so that he could look at the signatures and check the various books and I breathed a sigh of relief. At the conclusion of my cross-examination, Rumpole completed his case and the judge announced that he wished to hear from Eric. Accordingly I called him into the witness box and he gave a full account of his story, apologizing as he went on for taking his time over the answer. The judge was very sympathetic and I took the view that he believed what Eric was saying.

Before Rumpole could start his cross-examination, the judge asked Eric, "Is it true that you knew that you were signing for a loan?"

"Yes," said Eric, "I knew perfectly well."

"Did you know when you were signing the documents what the implications were?"

"I didn't know that if Linda didn't pay I would lose my house. It is all I have got, I cannot work any more and I only have my pension, I simply wouldn't risk my home."

"No," said the judge, "I appreciate that. Yes, thank you, I have no further questions."

Rumpole cross-examined Eric who at one point became extremely confused, getting rather mixed up with his answers.

"You appear to be rather confused Mr. Sharpe," said Rumpole.

"It's not surprising," interjected the judge, "your questions have confused me as well. Isn't it the case, that Mr. Sharpe was confused about the loan as well?"

"No," said Rumpole, "We do not accept that contention, but of course it is a matter for your Honour to decide where the truth lies."

"Quite so," said the judge, "Have you any further questions?" giving the clear impression that he had heard enough of the cross-examination.

"No your Honour," said Rumpole and he took his seat.

The judge was busily writing something and so I waited until he was ready. He put his pen down and took his glasses off and looked directly at me and said, "I would now like the various parties to address me in the matter."

We all gave our respective accounts, but the judge cut mine short saying that there were certain points which he did not require me to deal with.

He then retired for a short time to consider the matter and Eric and I went to the WRVS canteen. I was still wearing my gown, winged collar and tabs, which delighted the criminal fraternity who were waiting to go into the magistrates' court in the same building.

Jack was there and commented on how smart I looked in my 'Black frock', but before we could drink our tea the court usher called us back into the court room.

While I was confident as to the result, it did not stop the bats from flying round in my stomach.

The judge summed up the case carefully and it appeared as if there was a swingometer at his side while he was speaking. I had visions of the Court Usher pushing the swingometer towards us when we had a good point and then away from us when the other side countered it. Towards the end of his address, the swingometer had crossed into the loan company's territory but then he told us that he did not accept that Eric Sharpe knew the implications of what he had signed and accordingly he found that there had been a misrepresentation. His decision would therefore go in favour of the first defendant. I took a deep breath and stood and thanked the Judge and formally asked for an order for costs.

"Granted," he said. "Are there any other applications?"

No one spoke and with that the judge announced that he would retire before calling the next case.

There were some cheers from the back of the court and a round of applause. I turned to look at Eric, who had not understood a word of it.

"What's happened?" he said, "have I kept my house or what?"

"I am delighted to tell you Mr. Sharpe that not only have you kept your house, but you have won your case."

"What about the money I owe the loan company?" he said.

"That's their problem and they must resolve it with Miss. Sharpe."

Rumpole then joined us and insisted that his clients were a very reputable loan company and if their employee was at fault, in any way, they would deal with him accordingly. He tried to assure us that they did not want any member of the public, particularly an old gentleman to lose out in those circumstances. Therefore he confirmed that he would advise that they should not press Eric for any money at all, but Linda Sharpe, on the other hand, was a different matter.

When I left the advocates' room, I couldn't see Eric anywhere. The usher told me that he had gone outside where I found him on a wooden bench near the court with his head in his hands. He was in tears.

"I can't believe that it's over," he said, "I never want to go into a court again."

With that my winged collar shot out unceremoniously at the side and we both laughed.

"Here's a fiver," said Eric, "buy yourself some new collars."

One of Eric's friends came forward and shook hands with him

vigorously before leading him off to the car and back home.

That night Eric would sleep well in the knowledge that for the first time for many months the threat of being homeless had finally gone away.

As I walked to the advocates' room, I looked a peculiar sight with my wing collar stuck out at a funny angle. One of the other Solicitors came in and said, "Good morning Smithy, I didn't know that you appeared in the county court?"

"I don't," I said smugly.

"No I think that was obvious from the way that you dealt with that case," said the solicitor equally as smugly.

"Sod off, can't you see I'm under stress. But I have found the ultimate cure for constipation."

"Oh, what's that?" said the solicitor.

"I'll tell you another day, but just now I've got to pay a call."

"Too much red wine last night is it?" asked the solicitor.

"No," I replied, "I've just got to take the cork out."

"Take the cork out?" said the solicitor.

"Oh never mind," I said, "it's been a long day," and with that I left to see what appointments were waiting for me.

As I walked past the court room, I could see other advocates in heated discussions about their cases. There were expressions of disappointment and signs of complete joy. It is always a tremendous feeling to win a case, particularly when you believe in it and I liked to think that in Eric's case I had struck a blow for the little man. It was pleasing to see how 'Joe Public' could take on the big guns and beat them. In many ways, it was no marvellous discovery or magnificent effort on my part, it was a simple case of an unscrupulous loan 'shark' in pursuit of his commission payment at any price. In his greed, he obtained the forged signature and indeed if it had been Eric's signature the result might have been very different.

This case underlined my faith in our system. After all I was an idealist, doing a job that I liked and fortunately we had a Legal Aid system which although not perfect, was certainly better than anywhere else in the world. It gave 'Joe Public' a more equal chance than would have been the case had it not been available.

Over the next few years, I was to see an erosion of that right, where the possibilities of injustice were to become more of a reality with a legal aid system that was to fall into decay.

When I got back to the office, I looked around and saw that the staff rooms were full. We had three girls crammed behind the counter, three other people sharing a room more suited for two and Wilford and I were also having to share because of the overcrowding.

"I think it's time we moved on," I said to Wilf.

"I think you're right," said Wilf, "this place is simply too small."

With that I heard the familiar sound of the trombone and added, "It doesn't really give the best impression does it?"

"No," said Wilford.

Our thoughts were interrupted by some swearing from the toilet as I heard the words 'Bastard' and 'Ballcock' emanating from a much aggrieved Oscar.

Approximately one month later I opened the office door to find Eric Sharpe standing there completely out of breath.

He had a heavy shopping bag which I held for him while I ushered him into my room. He was extremely excited and gabbled out his story.

We sat him down and he handed me a letter. It was from the loan company which said, amongst other things.......'In all the circumstances of this case, we do not propose to seek any repayment from you in respect of this loan. We hope that this action will go some way to compensate you for what's happened.'

"Well done Eric," I said, and Wilf agreed.

With that Eric pulled out a bottle of champagne from his bag. Wilf fetched three containers; two glasses and one broken cup. We went through the charade of tossing a coin to see who got the cup.

"Heads," I shouted, and I lost.

I raised the broken cup to Eric's good fortune.

"Steve," said Eric, "I will never be able to repay you for what you have done for me, so I would like you to accept this little gift."

"I am not supposed to accept gratuities," I said.

"Oh well I am sure that you will accept this from one friend to another," and he handed me a nicely wrapped object. I opened it to find an expensive Waterman pen.

"I love pens Eric," I said.

"Yes I know," said Eric, "I have noticed you using a different pen every time I see you."

"It's a wonderful thought," I said to him when we shook hands.

"Whenever you use that pen," said Eric, "you will remember my case."

"I certainly will Eric, thank you again."

Eric drank his glass of champagne and then made his apologies as he had a pressing engagement.

"Are you going anywhere nice?" I asked him.

"Yes," said Eric, "I'm going out to lunch. The widow next door but one has asked me round for a meal."

"Oh yes, well make sure you behave yourself."

"Not likely," said Eric, "I'm 80 and with what time I have got left I am going to live a life to the full."

"Well best of luck then old fellow," I said as we shook hands again and Eric turned to leave.

"You want to get an office with a ground floor," he said. "Walking up and down these stairs is enough to kill me."

"That's a good idea Eric," I said. "In fact we are already thinking about it."

"Very well," said Eric. "Don't forget to let me know if you move."

As he left, he turned and winked and gave me the thumbs up sign. I filled my new pen with ink and tried it out. I still use it to this very day.

The last I heard of Eric was that he was happily married to his widow friend. They sold their respective bungalows and bought a beautiful ground floor flat in a complex specially built for old people. It has a warden and all the facilities they need. They have kept their independence and also have the benefit of a warden service.

Remarkably, Eric's health had improved enormously with the result that he was able to get about and enjoy life a lot more. Shortly after the house warming to which we were invited, I received a postcard from Barbados which read quite simply,

'Having a marvellous time - suggest you visit this beautiful island, but avoid limbo dancing like the black death - yours Eric and Violet - Thanks again.'

Chapter Eight
ALBERT STRIKES AGAIN

"The courthouse on line one," said a harassed Tracy in reception,
"Put them through," I replied still keen to create the right impression.

"You've got two this morning Steve," said the gaoler. "One is McIver and the other someone called Cusack."

"What have they done?" I asked expectantly.

"McIver - minor theft," said the gaoler rustling his papers, "and Cusack......... looks like drugs........ yes drugs, possession and supply.....a pleasant little mix for your delectation," said the cheerful gaoler.

"I'll be down by 9.30 am," I said, "I want a good clean start today."

"Always willing to oblige," said the gaoler, "our wish is your complete satisfaction."

"Well lend us a fiver," I replied and with that the telephone went dead.

I left the office with a spring in my step. I liked the idea of being self-employed, it really suited me.

"Morning Oscar," I shouted at the toilet door.

"Morning Steve, Kelso's Lad, Doncaster 4.30 has a fair chance but not much more. I'm having a fiver on it."

"A fiver? Do you think that is wise?

You know me I only like to bet on certs."

With that I became aware of a conveyancing client who was watching me having a conversation with a toilet door.

The client watched me as I walked down the stairs, only looking away when he heard what sounded like trombone sounds coming from the toilet.

When I arrived at the court, I banged on the large green door which led to the cell area. A makeshift sign had been placed on the door saying "Tradesman's Entrance". Some wags had scrawled 'Gents' underneath. Weeds had grown rather irreverently around the path leading to the entrance concealing a well-planted rose garden which was supposed to placate the inmate's visitors while they waited to go in. You would often see visitors picking the roses and placing them in their hair over their ears. Women, on the other hand, rarely bothered.

My first client was Michael Wellington McIver who was facing three charges of shoplifting. He had been released from his cell and was walking into the interview room opposite the cells looking rather downcast. He looked a poorly nourished youth with all the hallmarks of diabetes and chronic piles. He had short mousey hair, spots and an abundance of gums which dominated his large mouth. He was distinguished, however by the most appalling tattoos which covered his entire face. His forehead bore the words 'FORD CORTINA MARK IV' which was a favourite vehicle for local villains. The large tattoo which dominated his face was of a spider which was hidden in an even larger web which extended from his cheeks to his neck. There were small spiders around his chin completing a family portrait gallery.

"Sit down young man," I said trying to make him feel at home. "What can I do for you?" I asked without suggesting a plastic surgeon.

"I'm in bother," said the youth.

"Yes I believe so," I replied, "that's why you are in here. Let me get some details from you before we go any further. What is your full name?"

"Michael Wellington McIver, The Children's Home, Wilson Road, Rotherham" replied the youth.

"And how do your friends refer to you? " I asked.

"Tha what" said the youth missing the point of the question.

"What do your friends call you?" I asked.

"Spider," shouted the disfigured youth almost triumphantly.

"And why do they call you that?" I asked trying to break the ice with a joke.

"Because I have spiders tattooed on my face," said the youth again missing the point entirely.

"Very well," I said, " I will also call you Spider. Let me see your charge sheets."

He reached into his jeans pocket and pulled out four pink sheets. They were stained with gravy from the police issue mince and onion pie served up the night before in the police canteen.

I picked up the papers as if they had contracted a highly contagious virus. There were three charges and a bail sheet.

"Why are you in custody?" I asked "These are not the most serious offences in the world."

"I've not paid my fines so there's a warrant out for me. I'm hoping you can get me out."

I realized that Spider was not really a bad lad. He was certainly misguided but without malice and I actually felt sorry for him as looking at the state of his face he must have been the brunt of every wit and wag in Rotherham.

The cells, ten feet by eight feet with stone walls were early Victorian and in over 150 years of use I don't think that they had changed at all. There was a wooden bed which dominated the floor; and in a corner was one of the oldest wc's I have ever seen covered in graffiti among which was scrawled "Crippen crapped here". This toilet was even older than the office bog but in this case the flush didn't work at all so I couldn't tell if there was a ballcock or not! There were five cells in all. Cell 1 with the offending toilet was reserved for awkward prisoners. After two or three hours in there only the most obstinate or those with no sense of smell continued their recalcitrance. In summer the cells were cold and in winter they were freezing and only when they were full did the temperature increase and when it did they became like black holes of Calcutta. You only needed one prisoner with gastro-enteritis to add that certain ambience reserved for only the finest of torture chambers. It was hard to believe that they were still being used in the 1980's, and I wondered what the Home Secretary would have thought of this hole from Hell.

Just then the gaoler reappeared.

"Have you a minute Steve," he asked, "there's a phone call for you."

I excused myself, and went out into the main cell area. It is always annoying to get calls when you are in the cells. You have to break off and run the risk of someone nicking your interview room. There were only two available and if they were occupied, you had to use one of the cells and sit with your note book and legal aid forms perched rather precariously in your lap.

I was irritated to get the call and I think it showed in my tone to the caller.

"Yes," I demanded, "What is it?"

"Steve, is that you Steve?" he said "Steve Smith, solicitor?"

"Yes, I think so, let me just check, " I said sarcastically. "Yes I think it's me, but then who else could it be, General Jaruzelski, President Anwar Sadat or John DeLorean?"

I was interrupted from my outburst.

"Steve, is that you?" said the caller.

"Oh my God," I thought to myself, "WHAT DO YOU WANT?" I shouted slowly and deliberately. The police officers waiting in the cell area were amused at my misfortune,

"It's me – Jack."

My tone altered for Jack was one of my best clients,

"What's up Jack," I asked more sympathetically,

"It's Albert," said Jack, "he's done a runner, buggered off like, disappeared, legged it ......"

"Yes," I interrupted, before Jack treated me to the umpteenth version of "gone".

"E's not locked up is ee?" asked Jack.

"Not down here Jack," I answered, "Have you tried the youth club?"

"Ee's barred tha knows, ee can't go in there any more. Madge is doing her nut."

"OK Jack," I said, "keep looking and I'll meet you here in half an hour and I'll get the car out and we'll look for him."

"All right," said Jack, "I'll paste him when I get 'im."

What a peculiar statement that was. Jack was terrified something had happened to Albert and was desperate to find him only with a view to killing him when he reappeared.

I went back to the interview room to find Spider deep in thought busily picking his nose. He stopped as I entered the room,

"Will I get bail Mr Smith?" asked Spider.

"All being well Spider," I said. "Now sign these legal aid application forms."

Spider hesitated as I passed him a biro. "What's the problem Spider?" I asked.

"Nowt really, its just that....."

"Just what?" I interrupted.

"Tha sees I can't write reight good."

I didn't want to embarrass Spider any more than he already was, so I pointed to the place for his signature and Spider made a cross.

"I'm going to learn proper tha knows," said Spider, "when I get chance that is. Mrs Evans at the 'ome has promised me."

"Very good Spider," I replied. "That's a good idea."

I left the interview room and Spider walked back to Cell 1,

"Does he have to sit in there?" I asked Roy, the gaoler, "can't he go in one of the others?"

"Sure," said Roy, "come on me old cock, Suite 3 for you; in you go."

Spider went inside and the door was closed firmly behind him.

"Next please," I said to the gaoler and with that a young man of about twenty-five years came into view.

He was wearing the latest designer-wear tracksuit, expensive trainers and the obligatory gold medallion. He had blond streaked hair, well manicured finger nails and wore a gold earring. He had an air of arrogance about him that almost shouted as he greeted me. In a mere second or two I had formed an instant dislike to him.

"Gary Cusack," said the young man, who then rather piously handed me his business card.

"Now then Captain," he said, "You have got to get me out of here pronto. I'm sharing a cell with weirdos. Just look at that moron with the tattoos who has just walked in - where is he from? Christ what a wacko. Look, get me bail right and there's a drink in it for you. You look like a lad who likes a drink."

"Really?" "Let me see your charge sheets," I responded with little or no enthusiasm.

"Ripped them up old son," said Cusack, "they offended me so they went to Bogville."

"Who offended you?" I asked. "Anything human?"

"The pigs."

"Who?"

"The filth, the feds ..... Christ don't you know any of the names for the cops?"

"No of course not," I replied "I have only done the job for 17 years I must have missed those names," Cusack was bright enough to recognize sarcasm.

"Hey you're a cool dude," said the flash git. "Come on let's cut the crap and do the business. I want bail, you do your job and everything in the garden will be rosy."

"I need the charge sheets," I said. "Wait there and I'll see if the

97

gaoler has copies."

I left the interview room and went to the gaoler's desk. It housed an old Imperial 60 typewriter with all the e's, o's, p's, b's and d's bunged up with the remnants of rubbings out long past. The walls were decorated with pictures of football teams from the 70's and out of date memo's from a chief constable who had since died. Perhaps these had been left to honour his memory or more likely just left to gather dust. The only up-to-date documentation was the new 1981 Pirelli calendar with each of the preceding months marked out of ten by an avid voyeur. Then there was the sink which was an original, circa 1910, and at the side of the one large brass tap there was a pink plastic cup scarred with teeth marks and lime scale from years of use. The awkward bastards got Cell 1 and that cup.

The gaoler gave me copies of Cusack's charge sheets from the resplendent "out tray" on his desk. The "out tray" was a cardboard box which had housed Lurpak butter in its better days. However, no expense had been spared on the "in tray" which was an empty Andrex toilet roll box which had probably been emptied by people who had used the pink cup!

I read the charge sheets to myself,

1. Possession of cannabis
2. Possession of cannabis with intent to supply
3. Possession of amphetamine sulphate with intent to supply.

"What were the values of the drugs?" I asked the gaoler.

"£2,000 and £5,000 respectively," said the gaoler, "that's weed and speed. Hey that rhymes," said the gaoler triumphantly.

"Pour yourself a drink," I said pointing to the pink cup.

"Bollocks," said the gaoler who then commenced to wear out his index finger on his beloved typewriter.

I returned to the interview room to find Cusack sitting with his feet on the desk, showing off his expensive training shoes.

"Excuse me," I said waiting for Cusack to move his feet.

"OK Captain, stay cool," said Cusack in an attempt at being American.

"Well?" he asked.

"Well what?" I replied.

"What's the shit man?" he continued.

"What's the what?" I asked.

"What's the crack? Am I going to get bail or what?"

"Probably or what," I said. "Bail is not likely as these are very serious offences whether you like it or not."

I took as many details as I could and I was under the distinct impression that Mr Cusack was not well pleased.

"I'll do my best," I said shaking my head.

"Your best better be good enough," said Cusack, beginning to lose a little of his 'cool'.

I didn't reply, but as I was leaving I remembered noticing the sole of one of his trainers.

"By the way," I said, "I think you've stepped in something."

"You what?" shouted Cusack. "Oh fucking hell, what's that?" he said looking at the unwelcome deposit on the underside of his shoe.

"I think the expression is tough shit man," I said triumphantly.

Cusack was deflated and I couldn't conceal a smile.

As I got to the top of the spiral staircase, I bumped into the court sergeant who was having difficulties with his police radio.

"What's up Ted?" I asked.

"Don't know, someone's buggering about with the radio. Hello, hello, court sergeant, courthouse over. Bugger it," said Ted tapping the battery on his radio.

Emerging into the court room I realized that the Lord Chief Justice was sitting. This was the name I had given to the magistrate known to the local solicitors as 'Big Ed.' He was a paranoid schizophrenic who viewed his position as second only to God. He was the scourge of the Rotherham Bench, disliked by court staff and magistrates alike for being the biggest 'know all' in Rotherham. He was to manners and court decorum what Attila the Hun was to Origami. Ted the court sergeant described him as an 'Ignorant pillock'.

He ruled the court with a rod of iron and would not allow talking in court. Solicitors would be rebuked if they didn't bow deeply enough and he could not tolerate defendants no matter what they were charged with. Jack described him as an 'out and out bag of shite.'

He was the worst bench in Rotherham and I had got him that morning.

"Bloody marvellous," I thought, "I'll need a miracle to get bail today and I need my quota to help Jack find Albert."

I walked to the Solicitors' Bench only to find Philip Portman, the hardest of the Rotherham prosecutors prosecuting and big Geoff Clarke, another awkward bugger when that way out, was the clerk. What a hand I had drawn and I could have sworn that they were all related, with same mother but different fathers.

When the Bench retired to consider a case I approached the clerk.

"Yes?" he said sharply.

"Good morning Mr Clarke and how are you this bright sunny morning? How well you look."

"What do you want?" he asked equally as sharply.

"How about putting my case in Court 2?" I asked bluntly.

"Why on earth do you want to go there Mr Smith? It wouldn't be the choice of the Bench would it? Or perhaps it's the prosecutor that you are trying to avoid?" he said sarcastically,

"No," I said, "It's the bloody clerk."

"I beg your pardon?" asked Mr Clarke.

"No", I said, "It's the bloody dark - the light in here gives me migraine."

"You need a brain to get migraine," ventured Portman smugly.

"I didn't ask you for your contribution shit head," I shouted.

"Now, now Mr Smith, if you're looking for favours you will have to watch your tongue," Portman snapped.

"It's unlikely I'll get any favours from you isn't it?" I continued.

Portman smiled as he rubbed his hands together, preparing for battle. It was obvious he was looking forward to his morning's work as he enjoyed helping to lock people up and he actually liked the 'Lord Chief Justice'.

"Two prosecutors today then Philip?" I ventured.

"What do you mean by that?" asked Portman.

"Well there's you and there's him (pointing to the chairman's position on the Bench), you won't have to break sweat today will you?"

"What odious little pieces of waste are you representing today?" he asked.

"Just two, both agreed bail I would have thought," I suggested tongue in cheek.

"Not likely," said Portman, "they are both staying, you'll never

100

get them out, I'll see to that."

To say he was biased was an understatement. The main problem was that he was actually a clever prosecutor and with a Bench like the Lord Chief he knew he was virtually home and dry.

He did have a weakness, however, which was that he did have a tendency to go 'O.T.T.' and when he did, he completely lost his credibility. Therefore, the only chance I had of winning was to wind him up and make him lose his temper. I already had a knack of doing that without really trying. All I had to do was to accuse the police of something dreadful and he would bite because his extremely right wing views would get the better of him and a left wing Bench would react against him. It was certainly worth a try.

Just then Ted's radio started playing up again; he cursed it as he tried to speak to the caller.

"What's that noise?" shouted the Lord Chief.

"I apologize your Worship," said the sergeant, "I'm having a problem with my radio."

"Well turn it off in court," said the Lord Chief.

"I am supposed to leave it on for emergencies," protested the sergeant.

"TURN IT OFF," said the Lord Chief.

"Here comes a complaint from the Police Authority," I thought to myself. It is very easy to make enemies in the law and when you do you have to watch out because the depths to which some people will stoop to "get their own back" never ceases to amaze me.

The clerk to the court spoke quietly to the Lord Chief and at the end of the conversation he scowled at Ted over his horn rimmed spectacles.

"Turn it back on," I said to Ted, "round one is yours."

Ted did so scowling back at the Lord Chief in a repeat performance of his earlier show of rudeness.

"Will you call my first case," said the Lord Chief, much to the annoyance of the other members of the Bench who thought that they should be involved as well.

"If you please Sir," said the Clerk, "Michael Wellington McIver."

"Shit," I said to myself, there is always a fight to be first on except when the Lord Chief is sitting.

I saw Spider flanked by two burly police officers. Dwarfed by their considerable presence he looked almost insignificant apart from the tattoos. The Lord Chief looked at him with disdain and disbelief as the clerk went through the charges one by one. One by one Spider pleaded guilty to the charges.

"What an obscene object," said Portman. "What possible use to society could that senseless object be? He ought to be put out of his misery."

This was my chance.

"Of course the police have been less than honourable with this lad," I winced.

"What do you mean?" said Portman, "He's an out and out thief. The police caught him and that's an end to it."

"Not really," I continued, "you see they have forced a confession out of him. They have realized he is an inadequate and they have amused themselves by seeing what they could get him to admit to."

"How dare you?" said Portman grasping the bait firmly between his teeth, "I know this officer, his character is beyond question."

"Aye, beyond question by you," I said vindictively, "He`s a bully and a considerable shit."

By this time Portman was about to explode.

"Yes Mr Portman," said the Lord Chief, "we are waiting."

"More fuel on the fire," I thought.

Portman rose to his feet and set about the most vindictive character assassination I had ever heard.

"And the true nature of this person's character is to be seen from his positive denial of the crimes despite his full, complete and inordinately well chronicled admissions. I submit to you that bail is inappropriate in such a case."

Portman finished his address with a flourish, turned to me with a smile, a knowing smile as if to say, "Have that, you insignificant person you."

I rose to my feet.

"Your Worships," I announced, "I am at a loss to understand my friend's address in which he suggests that my client denies the offences. The well chronicled admissions are true and the police have recorded them correctly but in due course my client will plead guilty and so I find that my friend's remarks are not only unjustified but completely wrong. Perhaps my friend is making a mountain out of a molehill. These are minor offences of shoplifting not Grand Larceny."

Portman stared the stare that said ....you bastard ....

He was right in actual fact, but the best was yet to come.

Spider was given bail and returned to his cell pending confirmation that the children's home would have him back. Portman threw down his pen and The Lord Chief saw him do it.

"Mistake number two," I thought.

Seizing the opportunity for a fag and a tea, the Lord Chief Justice retired and I went into the Court corridor.

I was pounced on by four defendants,

"When am I on?" asked one.

"Fuck this waiting," said another.

"Lend's a quid," said the third and then there was Jack.

The grin had disappeared and for once concern was etched on his face.

"We can't find the little bastard anywhere," said Jack pathetically,

"If some bendo has got 'im, I'll kill, I really mean it."

For the first time I realized the depths of feeling which Jack had for his family.

"Don't worry Jack," I said reassuringly, "we'll find him. I have one other bail application and then I am with you."

I returned to the court. I was under pressure and was contemplating my next bail application when I was approached by a very attractive young woman. I guessed that she was about 20 years of age. She was blonde with the figure of a model and I was attracted to her pale blue eyes which dominated her magnificent face. Her clothes were expensive and had been chosen with considerable taste. A pair of Georgio Armani sunglasses adorned the crown of her most beautiful head resisting the weight of a platinum blonde fringe which hung perilously and yet intoxicatingly against a suntanned brow.

As she walked towards me the yobs in the court corridor wolf-whistled. She was oblivious to their prognostications as all her attention was focused on me.

"Are you Steve Smith?" she asked.

"Yes Madam, what can I do for you?" I replied.

"Get stuck in," said an envious onlooker.

A 'V' sign was appropriate as I guided my unlikely guest into the 'Rat Hole' interview room. We passed by a group of solicitors reading their briefs in the room adjoining the 'Rat Hole.' One of them, Paddy Hargan, looked incredulously at my guest as she entered but I merely looked at him and winked as I followed her into the room.

I was immediately deflated when she explained who she was.

"I am Siobhan Danvers, Gary Cusack's girlfriend," she said with an assertiveness reserved only for the bourgeois. "Are you Steve Smith his solicitor?"

I was deflated.

How was it, I asked myself, that such a beauty as this, with breeding and deportment, chose to associate with that shit bag. It was beyond me. I have found, in my not inconsiderable experience, that the 'good birds' always went for 'a bit of rough'. Cusack was indeed as rough as the proverbial 'bear's arse'.

"Will he get bail?" she asked, nervously twisting a Gucci watch around her left wrist.

"I'll do my very best," I said.

"Thank you Mr Smith," she said seductively. "Can I see him before he goes into court ?"

"I'm afraid not," I replied. "He is in one of the cells at the moment, but I am sure you can see him afterwards if he doesn't get bail."

"You mean he might not be released?" she asked. I paused before I answered. I wanted to say "Not likely," but she was clearly besotted with the flash git and I did not want to upset her more than was necessary.

"If it is a question of money," she protested, "I have money. I can stand bail but I cannot use my own address."

Everything fell into place She was a rich kid, who lived with her parents who were well heeled but too busy to check on their daughter. There's plenty of money on offer as long as she doesn't bring problems home! I had hit the nail on the head.

"What are you doing here?" I asked.

"I've come to see Gary," she replied, oblivious to the real meaning of the question.

I decided not to disabuse her of her obvious folly as I rather doubted that she would listen in any event. There are none so blind as those who will not see.

"Are you ready Mr Smith?" asked the clerk.

"As ever," I replied wishing I was somewhere else.

"Gary Cusack No. 45 to 48 your Worships," said the clerk.

I turned to the public gallery and watched as Siobhan entered the court.

Portman rubbed his hands together. "Vengeance is mine sayeth the Lord," I could almost hear him say.

Most advocates fight every case without fear or quarter, no matter who they are representing. Here was a defendant who no one could like, except perhaps the lovely Miss Danvers.

"Is your name Gary Cusack?" asked the clerk of the court.

"Yes Sir," said Cusack bending to respect the Bench.

The clerk read out the charges and then Portman went to work again.

He began a beautifully well argued opposition to bail, but unfortunately for him went a little too far in his opening.

He told the bench what they had to decide and no magistrate appreciates that. The Lord Chief was miffed. Of all the magistrates at Rotherham he was not the one to order about. Portman had made a considerable error and there was I, waiting like a predator who had not eaten for days.

Wallop! - A lengthy address appealing to the Lord Chief Justice's obvious good sense resulted in Cusack being bailed against all the odds.

"The man is a retard," exclaimed a disappointed Portman, referring to the Lord Chief Justice.

I smiled at him but did not speak. I did not have to as the court's decision said it all.

Portman was sunk but unfortunately Cusack was freed and I wished I could have saved that decision for a client I had liked. Even when you get a result it is not always the right one but a solicitor is not judge and jury.

Portman was distraught.

"I'm dealing with imbeciles," he cried.

"No," I answered, "they just think you're a shit. You are OTT. When will you realize you cannot tell magistrates what to do?"

Cusack gave me a 'thumbs up' sign which I did not acknowledge and he blew a kiss to his girlfriend. I bowed to the court, smiled at Portman and prepared to leave the court. Turning I saw the model blowing kisses to a delighted Cusack who appeared to be revelling in his success.

Outside, Cusack's girlfriend came up to me and thanked me enthusiastically as she thought I had performed a miracle. How I wished I could have told her the truth but I mitigated my dishonesty in the certain knowledge that she would not have accepted a word of what I had said.

When I returned to the cells, I found Spider and Cusack at the gaoler's table signing for their property.

Spider was mesmerised as he watched Cussack slip his Rolex watch over his wrist and have a bundle of £20 notes counted onto the table.

"Two hundred and forty, two hundred and sixty, two hundred and eighty, three hundred," said the gaoler.

Then Spider moved forward to collect his belongings.

"Twenty, thirty, forty, sixty eight pence," said the gaoler, "one watch without strap and a brass crucifix."

"Don't spend it all at once," said Cusack. "Here take this, get yourself a hot dinner!" Cusack handed him a £5 note. He was enjoying the hero worship that the money and his baubles had brought him.

"Come on ugly," said Cusack, "I'll give you a lift, where are you going?"

"To the children's home," said Spider.

Cusack then turned his attentions to me.

"Nice one Steve, I like your style. Just send me an appointment and I'll come to see you."

Spider put his cross on the property receipt form and Cusack smirked. He was amused by the attentions of this peculiar youth who had chosen to disfigure himself with the disgusting tattoos which had scarred his face and neck.

"Here is your bail sheet Spider, don't forget when you have to return to the court. If you don't show up you will be arrested and kept in custody," I warned him.

"OK Mr Smith," said Spider, "and thank you for getting me out. I won't let you down."

Within a minute or two Spider and Cusack were released. I returned to the court corridor to find the sergeant swearing into the radio.

"What's up Ted?" I asked. "Radio gone on the blink?"

"No, we've found the problem, some kid has broken into a police car at the compound and is buggering about with the radio."

"But I thought the cars were secure in the compound."

"They are supposed to be but it looks as if we have got an expert in there," said Ted.

"But why would anyone want to break into a police compound?" I asked.

Ted just shrugged his shoulders. "Nothing surprises me any more," he said. "Thirty years in the force removes any element of surprise."

Collecting my papers from the solicitors' room I looked out of the window to see the beautiful blonde in an open-topped MGB sports car, parked outside the rear entrance to the cells. Two young men got into the car, one in the front and one on the small seat in the back. It was Cusack and Spider. As the car set off at speed, Spider fell backwards onto the seat with his feet in the air. I doubt if he had ever been in a sports car before.

As the car disappeared from view, the court sergeant arrived.

"Steve, you are wanted at the police station. They have caught some young kid in a police car at the compound and he's asking for you. He won't even give his name without you being present so I can't tell you who he is."

"How old is he?" I asked.

"Oh about eleven or twelve," said Ted.

"OK, I'm on my way." Picking up my papers I walked into the court corridor.

"Jack," I shouted.

"Yes Steve," said Jack who sat nearby.

"You had better come with me, I think we've found Albert."

Chapter Nine

I FIND THE LAKE DISTRICT AND SPIDER FINDS DRUGS

After we had collected Albert, Jack took him home, pondering on how to deal with his son's fascination for police cars. Police cars were to become a constant feature of his life.

When I got back to the office, Wilf was busy on the Space Invader which had been rented from a local dealer. We used it to host competitions for our friends and associates and that day we were to start the first games of the Wilford Smith Space Invader Championship.

The names of forty participants had been drawn out of a hat for the first round. I was to play Oscar, and Wilf had the dubious honour of playing a mad Scotsman, Lewis Frame.

Eight matches were scheduled to commence that lunchtime in the 'Board Room' upstairs. The board room was air-conditioned as the roof still had a number of holes in it. Wilf always said that we left them to please the bird fanciers so that pigeons could have somewhere to die.

I set about opening some packs of beer which Wilf had already started. We were disturbed by Jarvis, who I firmly believe could smell beer at a thousand paces. He came in to tell me that he had got a brochure about a hotel in the Lake District which might suit us for a weekend break.

He invited himself into the board room and the beer cabinet and as we sat among the boxes of stationery and typewriter ribbons we discussed the idea of visiting the Old England Hotel at Bowness on Windermere.

The brochure described it as a 4 star hotel with a swimming pool and Jarvis extolled the virtues of the facilities. I found this rather odd because Jarvis couldn't swim and in all the time that I had known him I had never seen him near a swimming pool.

By the end of the lunch we had decided to book for an autumn break in the Lake District, which was to be my first break since starting the business.

The day soon arrived and we were to set off, Jennifer and I and Jarvis and Anne on the Thursday afternoon. Unfortunately, that day my court didn't finish until 1 pm and when I got back to the office there was an urgent Brief to Counsel to deliver to Sheffield.

I telephoned Jarvis and we agreed that I would pick him up on my way home and he would help load the car while I showered and changed. We would then all call at Sheffield with the brief on the way to the lakes.

The barrister's chambers in Sheffield was an 'olde worlde' building with a number of brass plates fixed to the wall by the side of the door. One of the plates near the top was for Peter M. Baker a barrister who was one of the busiest and indeed one of the best around. The brief I had to deliver was for him and we met in the reception area. Peter introduced me to a new pupil of his, a young and newly qualified barrister by the name of Alan R. Goldsack who had just joined chambers. Little did I know that I was to spend the next twenty five years or so working with him, learning a great deal in the process.

On leaving, I found that a traffic warden was focusing her attentions on my car. The race was on and I set off at some speed. As I quickened my pace, so did she with the result that we were both running down the street but I beat her to it, got into the car and shot off at a rate of knots.

We had only got as far as Leeds when Jarvis said, "I'm going to have to pay a call."

I thought that he wanted to use the toilet, but he wanted a drink. When Jarvis is on holiday, he likes nothing more than to avoid the sun, the beaches, the sightseeing and travel and spend his time concealed in an air-conditioned bar. To keep him happy, we picked a local pub and had a bar meal before we continued our journey. After a two-and-a-half hour drive, we arrived at Windermere.

Rounding a bend, I saw Lake Windermere for the first time. It was a magnificent sight with the sun glittering on the water. I asked Jarvis what he thought of the incredible view, but there was no answer. As I looked in the mirror, I could see that Jarvis was fast asleep.

Within fifteen minutes, we were outside the Old England Hotel in Bowness and, having parked the car and unloaded our belongings, we made our way to the front desk. It was an old traditional hotel and I liked it immediately. The dinner menu was displayed in the foyer with a notice board explaining the events of the day. We were shown to our rooms, which were on the same floor and having unpacked we met Jarvis in the bar downstairs.

The bar led to a veranda, overlooking the lake. It was a magnificent view with all the boats bobbing about in the water and there and then I told Jarvis that one day I would have my own boat on that Lake and I meant it. The four of us spent the afternoon browsing around Bowness itself. Inevitably, we ended up at one of the boat yards where I was totally captivated by the cabin cruisers. I suggested to Jarvis that we should go into partnership and buy one. Although Jarvis laughed, I was deadly serious and told him so. Making our way back to the hotel past the quayside, we saw that one of the large boats that ply the lake was mooring up. We all agreed on a boat trip, particularly Jarvis who had seen a sign indicating that the boat was licensed. I left the group in the bar while I went to the front and absorbed the *je ne sais quoi*.

As I looked out to the shore line on our way to Ambleside, I saw cottages dotted around the lake's edge, raised slightly above the level of the water.

I had been in the Lakes for little more than two hours and I had already decided that one day I would buy a boat and a cottage. All I had to do was to convince Wilford, a building society and a bank.

The boat we were on was called the *Swan* and it travels the lake at regular intervals from Ambleside in the north down to Lakeside in the south. As we arrived back at Bowness, we could not find Jarvis so I went down to the bar area to find him fast asleep, having missed the whole of the boat journey.

Shaking him awake he said, "Marvellous that, I thoroughly enjoyed it."

Getting back to the hotel at about 6 pm we arranged to meet at 7.30 pm for dinner. Jarvis said that he would take the opportunity to have a nap, but I sat on the veranda watching the boats. At 7 pm I went down to the dinning room to book our table. I was desperate to get a table near a window so that I could continue with my new found hobby of boat watching. Unfortunately the window tables were all booked, but after giving the head waiter a £5 note and telling him Michael was the first son of a baronet, I got the window seat I wanted.

I went back to the room and took up my position on our verandah. I spotted Jarvis on his, seemingly enjoying the view or at least he would have enjoyed the view, but for the fact that he was asleep. On the stroke of 7.30 pm however, he was wide awake and ready for action.

At thirty one minutes past the hour, we all met in the foyer.

"Time for a quick one?" he asked and off we went to the downstairs bar and the verandah overlooking the lake.

We ended the evening with the head wine waiter bidding Sir Michael "Good night."

Jarvis was confused and simply said,

"He called me Sir Michael, is he taking the mickey?"

"Probably," I said and helped Anne get Jarvis back to their room.

The following morning, Jarvis was dragged to a lake view seat for breakfast by an ingratiating waiter who referred constantly to Jarvis as "Sir Michael". I noticed we were the only guests who had our luggage carried out to the car when we left!

On the Monday morning, I was back in the office bright and early to find that I had a very large list of cases involving a number of prisoners all of whom were demanding bail. I was disappointed to find that Spider was locked up again, but this time the offence was much more sinister. He had been caught in possession of some amphetamine sulphate and the drug squad did not believe that it was for his own use.

Amphetamine Sulphate is commonly known as 'Speed' and is taken among other things to fend off tiredness. It is used quite illegally by those so motivated.

The prosecution wanted a local remand, which is used at court to secure the detention of a prisoner in the local cells for the purposes of interviewing. Spider was out of his depth and the police knew it.

The case was adjourned for what we call a three day local, to facilitate interviews. It was an excellent device that the prosecution had in their armoury to gather evidence and seek confessions. Spider was not equipped to deal with this situation and while he was in court he looked nervously around the public gallery to see who was watching.

I found this rather sinister because it was not Spider's usual way of doing things. I then saw his gaze fix in one position and there was a marked look of fear in his eyes. He was looking at one man with dyed blond hair. He was wearing an expensive designer suit and had a diamond in his ear.

It was Cusack and he was showing a little more than a token interest in the case. I turned to the front and looked again at Spider whose eyes were still firmly fixed on the public gallery.

During the adjournment I went to the cells to see Spider.

"What's going on Spider?" I asked. "Why were you carrying all those drugs? That's not your game."

It was almost as if Spider had been programmed as he addressed me in a slow and monotonous tone, "They're my drugs for my own use."

"You don't use drugs and if you did, you had enough there to supply the whole of your estate. What's going on Spider?" I asked again.

"They're mine," he repeated. "They're mine I tell you, I'm taking the rap."

"You know the police are suggesting that you can only have that quantity if you are going to supply it. They are going to charge you with possession with intent to supply which is very serious. I don't believe that they are yours, I think that you are carrying them for someone."

"I can't grass," said Spider.

"So it is true," I continued, "you were carrying them for someone," and without any doubt I knew who.

"I am not saying that you should grass on anybody Spider, but if you are saying that they were for your own use, the court won't believe you and I think that they will convict you of possession with intent to supply and on that amount of drugs it means the Crown Court and a big sentence."

"What do you call a big sentence?" said Spider.

"Well even though there are no drugs matters on your record, I think you are going to be sent away for at least two years."

Spider gulped, he was clearly shocked and had not realized the implications, but he refused to change his story.

I left it at that and agreed that I would come to the police station when the drug squad were ready to interview him.

I went back into court and finished my last case. When I came out into the corridor, there was Cusack with his pretty girlfriend waiting to speak to me.

"I see poor old Spider's in bother then," said Cusack.

"What's that to do with you Mr.Cusack?" I asked.

"Just interested," he said, "he works for me now."

"Doing what?" I asked.

"Well I'm selling cars now, I have a little sales pitch and he valets the motors, he's good at it, admittedly he can't do any more than that because he has only half a brain. He fetches parts for me and generally runs about."

"Well," I said, "you are right he is in bother," and turned to walk away but I was aware that Cusack and his girl-friend were following me.

"Well," I demanded, trying to face him, "what now?"

Cusack then tried to put me on the back foot and asked, "You don't like me Mr. Smith do you?"

"I'm not paid to like people Mr Cusack, I do a job and I do it to the best of my ability whether it be for you, Spider or anybody else."

"Yes, OK I accept that, you got me bail good style and I was impressed, but it's as a person I am talking about," said Cusack continuing his offensive.

"I don't make decisions as to whether I like or dislike people. If I worked in a supermarket I wouldn't consider everybody who bought a tin of peas and decide whether I liked them or not, it doesn't enter into it."

"OK Captain," said Cusack, "By the way, has he said anything about me?"

I wondered when we would get to the point but I was not prepared to enter into discussions with filth like Cusack.

"Spider has not been interviewed at length yet, but that is what is going to happen over the next two or three days."

"Oh, I just wondered," said Cusack. "Somebody's got to have a bit of time for the dick head. Listen, call me if you need anybody to stand bail for him." This time he produced a metallic card with the words 'Cusack's Cars' and in brackets after it 'Value for money, every car guaranteed.'

"I will bear it in mind," I said, and turned to walk away.

As I moved downstairs to the entrance, I saw Cusack getting into a flashy sportscar, he drove off at speed screeching his tyres as he left. "Flash Git," I thought and went about my business.

After lunch I was back at the office to start my appointments for the day. Jill told me that the first clients had arrived at 2 pm and were waiting in the reception. Calling them in, I was greeted by two men and a woman, all middle-aged and by the look of them, related. All three were extremely well-dressed and had the air of respectability. The woman, who introduced herself as Mrs. Cartwright, was extremely businesslike and presented a leather folder with a file of documents inside. She told me that she wished to obtain a Power of Attorney over their absent brother's estate so that it would be administered while he was unavoidably absent.

I ventured to say that this was not a difficult job and could be dealt with quite quickly, but would require a visit to their brother for his signature and a discussion as to his understanding of the position.

I asked the reason for the brother's incapacity and she explained the story to me quite concisely. The problem was that the four of them were partners in a thriving and very profitable business. Their elder brother, Brian, was the senior partner/managing director and played a very substantial part in the development of the business. Unfortunately, the previous year he had begun to exhibit certain behavioural problems and bouts of depression. The upshot of this was that he was eventually out of control and was committed to a mental institution for his own welfare. Owing to the construction of the partnership, it was not possible to carry on the business properly unless the partners were able to act on Brian's behalf on the day-to-day decisions of the business. Consequently the banks and various creditors had suggested that the family obtain a Power of Attorney. My job was to prepare the documents and to visit Brian in the hospital and obtain his signature. I was told that Brian was in full agreement to this course of action and the doctors had agreed that he knew and understood what was happening.

However, I didn't feel comfortable possibly because I didn't know the people who were from out of town and I couldn't understand why they had sought me out.

Something, somewhere did not ring true.

They explained that I had been recommended by another client of mine who they knew and they had ventured out of their normal area because of the embarrassment that this family difficulty had caused within the local business community. It seemed a satisfactory explanation and so I agreed that I would prepare all the documentation and then visit their brother and report to them on the meeting.

At this point the telephone rang, telling me that the police, were ready to interview Spider. With clients queing up outside I had to leave the office, taking my next client with me to discuss his case as I walked to the police station leaving Wilford to deal with another.

The criminal law does not work to solicitors' convenience. One day you can have a very light diary and the next you are hit with everything all at once. At this stage I felt that I was lucky to be working and so consequently I shrugged my shoulders and tried to make the best of it.

I was met by the detective inspector of the drug squad wearing a bomber jacket, jeans and training shoes. I believe that they dress in this way so that they can blend in and give the appearance of being someone other than who they really are. On brief scrutiny, he appeared to be a police officer in bomber jacket, jeans and trainers. I was a little surprised to see someone of that rank waiting for me, but we went into a side room and the Inspector explained the reason for his presence. He was extremely courteous and told me that he was investigating what he believed to be a large drug ring operating in Rotherham. Large quantities of amphetemine were being shipped into the town and were circulated by young people at various functions. He told me that Spider was involved.

I thought it rather unlikely that anyone like Spider would be involved in something like drugs but the inspector had done his homework and told me that while he agreed that Spider did not have any previous convictions for drug offences, he was still nevertheless involved.

I am always worried when police officers say to me "I'll be frank with you on this occasion". It tends to suggest that they are not frank with you on other occasions, but I listened to what he had to say.

"We are not sure about McIver's involvement at this stage, but he was seen to collect a large parcel in Sheffield and travel over the Rotherham boundary. The officers who were following him became concerned that they had been observed in their surveillance and so we had no option but to stop the car and arrest the man before he got any further. What we really wanted to do was to follow him to his final destination and make a number of arrests, but we were worried that they may have tried to dispose of the drugs in some way."

The officer could see me looking in amazement, for I simply did not believe that Spider could have got himself involved in such business.

"I simply do not accept that Spider is a drug dealer," I said to the officer.

"We are not saying that he is," said the inspector, "but what we are saying is that he is involved and we want to know to what extent. He is either shipping the drugs out to sell himself, or he is bringing them back for somebody else. He is either an errand lad or the real thing. The problem is that your client won't tell us and in the absence of any explanation, we have to conclude that he is a dealer."

I ventured to ask why the officers thought that, in the absence of anything else, he had to be a dealer. "In the absence of anything else, why couldn't he just be a user or an errand lad?" I asked.

The officer smirked and said, "Well, it's for him to convince us that he is not the main man."

It was obvious in my view that the inspector knew that Spider was an 'errand lad' as they put it, and that he was going to help him catch bigger fish.

I was allowed a few minutes with Spider before the interview took place and so I immediately waded into the attack.

"What in God's name are you playing at Spider?"

"I ain't done nothing Mr Smith," said Spider. "All I did was to do as I was told."

"What do you mean?"

"I can't say, can I?" said Spider nervously.

"Well I'm asking you," I said forcefully, but there was no reply.

"The police are going to want to interview you about this, Spider, and I am going to tell you that you are not obliged to answer any of their questions if you do not wish to do so, but obviously if you do answer any questions, then the police will be entitled to use what you have said in evidence later."

At this time, the police were not using tape recorders for interviews and usually when a Solicitor was present, the questions were put and the subject's replies were written down contemporaneously. It was a very slow and laborious process and the police took the view that it was unfair, because it gave the defendant time to think of his answers.

"Exactly what is your case?" I asked Spider.

"I have nothing to say," he said.

I asked him if he was afraid of anyone and he said that he didn't want to say but it was obvious that he was an extremely frightened young man. There seemed little point in continuing our conversation, because Spider continued with the same pathetic story.

The inspector came in with an aggressive looking detective sergeant who sneered as he spoke. He had the job of note taking, and the inspector asked the questions.

"Where did you get the drugs from?" said the inspector as he stared into Spider's eyes.

Spider was uncomfortable and looked away. It was standard police procedure to stare their subject out, because they worked on the basis that if someone lied they could tell by the reaction on their faces. The object of the exercise was to unnerve the person being questioned and thus get the answers.

The interview continued, "Well, if you don't explain to us what you know, we will take the view that you are the main man," said the inspector.

I objected to the line of questioning and I told the inspector that I wished my objection to be registered. The detective sergeant was not impressed with my interruption and told me that if I interrupted again he would have me excluded from the interview.

It was a very unpleasant situation to be in, but I believed that I was right and told him if I was excluded, I would advise Spider not to answer any more questions. The inspector realizing that there may be something in what I said, began to ask questions in a more pleasant and sympathetic manner, but the detective sergeant continued to sneer. The officer did his very best to catch Spider out and I was most surprised at the way Spider conducted himself in the interview. It was almost as if he had been told what to say and because he wouldn't say who the drugs were for, he gave the general impression that they were for his own use, denying that he was going to sell any of the drugs. The officers put to him that the amount of drugs could not possibly be for his own use because of the huge quantity.

Spider refused to answer and I winced in the certain knowledge that he was going to be charged with possession with intent to supply.

The interview took two hours and I had been listening so intently that I had forgotten about the appointments waiting for me back at the office. I was allowed to use the telephone to find that there were one or two aggrieved clients still waiting. Anne had done the best that she could by trying to give them other appointments, but some were not happy and had waited to complain. I was soon back in the office making my apologies to a waiting-room full of disgruntled people. One of them was an old lady from a local old people's home complaining about a man living in the next room to her. Unfortunately, the man suffered from Alzheimer's disease which somehow prompted him to expose himself on a fairly regular basis and my aged client was sick and tired of it.

This was a very difficult situation as I could hardly consider taking Court proceedings, so I decided to speak to the owner of the home in the hope that they might be able to sort something out. I made some telephone calls and was fortunate enough to speak to a very sympathetic matron who doubted the veracity of my client's claims.

Nevertheless she agreed to move the ageing Romeo to another floor, in the hope that the problem would be resolved. I was to hear from this old lady about a month later, when she rang me to express her delight that her problems had been solved. I asked her if he had mended his ways, but apparently he had not and was busy doing the same thing on another floor, but his new neighbour apparently enjoyed it and had made no complaint. One satisfied customer I thought to myself.

The following morning I was back in the office, making arrangements to see the gentleman in the psychiatric hospital when the police telephoned me to say that they had completed their enquiries in relation to Spider and they were placing him before the court that morning. Despite having a case on in Sheffield, I was able to dash back in time to see Spider in the cells before his case was called on.

Spider looked dreadful. He was pale and drawn but appeared to be highly excited, twitching and behaving in a rather bizarre manner. I realized that he had got an addiction to amphetamine and was obviously in a state of withdrawal. When I got into the court corridor, I noticed Cusack who was involved in a very intense conversation with a man who looked like a heavyweight wrestler.

I dodged past him and went into the court.

I asked the prosecutor what application he had intended to put forward and I told him that I would be agreeable to any conditions of bail. Unfortunately, he said that he could not agree bail and explained that Spider had been re-interviewed in my absence. I was furious and told him that the police had absolutely no right to do that, but the prosecutor pointed out that it was Spider's own decision and he had not made any request to have a solicitor present. He told me that Spider had accepted that he had purchased those drugs and that he was going to sell them himself. I was totally and completely horrified.

"But the police told me that they didn't believe Spider was a supplier."

"Yes, I understood that to be the case, but Spider apparently was most insistent that they were his drugs and because there was no evidence to the contrary, he has been charged with mainstream supply."

I wished that the police had followed him to his destination point and then perhaps he wouldn't have been in such a mess, but there was little that I could do. The prosecutor showed me a copy of the interview and it was clear that Spider had indeed admitted it. I went to the cells to see him and he could not look me in the face.

"I'm sorry Mr Smith, but it was me, so I have admitted it."

"Who were you going to supply?" I asked him.

"Anybody." said Spider. "Round the pubs and youth clubs like."

He made the answer with so little enthusiasm that he was clearly lying. I realized when I read the notes that he might have given the same impression to the police, I just looked at him and asked,

"What have you done?"

Spider looked back at me and simply said, "I have saved my neck".

I didn't bother to ask him what he meant, because I realized that he was taking the blame for somebody else. If he had told the truth to the police and implicated the real people responsible, then he would have had to face the consequences from them. I was annoyed that this could happen and, more importantly, that there was nothing that I could do about it.

When I came up to court, I saw the detective sergeant and asked him, "You know those drugs are not his don't you?"

"Mr Smith," said the sergeant, ingratiating himself, "your client says they are and we can't prove anything to the contrary. In those circumstances he has been charged with what he has admitted and therefore will have to face the consequences. I am as unhappy about it as you are, but there it is. I acted upon what your client had to say. If we ever find any evidence to the contrary we will act upon it and then he can be prosecuted for perverting the course of justice."

I didn't stop to argue, but simply said, "A brilliant bit of detective work Sergeant, you should be very pleased with yourself," and walked off.

This was a very difficult situation to be in. Spider was telling me what he had said to the police was the truth. I was not in a position to act as Judge and Jury and question it. I did all that I could to try to persuade him against the course that he was adopting, but Spider stuck to his guns and there was little that I could do. I went into court a most unhappy man and as the prosecutor read out the facts, I realized that I was not going to be in a position to argue. I took the decision, however, to apply for bail, although I didn't believe that Spider had much chance. I pointed out to the court that he had no previous convictions for any drug matters and that all the drugs in his possession had been recovered. I went into some considerable detail about his background and I must say that I ventured the opinion that he was nothing more than an errand lad, despite his admissions. The court were unimpressed and promptly remanded Spider in custody. He was led away to the cells and I noticed Cusack nod to him as he disappeared through the doorway.

I went back to the office to find a telephone message from the children's home, who were enquiring about Spider's welfare. Having been given some of the facts by a probation officer they were very distressed about the allegations. The matron gave me a potted history of Spider's life, telling me that he was taken into the home at six months old, when his unmarried mother was unable to keep him. Spider was highly regarded at the home and, while he had involved himself in the stupid tattoo business. he wasn't thought of as being a bad lad. She believed that he had been used, saying that he was easily led and often fell prey to unscrupulous people. She offered her help by guaranteeing Spider a home and offered to come to court the following week to confirm this.

Chapter Ten

AM I GOING THE RIGHT WAY TO GET INTO
THE PSYCHIATRIC HOSPITAL?

I had never been to this hospital on a business appointment before and I could not remember being a patient but despite plotting the route and being a seasoned traveller, I lost my way. Coming across two old locals drinking beer outside a pub, I decided to ask them for directions. The one who did all the talking was a man who looked to be in his early 70's, with long shoulder length, iron-grey hair and matching eyebrows which joined in the middle and which appeared to be about the same length as his hair. His face was highlighted by a jet-black moustache which looked as if it had been dyed. He wore a tweed sports jacket with green cavalry twill trousers and well-worn brogue shoes. However, he had the bearing of an educated man.

"Am I going the right way for the psychiatric hospital?" I asked.

"It depends, do you hate your mother?" asked the man seriously.

"I want to get to the psychiatric hospital, can you point me in the right direction?"

While the man explained the route, his friend just looked up into the skies above as if waiting for some visitation. He was younger than his friend, with short hair and was clean shaven. I always believed that I was a good judge of character and I assessed that this man had the mark of a doctor about him.

He was smartly dressed with highly polished black shoes and a pair of horn-rimmed spectacles only partly concealing steel blue eyes which continued to watch the sky with great intensity. Having got some information, I thought it best to ask somewhere else further down the road because the old fool didn't seem too sure of himself.

About half a mile down the road I saw a man on my off-side walking towards me along the road. Pulling up and winding my window down I simply asked, "Am I going the right way to the psychiatric hospital?"

The man burst into manic laughter and ran off. I wondered if he was related to the old man at the pub but as I was thinking about it, I spotted a rather dark and austere building set in some trees in the distance. It was a dark forbidding place and I thought that it might be what I was looking for. I turned up the drive only to find that it was a private house. The owner was none too pleased to be asked if his home was a psychiatric hospital, but he eventually put me in the right direction and at last I came across a rather splendid looking building in its own grounds with a long winding drive leading up to it.

It was an extremely pleasant place with immaculately laid out rose beds set in a sea of emerald green grass.

At the reception area I was greeted by a lady in a very smart suit, to whom I gave my name and showed my driving licence and a letter of introduction from the office. She said that I was expected but asked me to fill in a form comfirming my identity and the reason for my visit.

Having been accepted, I was asked to wait in the beautifully decorated reception area. There were flowers set out very artistically in crystal containers which caught the sun as it shone through the window. The receptionist confirmed that all the flowers on display were from the hospital's own gardens and she explained with great pride how some of the 'non-risk' patients worked in the gardens and kept them beautifully neat and tidy. There can be absolutely no doubt that first impressions do count and the gardens together with the very neat reception made me feel most comfortable.

On the walls there were a number of excellent sketches and paintings.

"Are these done by the residents as well?" I asked.

"Oh yes, all the paintings that you see in the hospital are by the patients."

My attention was drawn to a neatly printed sign which offered tea and coffee for people who were waiting.

"Do you have catering staff for the refreshments?" I asked.

"Oh no, all the refreshments are prepared by the patients. Would you like something?" she queried.

"No thank you," I replied not wanting to cause offence but realizing that the last murder case I dealt with involved poison and a defendant who ended up in a psychiatric ward.

I picked up a paper from a beautifully veneered and highly polished coffee table. I turned to the receptionist and gave her a questioning look. "Oh yes" she said, smiling. I just nodded in agreement. The paper happened to be the *Nursing Times* and the headline was referring to Government cut backs.

About five minutes later I was greeted by a young lady in a nurse's uniform. I followed her through the main doors leading from the reception into the hospital itself and within a matter of feet, the atmosphere changed completely. We then went through a series of security doors, all of which had to be locked.

We arrived at an hexagonal reception area, which was surrounded by wooden panels and plate glass windows. It housed a series of television monitors with the names of the wards underneath.

One man was watching the monitors, another was watching him and another watched me as I was 'booked in'.

"Sign here," demanded a gruff and unfriendly voice.

"Only if you let me out," I said, trying to bring some levity to the proceedings but there was no reply and the man just looked at me as I walked along with the nurse.

"I wonder if the patients work the reception as well," I thought to myself as I followed on through the security doors.

Eventually, I arrived at the Trueman Ward where I was eyed suspiciously by two orderlies in white hospital jackets.

I explained who I had come to see and the reason for my visit and I was asked to wait in a small interview room at the head of the ward. As I sat down I saw a closed circuit camera focusing its attention on me. I realized my friend from the booking-in point would be watching me and I couldn't help but smile, "Watch it Smithy," I thought to myself, "you'll be kept in here if you're not careful."

As I waited, a man who looked like a patient walked past the door, peered in and advised me not to take the medication as it had 'gone off'. Someone shouted "Bernard" and he left. I was finding the place a little intimidating when a gentleman, who appeared to be in authority, approached me. He was most courteous and told me that my client would be brought to see me within five minutes.

He then offered me tea and a scone which I politely declined. "They must work these patients to death," I thought to myself. Either that or they are all cooks.

However, he was as good as his word, and my client arrived within a few minutes. Introducing myself, I shook his hand and invited him to take a seat.

He was in his early 50's with sandy coloured hair, streaked with natural grey. He had pale blue eyes which were discoloured, giving me the impression that this man could be an alcoholic. He was over six feet tall with a deep resonant voice and had the bearing of someone who had served in the Forces. He appeared very relaxed and I decided to get down to business straight away. I explained the reason for my visit and he told me that he had been expecting me because his brothers and sister had called earlier that week. He thanked me for coming and with some embarrassment explained that it was with regret, but in the interests of the business, that he was to sign the Power of Attorney.

This man seemed perfectly sane and rational to me and, based on this opinion, I began to chat to him and asked him about his health.

He told me that he was making extremely good progress because of the drugs he had been given, the lack of pressure from being away from his job and the realization that he had been making himself ill with too much work and worry. He explained that he thought that the prognosis was good and it might not be too long before he could leave here and get back to work.

I suggested that if he were to return to work he might be putting himself back in the same position as before, but he told me that he intended to take on extra help to ease the workload. He spoke a good deal of sense and I couldn't help thinking that if he was crackers then I was a 'Dutchman'.

I took the documents out of my briefcase and explained them to him in detail. He asked me one or two questions surrounding the matter generally and when he was satisfied with my explanations he told me that, if he could borrow my pen, he would sign the documents. Looking out at the beautiful gardens I asked him if he had been involved in any of the work, but he told me that the gardens were out of bounds for him. He explained that it didn't worry him because he suffered from hay fever and avoided gardens like the plague.

Reaching in my pocket, I brought out my Parker fountain pen which had been given to me by my colleagues at the old firm as a leaving present. I told him that I would pay him the compliment of letting him use it. However he declined at first, saying that it was not wise to let anyone else write with one's fountain pen because the pressure would not be the same and neither would the writing position, consequently it could ruin the nib. I told him that I did not think that a signature would matter and handed him the pen.

I gasped with astonishment as he took the pen in his hand and scraped it up and down the paper, splitting the nib in the process. Ink went everywhere. He then calmly handed the paper back and asked, "Have you any blotting paper ?"

I was open mouthed. At this point, a male nurse who had been watching from outside came into the room and took the pen off the client, who was looking a little perplexed.

"What's wrong?" he asked.

"Nothing Brian, but I think that you ought to come with me," said the caring nurse.

"But I was talking to Mr Smith and we were having a very interesting conversation."

"Yes," said the nurse. "but it's time for your medication."

"Oh, all right," said Brian. He stood up offering his hand, and said, "Well thank you very much for coming Mr Smith, I am most grateful to you for your kind assistance. I do hope that we will have the opportunity to meet again and perhaps you would like to undertake all my legal work in the future. Bye for now."

I was on automatic pilot, albeit open mouthed, as we shook hands.

He turned and left the room. I looked at the pen nib which was damaged beyond repair and looking at the door I watched my unusual client disappear down the corridor behind the locked gate. I glanced at the piece of paper with the scrawl and puncture marks upon it and got up to leave.

I was escorted back through the same doors and along the corridors to the booking-in area.

"Going out?" said a gruff but familiar voice.

"Yes," I replied, still holding the wounded pen in my hand, "Yes, I'm going now."

"You're not stopping then?" said Gruffy.

"No, not today, maybe next time," I said entering into the spirit of the occasion. "Not on your life," I thought to myself as I tried to repair the remains of my pen.

As I was waiting at the gate, a patient who was accompanied by a male nurse walked past me.

"Who are you?" said the patient.

I was still in shock but in a slow, deliberate action I turned to face him and I just said, "My name is Van Dam, I'm from Holland".

He congratulated me and said, "Lovely place Holland, I used to do a lot of climbing there".

"Of course you did," I said and went to the reception desk.

I handed in my visitors' card and walked into the reception area. I thanked the lady who had greeted me earlier and courteously declining a cup of tea and a scone, I left.

As I got outside into the garden, I noticed an old man with iron grey hair who was picking himself a rose for the lapel of his jacket.

"Found your way then old chap?" said the man.

"Yes thank you," I said as I tried to walk past him as quickly as possible, with my earlier experiences of strange people rattling around in my head.

"Have you been to see an inmate?" he said, trying to get me into conversation.

"Yes, I have," I said as I tried to walk away from him. He joined me en route to the car park and I must admit that I was getting a little concerned at this point, because it looked as though I had inherited another hanger-on. As I was about to get into the car, I was thinking of ways of shrugging him off when a nurse shouted, "Doctor, doctor, will you come quickly we have an emergency".

As she approached us, I looked around to see who she was speaking to and I saw to my surprise that she was addressing the old man in a most respectful manner.

"Very good nurse, we will go straight away. Cheerio old chap," he said to me.

"Cheerio," I said and whispered under my breath, "My name is Mr Van Dam and I am a mountaineer from Holland."

Chapter Eleven

I MISS THE CHRISTMAS PARTY BECAUSE
JIMMY SHOT HIS WIFE

Christmas is a most special time of the year and in 1981 it was my first as a self-employed man.

Wilf and I, deciding that we would have a superb time, had planned all sorts of events. By this time, there were six of us in the office as we had taken on another typist.

We had organized another Space Invader Championship which had grown in popularity and to add to the festivities we had decided to invite guests on Christmas Eve morning to the office for a drink, to show our appreciation for the way that we had been supported during the year.

"Who do you think we ought to invite, apart from Pagey?" said Wilf in a reflective mood.

"How about Pagey?" I said.

"Not likely," said Wilf, "we'll get barred."

"Oh, he's not as bad as all that," I said, "and if we speak to him politely and ask him to behave...."

Wilford interrupted, "He'll do exactly the opposite, yes I know".

"We've got to invite Jarvis," I said. "Let's draw up a guest list."

With that we walked across the landing into our shared room and as we did so I heard the sound of the trombone.

"Morning Oscar," I shouted.

"Morning Steve," came the voice from within.

A further sound of the trombone.

"Morning Oscar," said Wilf.

"Morning Steve," said Oscar. "3.30 Haydock Park, the 'Windygultch Kid'.

"How very appropriate," I replied, walking into my office.

We checked our pockets to find that we had almost £5 between us and we decided to put this princely sum on Oscar's horse.

"We've got to invite Bodge," said Wilf, "and anyway I want him to look at that roof."

"That's fine, so long as you don't let him repair it," I said, "Look at it by all means, give him a chair in fact and let him sit there as long as he likes, but don't let him touch it. What about the Mad Scotsman?"

"OK," said Wilf, "but we had better call it a day at that, otherwise we will have more guests than staff."

"Right," I said, "I'll draw up invitations and we will send them out tonight."

Later in the day, as I was making the arrangements for the office do, the barrister's clerk in Sheffield rang me.

"You have the attempted murder case of Riley, Mr Smith," said the listing officer.

"Yes," I said cautiously, "what about it?"

"We're thinking of putting the case in on the 23rd of December."

"That's our office party," I said. "We've got all our friends coming during the day."

"Oh," said the listing officer in a wounded tone, "You're asking me to leave this man in prison and delay his trial until after Christmas so that you can have your office party, is that it?"

"I don't know why you're moaning Tom, you have been invited," I replied.

"Oh," he said, "I didn't realize that. In that case we will start it in January."

We both laughed, but in the event it was our party that had to take second place to an attempted murder trial which was set for the 23rd December.

One positive aspect of the case was that I would be meeting a Barrister whom I had admired for many years. His name was Wilfred Steer QC, from Newcastle, who was a most highly regarded Counsel in his mid 50's and at the peak of his profession.

I had briefed him for the attempted murder case of Jimmy Riley sometime before in an attempt to guarantee his attendance. On this occasion I had a promise from his clerk that the case would not be listed unless Mr Steer was available.

The junior counsel on the case was Alan Goldsack who was beginning to carve out a niche for himself in the local Court scene.

Jimmy Riley was on remand in custody at Armley Prison in Leeds and I had been making regular visits to see him. He was charged with attempting to murder his wife and his best pal Patrick Guthrie who it seemed had been carrying on an illicit affair.

Although Jimmy had been tipped off that this was going on, he had chosen not to believe it as Patrick was his best pal and he trusted him.

However, after some considerable time and on the night in question Jimmy had decided to go home unannounced to satisfy himself that the rumours were untrue. Unfortunately he took along a twelve bore shotgun which, regrettably, was loaded.

The prosecution case was that, fearing that the rumours were true, Jimmy had gone to the house with a view to shooting them both and when he looked in through the lounge window he found his wife locked in a passionate embrace with her lover, Guthrie.

An aggravating feature was the fact that Mrs Riley was naked and that Patrick was in a similar state except for a black teeshirt which bore the initials N.C.B. (a company, then known as the National Coal Board).

Jimmy had told me that his wife had run off before with a chap from the circus but the relationship had only lasted a month and when she came back he had forgiven her. I asked him if the man concerned was a lion tamer and very much to my disappointment I found that he was a juggler, sending my developing psychological profile of his wife through the window.

The prosecution went on to contend that in a fit of rage, Jimmy had pushed the shotgun through the window and had fired at the loving couple, in an attempt to kill them both.

Learned Counsel for the prosecution was to add, "It was the most callous and calculated act and rest assured Riley intended to kill them both. Why else would he fire such a weapon at such close range?"

Our defence was fairly simple; Jimmy contended that it was his intention to push the gun through the window and simply frighten the parties, but unfortunately the gun had gone off. Regrettably his wife and his friend were in the line of fire but he stated that there was no intention to cause any injury, but simply to put the fear of God into them. He had certainly done that and also put a degree of buckshot into them as well. What Jimmy did accept, however, was that his actions were extremely reckless and because of this he accepted that he was responsible for the injuries to the complainants. On that basis we suggested to the prosecution that he should plead guilty to a lesser charge of wounding.

The prosecution had refused to accept this plea and therefore there had to be a trial for a jury to decide where Jimmy's guilt lay.

If Jimmy had been convicted of an attempted murder, he would have gone to prison for between eight to ten years, whereas for a lesser charge, namely Section 20 Wounding, taking into account all the mitigation that he had, eighteen months to two years would have been nearer the mark.

During the preparation for the trial, I hit upon the idea of obtaining the help of a firearms expert to see if he could assist with any information concerning the weapon. I knew a little about guns and it seemed fairly obvious to me that if Jimmy had a finger on the trigger when he pushed it through the window, the impact of the window could well have caused the finger to pull the trigger, but it would depend upon how taut the trigger was. We had therefore to gain access to this weapon, which was being retained by the police at headquarters as an exhibit

We obtained the help of a retired Army officer who was an expert in the use of firearms and he performed a number of tests on the weapon, simulating the incident which had taken place.

Surprisingly, he was able to show me that the weapon had a very loose trigger, which he described as a hairline trigger, meaning that the slightest pressure on the weapon would result in the gun going off.

This was a major breakthrough and I telephoned Wilfred Steer QC with the news. He was delighted, but being the wise man that he is, he urged a word of caution. He pointed out that if the defendant was only going to frighten his subjects, then why was there any need to put his finger on the trigger at all.

I realized the sense of his caution, and decided that I had to set off for Armley at the earliest opportunity to put the question to Jimmy.

Just before leaving, I checked my morning post and found that one of my other clients, who was appearing at Crown Court that week, had written to me. He had enclosed with his letter another envelope which was unsealed and addressed to "JUDGE". His covering letter explained that he had a medical problem which he felt might help him get bail if the judge was made aware of it. It was obvious that "friends" had advised my client to appeal to the humanity of the judge. I reproduce the letter to show the lengths some defendants will go to, to get bail.

Dear Judge

As you see I have put an application in for bail, today Because for round about two months Ive had lumps and like a Cramping pain in my testicles I have been worried about this because Ive started getting realy bad pains now sometimes bad enough I cry. I went to see the doctor in prison and he said it was nothing to worrie about what kind of doctor is he, because its realy painfull if you grant me bail I will fetch all the tests in to show you to show I am not a liar. I will go on eny conditions what so ever Just to find out wot realy is up with me if you will not give me bail to the faniely of mine I will go in a bail hostel in shetfield because then I wont be near eny of my friends and as well I dont know enyone up shetfield to try and get me into troubles

Please grant me bail as I am so worryed about my testicles.

Yours

THANKYOU!

132

I was thinking how to deal with this on my way to Leeds because if I decided not to submit it and the defendant had got a bad result he would have blamed it on to my failure to produce this letter. Some defendants feel that if they get a bad result, it is entirely the barrister's fault and has nothing to do with the fact that they may well have committed a grievous crime. Consequently it is a very difficult profession in which to gain total customer satisfaction!

Before I could come to any conclusion about the letter, I arrived at Armley prison, where Jimmy was waiting for me. I asked him about the trigger and his reply was simple.

"There was nowhere else to put it, and that is the normal way in which I hold a gun. My mind wasn't on how I was going to hold the weapon. I was just thinking about them and not what part of the gun to touch. I never gave a thought to the trigger. I also knew that the safety catch didn't work but   it certainly wasn't on my mind that night."

I had got my answer and now it was up to Wilf Steer.

I attended at the court and waited to meet our counsel. Mr Steer appeared, wearing an old and well worn coat, carrying a worn-out bag, which held a tatty wig and gown. He was tall and distinguished looking, with a deep resonant voice. He had an RAF type moustache and sharp eyes that eagerly took in all around him.

When all our team had assembled, we went down to the cells to see Jimmy. As one might expect, he was extremely nervous and fearful as there was an awful lot at stake.

Walking down to the cells, I drew a contrast between the clothing of Mr Steer and our junior counsel Alan Goldsack. On the one hand the older man with the huge experience and all the tricks of the trade at his disposal and on the other, the young man, with the new gown and white wig.

As we were waiting for the defendant to be brought into the interview room, I recalled one of the famous stories about Wilf Steer, concerning an appearance that he made in the Leeds Assizes, as it then was.

Wilf was a man who enjoyed a lunchtime drink and a meal with his colleagues and on the Wednesday of the trial in question the lunchbreak was no exception.

He had been to mess the day before. (A gathering of all the barristers when they dine out together and take wine.) It had been a particularly good mess for Mr Steer, who had thoroughly enjoyed himself, but the following day the effects had lain heavily on his stomach.

On his return from lunch he felt it necessary to pay a call of nature and so went into the barristers' toilets and found himself a cubicle. Unfortunately the court was due to start at 2.30 and at 2.35 Mr Steer had not made an appearance. The case was before a High Court judge who, it was rumoured, was of an unpleasant disposition. He instructed the usher to go to the robing room, present his compliments to Mr Steer and ask that he come to the court straight away.

The embarrassed usher went downstairs into the robing room and into the area of the cubicles within.

"Are you in there Mr Steer?" shouted the harassed usher.

"I beg your pardon," said Mr Steer abruptly from the cubicle within.

"His Lordship presents his compliments and asks that you come into court straight away Sir," said the usher.

Quick as a flash and as only Mr Steer could, he replied "I'll be with you as soon as I can but I can only deal with one shit at a time".

I was brought back to the present with the arrival of Jimmy Riley who was wearing traditional prison issue.

Mr Steer went through Jimmy's evidence very thoroughly before leaving to appear in the court.

We all took our places and the judge of the day walked in. It was a sombre setting in Court Number 1 at the Sheffield Crown Court. It was a traditional courtroom with a dock decorated with brass fittings, unlike the modern 'plastic' courts that are now being built. The jury were sworn in and taking their places they stared at Jimmy, doubtless out of curiosity concerning what was to follow.

The clerk of the court then put the charges to Jimmy, who pleaded not guilty in a loud clear voice. The prosecutor opened his case and then called the evidence.

I suppose we could have agreed the evidence of his wife but we knew she would be a bad witness and would not impress the Jury and indeed we were right. We did have certain points to put to her, not least that the gun went off at the moment it went through the window. I doubt if she knew the relevance of that question but she agreed with the proposition, making our explanation more likely.

Jimmy's best pal had not turned up and, despite an attempt by the prosecution to adjourn the case, they were ordered to proceed because information came to the court that he had left the country to work abroad and had not left a forwarding address.

The pendulum began to swing our way and at the end of the prosecution case we were doing very well indeed. The defence then had to make a decision whether or not to call Jimmy to give evidence. He had given an account of the incident to the police and we did not disagree with what had been said so there was not much more that Jimmy could add. There was of course the explanation as to why he had the finger on the trigger but Mr Steer felt that he could deal with that in his final speech to the Jury.

If Jimmy did not do well in the witness box the whole case could be ruined and so the decision was taken that Jimmy would not be called. He was very relieved because I think he was rather frightened of giving evidence. We did call the gun expert, however, who did an extremely good job, pointing out that in his opinion and based upon experiments he had carried out with this weapon, our client's version was quite credible.

The best of the case was saved until last, which was Mr Steer's speech to the jury. Other younger barristers who were in the courts at that time came in to listen to the great man. He had a smooth, almost laconic style and he treated the jury as though they were dinner guests who appeared to hang upon every word.

The speech ended with Mr Steer suggesting that whilst Jimmy was guilty of wounding by reason of recklessness it was certainly not an attempt to murder.

As he sat down I could almost hear people in the gallery standing and applauding, such was the impact of his address.

The timing was first class because we had reached 1 o'clock and it meant that the jury would adjourn for an hour's break with Mr Steer's words ringing in their ears. The afternoon was taken up with the judge's summing up, which everyone felt had a very heavy prosecution bias.

I have found in jury trials that if a judge sums up heavily on one side, whether it be prosecution or defence, Juries tend on occasions to go the opposite way. In this case they had been given a pro-prosecution summing up and indeed Jimmy commented on it in the cells afterwards.

The jury went to consider their verdict that afternoon but by 6 o'clock they had not reached a decision.

The court decided to adjourn until the following day and the next morning at 10.00 am I paid one of my many visits to the cells to see my client. He was in reasonably good spirits and was most grateful for the work which had been done on his behalf. Waiting for the Jury to come back is a very difficult time and it is when the recriminations can start.

The time began to drag and by 12 noon the jury were still out.

I went down to see Jimmy again and he took a deep breath when he saw me because he thought that a decision had been made. I put his mind at rest about that by simply saying no news is good news. I used the time to complete some dictation and I made a number of telephone calls to the office only to be told that the Christmas party was in full swing and Sean Page was delighting the audience with a selection of tunes from Gilbert and Sullivan's the "Mikado" sung outrageously out of tune.

"It's a shame you're missing it," said Wilford, his speech slurring as if he had had a stroke.

"I think that's a rather unfortunate and totally inept comment to make Wilford," I said, or words to that effect, and ventured back into the court corridor, where I continued to wear out the soles of my shoes walking the well worn path up and down outside the courtroom.

I had a conversation with Alan Goldsack about 3 o'clock and he told me that the judge wanted to conclude his business for the day at 4.00 pm and if the Jury had not returned a verdict he was going to check the state of play. I completed my dictation and, feeling the onset of cramp in my left foot, I decided to visit Jimmy once again.

I found Jimmy playing cards with two of the prison officers. He wasn't really concentrating on the game but he did not want to throw kindness in their faces. I got the impression that, having listened to the trial, they hoped he would not be convicted of attempted murder. Despite the fact that he was not on his own, Jimmy looked a lonely and desolate figure who blamed himself entirely for what had happened. I have to confess that I felt sorry for him. He was not a criminal but life had played him a bad hand and he was now paying the price. I really hoped he would get off.

I could feel the tension mounting as the judge came into court and watched the Jury as one by one they took their places in the jury box. I believed the foreman was the rather snipe-nosed gentleman in a business suit sitting at the front. I had noticed him in the trial writing a considerable number of notes. The clerk to the court asked the foreman of the jury to stand and indeed it was him.

The clerk of the court addressed the jury.

"Members of the jury, have you reached a verdict upon which you are all agreed?"

"No," said the foreman of the jury.

My heart sank. The clerk of the court then asked, "Members of the jury have you reached a verdict upon which at least ten of you are agreed?"

"Yes," said the foreman of the jury. I should add that juries are entitled to bring a majority decision of not less than ten to two.

The clerk of the court added to the tension by shuffling his papers and then he asked,

"Members of the jury, on the count of the indictment relating to attempted murder, do you find the defendant guilty or not guilty?"

There was a long pause and I swear you could have heard a pin drop. We all listened with bated breath as the foreman of the jury announced, "Not guilty of attempted murder, but guilty of wounding".

Jimmy fell back into his seat and there were gasps from the back of the court where Jimmy's family were seated. One or two of them began to clap, but the clerk of the court ordered silence and Jimmy was told to stand.

Mr Steer's face did not flinch for one minute as he continued to write a note on his brief. The judge asked Mr Steer to address him in mitigation, which he did most eloquently, and then the judge proceeded to sentence.

The judge then told Jimmy to stand and he prolonged the agony by telling him that despite the fact that the jury had found him not guilty of attempted murder, wounding was still a very serious matter and one in which he could only consider passing a sentence of imprisonment.

He said that he had mitigated the sentence somewhat by reason of the circumstances surrounding the case, but the least sentence that he could pass was one of eighteen months' imprisonment. The judge's final three words were "take him down".

With remission for good behaviour, an eighteen month sentence then was worth twelve in all and Jimmy had been in custody on remand for about eight months. That meant that he only had four months left to serve. As Jimmy was taken down he gave me the thumbs up sign and I smiled, not wishing to upset the court by reason of over-familiarity with a client.

Jimmy was as delighted as any man could be who had just been sentenced to eighteen months' imprisonment but had possibly avoided eight years. He knew that had he been convicted of attempted murder he would have been sent away for a very long time and not surprisingly he was most grateful. Of course he could not take the law into his own hands and if that was allowed then we would have complete anarchy, but there are those cases where it can be argued that the injured party had substantially provoked the situation. We found out later that this woman had had a string of affairs while Jimmy was working nights with everybody in the village knowing except him. It was a lesson to us all that you cannot take the law into your own hands but Jimmy was the loser in the long run.

As I was leaving the court I looked at my watch, it was after 5.00 pm. The Sheffield Christmas shopping traffic would be at its worst and I saw flakes of snow beginning to fall. As I left the entrance I saw Mr Steer walking down the steps.

"It looks like snow," said Mr Steer and he was right again.

The office party was due to finish at 5.30 and I saw little point in rushing because I was not going to make it in time.

I walked past a Salvation Army band who were playing Christmas carols. The tune was 'God Rest Ye Merry Gentlemen' and at that moment the prison bus pulled out into the main stream of traffic and I spotted Jimmy who was waving from the back seat. As corny as it may sound it was a poignant moment.

I used a public telephone to ring the office. It was answered almost straight away and a voice said, "VD Clinic Rotherham, are you phoning about your tests?"

"Merry Christmas, Pagey," I said. "What's happening?"

"We're just leaving old chap," said Pagey. "We're moving on, I'm going to a bit of a do with the Halifax Building Society."

"Where's everybody else going?" I asked.

"Round the twist old chap, round the twist, all the beer's gone, all the sausage rolls have been eaten and all that's left is a gherkin and a bottle of vinegar, but lovely thrash dear boy, have a nice Christmas and thanks for the invite." Before I could say anything else, Pagey had put the telephone down and that was it.

I walked to the car park amidst the comings and goings of last minute shoppers. A man and woman with five children were walking in front of me and each of them was carrying a piece of Christmas tree to their vehicle. How on earth they were going to get a 12ft Christmas tree into their car was beyond me. The children were all excited and I kept hearing references to "Father Christmas" and I wondered what he was going to bring me.

I got back to Rotherham just before 6.00 pm to find that the office was in darkness. As I walked up the stairs, I could see Christmas trimmings and plastic string adorning the stairway. At the top of the stairs I held the little wooden decorative door stopper which was always loose. As I put my hand on to help me around the twisting staircase, I was aware that I was touching something soft and horrible. It was crazy foam, green in colour. Again I gave out a begrudging laugh as I walked into the reception area. It looked like Hiroshima just after the bomb.

The walls were covered with trimmings and there was a Christmas tree in the corner which had fairy lights flashing on and off. As I went into our interview room I found a number of Christmas cards on my chair. I picked up the cards and slumped into the chair. I don't think I'd ever felt as lonely.

I opened one or two of the cards and found that one had a picture of a man dressed as Santa Claus. He was on a roof but he was not delivering presents, he appeared to be removing lead. On the inside the caption read 'All the very best from Jack, Madge and the kids', and at the bottom was the scribbled signature of Albert with a swastika next to it. There was a card from Mrs Yardley and Louise. I opened another which was a very large card with the legend 'Happy Birthday, Granny'. It was unsigned with the price label still on it and when opened there was a Marks and Spencers voucher for a Pyrex dish inside. I shook my head, put them all on my desk and decided to call it a day. I got all my things together and realized that the cleaner would be in on Monday so I picked up my keys and moved to leave. As I got to the top of the stairs I surveyed our office. So this is my first Christmas. They could have at least let me know where they were going - bastards, I thought again and went to leave. As I did so the door to Oscar's room burst open and all the gang jumped out blowing party trumpets and throwing streamers and shouting "Surprise Surprise". I was shocked.

Someone then announced that Pagey was going to make a presentation and he walked to the front wearing a Flower Pot Man's hat and an extremely lifelike pair of rubber breasts.

"Merry Christmas and congratulations on your first Christmas in practice Steve," he said and handed me a small box.

Inside it was a little wooden plaque with a silver plated mounting which read, 'Wilford Smith & Co inaugurated May 14, 1981'.

I would have been deeply touched and moved were it not for the fact that I had purchased this plaque the week before for the reception area but I suppose it was the thought that counted.

The cassette player started blurting out with the hit record of the day called 'The Land Of Make Believe' by some group or other. Pagey was dancing in tune to this music by the front window which looked onto the street. He appeared to be simulating the national dance of Nigeria in a rather offensive gyrating fashion.

As he did so two policemen on patrol outside looked at the window and simply shook their heads.

"Merry Christmas," shouted Pagey, giving his front end a squeeze - God bless us all and everyone.

Chapter Twelve

MONEY IS NOT EVERYTHING - IS IT?

It was late February, 1982 and it was freezing cold. The air-conditioned roof was the next thing on the agenda.

I had finished my court at about 3.00 pm and Wilford and I were having a partners' meeting to review our finances. Tracy, the receptionist, telephoned to say that Sam Trueman was in reception wanting a quick word. I had known Sam for ten years as we had played in the same football team until he retired at 40, because his knees had started to go.

He could best be described as a decent bloke, with no enemies, spending most of his life either at work or on the football field. Indeed, football was his life and after his second cartilage operation he realized that his body would not stand the rigours of training four nights a week and two afternoons playing matches. I remember his retirement party very well because I could not remember anything about the party due to alcohol induced facial paralysis, but I am told that I gave a speech and made a presentation.

Sam was upset at having reached the end of his playing career but he kept in touch with local football through managing one local side and helping to train the factory team for whom he used to play. He spent the rest of his time working in his garden and studying at the local technical college, acquiring skills in DIY. Sam was immensely popular and being a bachelor he often shared evening meals with the families of his friends. In all he was a thoroughly likeable chap.

Therefore I was surprised that he had called to the office to see me because he had always believed that social visits should not interfere with working hours unless there was a problem.

After my meeting with Wilford, I invited him in. He looked troubled and I could see quite clearly that this was not a social call.

"What's to do Sam?" I asked him cheerfully.

"I don't know where to start Steve but I've got a bit of a problem. I'm not sure what to do and I wondered if you could help me?"

After offering him a glass of Canadian Club Whisky, which was our favourite tipple at the time, I turned up the gas fire and pulled two chairs up in front of it. As I was doing so, I realized that despite having known this man for ten years, I knew remarkably little about him, apart from the fact that he was a steel worker, a sportsman and single. Beyond that, all I knew was that he had the appetite of a horse and the ability to run Jarvis a close second on drinking a pint of Guinness in just over four seconds!

Sam was holding some papers and a large envelope with a stamp which caught my eye because it was unusual.

"Where's the stamp from Sam?" I asked.

"Australia," he replied. "This is what I have come to see you about."

I was intrigued and wanted to know more.

"How much time have you got?" asked Sam.

"As much time as we need," I replied.

Sam took a deep breath and told me that he would need to explain some of the background before his story would make any sense.

"You see Steve I'm adopted, I never knew my parents."

I was taken aback. "But I thought your parents lived in Rotherham?" I queried.

"True," said Sam, "but they're my adoptive parents, although as far as I am concerned they were my real mum and dad."

Sam was rather uncomfortable and I could see it upset him to divulge personal details so I encouraged him a little by saying how lucky he was to have had two such splendid people to support him. He agreed and went on with his story.

"All I know is that my real mother was 'well to do' from a very good family but in those days to be pregnant and unmarried was frowned upon, and she was pressurized into putting the children up for adoption."

"Children?" I queried. "Did you say children?"

"Yes I found out that I was a twin but I will tell you more of that in a minute. My real father was the eldest son of the family's gardener. There had been a whirlwind romance but my mother's family had stopped her marrying him. She was sent away in disgrace and I and my twin were split up and adopted. When my real grandparents died they left all their money and property to my mother's very eccentric sister who had emigrated to Australia just before the war. This sister invested it in a farm in Australia but had no contact with my mother. At this point the picture becomes a little hazy and I'm not sure about what happened next but I settled with my adoptive parents in Rotherham, unaware that I was adopted until I was about ten years old when they thought that I should be told. From then, I often wondered about my own parents, particularly my mother, and my adoptive parents told me that they wouldn't mind if I wanted to find her. I chose to leave it at that although I often wondered what she was like.

"About a year ago I received a telephone call from a man called Mr Shoreham who said that he was acquainted with one of my family and that he would like to see me. His connection was from many years ago at the time of my adoption when he had married a member of my family, who had now died but who had made him promise that one day he would seek me out.

"I must say Steve that I was shocked, confused but also intrigued and so I agreed to meet him. A few weeks later he rang again from a hotel in Rotherham and invited me to join him for a meal. He wouldn't give me any further details over the telephone as I suppose he wanted to keep my interest and ensure that I turned up."

"Sam, it could have been anybody," I said, "someone with a grudge," realizing almost before I had said it that Sam had no enemies and he wouldn't even be suspicious. "Please go on," I said.

"Well I went to the hotel reception and almost straight away a man came up to me.

'You're him, you're Sam aren't you?' he said without a hint of doubt in his voice.

"I didn't know what to say. He could see that I was very confused but he led me to a table where we had a drink together.

"He said that he didn't think that there was an easier way of telling me than to get straight to it."

"That will do for me," I said, "I prefer straight talking."

"However, you could have knocked me over with a feather when he said that I was his brother-in-law."

"The twin?" I said.

"That's right," said Sam, "but I was still confused and he went on to tell me that he had married my twin sister. He could see the shock register in my eyes, and said, 'You didn't know, did you, that you were a twin?'

"I told him that I didn't even know who my mother was and I certainly didn't know I was a twin as my adoptive parents had not told me.

'Ah well they didn't know,' said Shoreham. 'They only knew about you. The twins had been parted at birth and Janet (that was the name of his wife) had been taken straight away whereas you were left until some weeks later. It was thought best at the time to do it that way. After all, we are talking about forty years ago'."

It was obvious that Sam was clearly moved by that revelation, as he related the story to me.

"So I had a sister you see, she was born ten minutes before me and she too was adopted but lived in London. She had never enquired about her birth until she found that she was suffering from cancer. By that time, she had married Shoreham, but she had no children of her own. It was when she was told that she only had a short time to live that she decided to trace her mother. It became quite a quest, and they did their best to find her before it was too late.

"By a number of twists of fate, they found that my mother had married and ended up in America but unfortunately she had died five years before my sister's quest had started.

"Quite by chance they found that our only surviving relative was our aunt who was living in Australia. She was still alive but was something of an eccentric and did not wish to have contact with them.

"The correspondence with our aunt did reveal one thing and that was my existence but as you can imagine it was a very difficult task for them to track me down.

"Unfortunately, Janet became very ill and just a matter of a few months ago she passed away. Her husband promised her that he would trace me and tell me that she did all she could to try to find me before she died.

"It was his sort of tribute to her that he carried out her wishes. He said that I would never know the lengths to which he had gone to try to find me."

Sam was clearly moved by the man's plight and he told me that he had kept in touch with him ever since and had been to stay with him one weekend. This had been an incredible learning experience discovering his family history, something he knew nothing about for over forty years.

"I had always wondered you know," said Sam, "if there might be somebody out there who I belonged to. I just wish that she had lived long enough for us to meet."

"But you never told us anything about this, Sam," I said inquisitively.

"No I didn't bother anybody with it, it was kind of personal if you know what I mean."

"Yes I know exactly what you mean," I said agreeing with him, "but what now Sam?" I asked.

"Well it doesn't end there, because yesterday I received a letter from some lawyers in Australia saying that they had managed to track me down following my aunt's death."

"Your mother's sister?" I queried.

"Yes that's right, my Aunty Kerry."

"Well you're probably a beneficiary," I said.

"Well they need to establish that I am actually her nephew and then I suppose they will tell me what they want. I hope I'm not going to be asked for any money."

Sam produced the letter which was simply enquiring into his identity and requesting a copy of his birth certificate.

Sam asked me if I would check the matter out for him and I agreed that I would do so.

I was of the opinion that the old lady must have died intestate, that is to say without a Will, and in those circumstance her estate would pass to the next blood relative or relatives. There was no likelihood of Sam being asked for any money so it was clear that something in the nature of a small windfall might be coming his way. I never realized what a windfall it was going to be.

Sam drank his glass of Canadian Club before going on his way.

"It's a fantastic story Sam, I hope there's a happy ending."

"Well Steve," said Sam, "there would have been if I had been able to meet her, but I am not really interested now because the old lady obviously didn't want to know me, but will you answer the letters and see what they want?"

Sam refused a further glass of whisky. We shook hands and he picked up his belongings and made to leave, but before doing so he turned and almost apologetically said, "There is one thing Steve...."

"What's that Sam?" I asked.

"If there is a picture of my mother I would like to see one."

"Of course Sam," I replied."If there are any pictures you shall have them."

"I've already got some from her husband," he ventured, "but it would be interesting just to see...." his words trailed off as he left the room. I was determined to help him and wrote to the lawyers that very day.

About a fortnight later, I received a reply from the Sydney based firm informing me that they were satisfied that Sam was Kerry's last remaining blood relative and, as she had died intestate, he was the sole beneficiary.

They were in the process of calculating the value of the estate and would send further information as soon as possible. They were also to telephone me on the Friday and explain the background more fully.

Friday arrived, the call came and I was given the full story by an extremely pleasant chap called Newbury.

Kerry was the older sister and was an eccentric. She had emigrated to Australia having fallen out with her family, never to see them again. However she did inherit some monies, which she put to good use buying a sheep farm. As more land became available she bought it, acquiring a vast estate. As she grew older, she became more and more eccentric with the result that the farm got into financial difficulties, forcing her to sell part of the land to pay her debts.

She had never married and indeed from what I could gather marriage would not have suited her.

Living in the outback she formed a great friendship with the Aborigines, and over the years gave them a considerable amount of land. It seemed that she was going to make a Will, but she never got round to it.

Mr Newbury told me that she had disposed of all but a quarter of the acreage to pay off debts and to ensure that the Aborigines, who farmed the site and looked after the sheep, had a permanent home and some security.

It would be a matter for Sam whether he kept the farm or sold it. However, I couldn't see the logic in keeping it and trying to manage it from the other side of the world, I advised him to sell.

Mr Newbury then told me that there was another asset that might be more appealing. It seemed that for the past forty years, Kerry had been visiting a villa, which she owned, in the northern part of Majorca. It was in a very prestigious area and one of the neighbours was none other than Sir Harry Secombe. The villa was set in three acres and had the benefit of two swimming pools and boasted a Bentley in the garage. The grounds housed a bungalow which was occupied by the maid/housekeeper and her husband, the handyman, who had been employed for almost thirty five of those forty years. The villa was fully furnished and a valuation of some £700,000 had been placed upon it.

The only other asset appeared to be a collection of one hundred and fifty didgeridoos of questionable value.

I was shocked and couldn't believe the fortune that Sam had inherited.

I thanked Mr Newbury for his clear explanation of my client's position and concluded by saying that I would write with Sam's instructions as soon as I could.

I put the telephone down, sat back in my chair and thought about the magnificent country of Australia with its warmth and space and then about Majorca with its discreet little coves set in an elegant coastline which made me drool at the very thought of it. I then realized that I had the rather pleasant duty of informing Sam of his good fortune. Without further ado, I telephoned him, but there was no answer. I telephoned his work and left a message for him to contact me as soon as he could.

That night, as I was leaving the office, Sam came round the corner in his car. He told me that he had got my message and had called on the off chance that I would still be at work.

"Go and park up and meet me back here," I said, unlocking the office door.

When he arrived I took him back into the office and poured him a large Canadian Club whisky.

"Sam you're going to need this," I said. "Prepare yourself for a shock."

"I'm not paying out a penny piece," said Sam.

"You're dead right there old cocker," I said to him, "now just listen to what I have to say."

I related the telephone conversation with Mr Newbury and

showed Sam the correspondence which I had received. Sam listened intently.

"You mean, there's a farm, and how many acres?"

"Ten thousand," I replied. "Most of the land has been sold off or given away to the Aborigines who lived there. Apparently the farm is a bit ramshackle, but the land is quite valuable."

Sam sat back in his seat and asked me to venture a guess as to how much it would be worth.

"At least one hundred pounds an acre I believe, but there are some duties to pay and taxes which will probably reduce the value."

"Bloody hell Steve," said Sam. "It's too fantastic to think about."

"Well that's not all," I said to Sam with the air of a know-it-all, "There is also a villa in Majorca with three acres and a swimming pool."

"Bloody hell," said Sam, clearly running out of superlatives.

"Actually, it has two swimming pools with a housekeeper's bungalow in the grounds, but I saved the best until last, and that is the Bentley in the garage."

"Bloody......," this time Sam couldn't even finish the comment. He looked to the ceiling and scratched his head and then looked at me rather suspiciously,

"This is not one of your little jokes is it? Because if it is......"

"Look Sam," I said, "this is not something to joke about. You have to face facts and the facts are that you, Samuel Trueman, are a millionaire."

I poured Sam another large glass of Canadian Club as he attempted to take in what I had said.

"Oh, and of course, there is one thing that I have forgotten, you own about fifty thousand sheep."

I laughed, but looking at Sam he didn't know whether he wanted to laugh or to cry.

"You are being serious aren't you Steve?" said Sam.

"I have never been more serious in all my life and in view of the fact that you are a millionaire, I am even going to be nice to you."

"It's all like a dream," said Sam. He still couldn't take it in.

"You are probably the richest man that I know Sam, and I would like to shake your hand because it could not have happened to a nicer fellow."

Sam scratched his head again and said, "If you weren't so ugly, I would kiss you."

"Oh kiss me anyway you rich bastard," I said.

We laughed and I poured Sam another glass of Canadian Club.

We discussed the merits of owning a sheep farm but Sam was determined to sell it. He was anxious to ensure that the residents who lived on the land would have a home, so he decided that he would donate the farm house and some of the land to the people who had worked for his aunt, to ensure their security.

This was typical of Sam, but nothing less than I expected.

The only difficult decision was the house in Majorca. We decided that Sam would go home and consider the matter and make a decision at a later date.

We agreed a meeting and Sam offered to buy me a champagne dinner. I accepted gladly because I did not wish to offend him and of course I wasn't going to turn down a free meal.

Over the next two or three days, Sam considered his position and at dinner he told me that he was going to Majorca to see if he liked the villa. If he did he was going to move in and sell his house in Rotherham.

I wondered if Sam was subconsciously trying to have some form of contact with his new found family, because I thought it odd just to up and leave. However, Sam had no family and when he asked me to go with him in an advisory capacity, any doubts I had quickly disappeared.

By the end of the evening, I had drunk more than was good for me. At 1.00 am I had agreed to arrange for 50 of Sam's sheep to emigrate to Majorca as well, so that he could start a sheep farm on his villa. Fortunately, we called an end to the evening before things really got out of hand but not before we had decided to buy some pigs to keep the sheep company.

A fortnight later, after juggling my work commitments, Sam and I were sitting at East Midlands airport waiting for the 8.40 am flight to Majorca. Four hours later we were crossing the tarmac at Mahon airport.

It was 15th March, and it was raining as we left but on our arrival there was bright warm sunshine to greet us.

Transport had been organized to take us to the northern point of the island, where the villa was situated, and within two hours we were there. All we could see were wrought iron gates which looked to be newly painted and a terracotta tile driveway which twisted and turned invitingly into the distance.

As the gates were locked we used an intercom mounted on the gatepost at the front. A woman's voice answered and the electrically operated gates opened. We paid the taxi and decided to walk up the drive. It went on forever and at each side of the path there were shrubs and flowering trees, many of which I had not seen before.

The whole driveway was a blaze of colour and the perfume from the plants almost anaesthetized us, the scents and aromas were so strong. As we rounded the final bend, we saw what was probably the most beautiful building I had ever seen. It was the colour of terracotta. The house was enormous and had two separate patios at different levels, both of which housed magnificent swimming pools.

As we reached the first patio, we could see beyond the trees to the coastline and a pale blue sea that shimmered in the sunlight. The view was breathtaking and almost rivalled the Amalfi coast for beauty. We both stood and looked at the view without speaking. Our silent deliberations were interrupted by a female voice shouting "Hello, hello".

I looked round to see a grey-haired lady in her sixties. She had a dark skin, lined by the ravages of the sun and she was wearing a black dress and oven gloves.

"It must get cold in March," I said to Sam nodding towards the gloves.

"No," said Sam, "she's probably just had a boxing lesson."

As she drew nearer, I saw a most welcoming smile on a still beautiful face. She shook hands with us both and curtsied as she did so.

"My name is Isi," she said with a giggle and, turning to the villa, bid us welcome. She asked us to follow her and we were taken to the second patio which had a number of stone urns placed here and there containing bright red and yellow flowers which had been freshly watered. My attention then focused on a man, who looked like a farmer, wearing a red teeshirt, shorts and sandals. He was of about the same age as the woman and it was clear that here was the handyman. As we were introduced, he lifted his hat and we shook hands.

We were shown into the house and given a conducted tour with Isi showing us around with great enthusiasm. She spoke fairly good English which was fortunate because we had no Spanish at all, other than Paella, Chianti and moucho gracias.

The house was beautifully decorated and had been extremely well maintained and it was clear that Isi was justifiably proud of her charge.

The gardens were beautiful and there were a number of hoses watering the lawns. Many of the flower beds had been freshly dug, ready for the new influx of flowers for the forthcoming season.

At the rear were further gardens and in one area there was a wooden arbour which housed bougainvillaea for a distance of at least fifty yards. Beyond this there was a wonderful little cottage with its own gardens. There were vegetables, herbs and fruit trees of all descriptions. This was where Isi and her husband lived and the view was magnificent.

We sat on the patio and looked out to sea. There can be no doubt that it was an idyllic spot and I could understand how Kerry would have been intoxicated with the place.

Isi had prepared a meal for us which we ate and washed down with a litre of local wine.

We had all but forgotten the Bentley when Toni showed us a large three door garage and there was the car in all its splendour. It must have been twenty-five years old but in mint condition with only twenty thousand miles on the clock. It was a white open topped car, but we discovered that it had not been used for some considerable time and would need a mechanic's eye over it before we were able to drive it.

Isi explained that the local village was only a walk of some two kilometres away. It had two restaurants, a mini-market, an electrical shop and something in the nature of a newsagents/post office.

"What more do you want?" said Sam enthusiastically and I realized that he was smitten.

The next two days were spent enjoying the house and the local terrain and we even assisted Toni in the garden.

The early evenings were spent in the pool, although Sam seemed to suffer some skin reaction to the substance in the water which was equivalent to our chlorine. The evenings were spent dining in grand style on the patio. The cellar had a marvellous wine collection with a large number of bottles of expensive champagne.

It was still warm enough to sit out in shorts and teeshirts and we took full advantage of the weather. I was sorry when it was time to leave as although we had only been there two days, it was easy to get used to the life.

On our last evening we sat together and watched the magnificent sight of the setting sun. A yacht sailed by, followed by a solitary seabird which dived in and out of the empty rigging with the sound of an outboard motor as the only competition for the rustling of the mimosa tree in the gentle breeze.

As we looked out to sea Sam confessed to me that he wanted to stay and I even had a job persuading him to return to England and settle his affairs. His two new employees were clearly delighted with their new employer and he with them.

Sam gave them full assurances that their jobs and future were secure and so, on the day we left, everyone was happy.

On the flight back home, Sam told me that he intended to put his own house up for sale and as soon as he had dealt with his affairs he was going to catch a plane for Majorca and make the Villa 'EL ANOS POCA' his new home. I couldn't blame him.

Three weeks later I was waving Sam off at East Midlands airport with a standing invitation to visit him. Watching him as he boarded the plane, I realized that I had never seen him so happy.

Driving back to Rotherham, it was raining and cold and as I passed the 'Welcome to Rotherham' sign it began to hail. I could not help feeling a touch of envy. The car radio started playing Julio Iglesias' 'Quierene Mucho'. I jabbed at another pre-set radio button thinking what a lucky bastard Sam was. The warm continental music was gone and a newsreader was announcing that a 200 mile Exclusion Zone around the Falklands was coming into force. I was back in the real world. When I got back to the office, I was told that Spider's case had been listed before the Crown Court and had been called in as a reserve and would be heard the next morning. Reality was certainly waiting for me with open arms and I embraced it reluctantly.

Chapter Thirteen

PAGEY GETS DRUNK AND GOES TO BED WITH A HIGH COURT JUDGE

A few days later I had arranged to meet Sean Page for lunch to see if I could help him with the insurance brokerage business he had recently set himself up in. Having completed my morning court I had rung the office to find that there was a message from Pagey telling me that he would have to miss our lunch appointment. As I left the court I ran into Paddy Hargan, a fellow solicitor in Rotherham who I had not seen for some time and we agreed to eat together and bring each other up to date with our social lives.

I happened to mention Pagey missing lunch and Paddy smiled a knowing smile.

Paddy had gone to the same public school as Pagey and he had invited him to an old boys' reunion the previous night in the hope that Sean could make some good contacts for his new business.

The function was held at the old school itself and began with early evening cocktails followed by a dinner with many courses. Inevitably there were large quantities of alcohol to drink and by the end of the evening, Pagey was drunk and had also spent all his cash.

With no money he was unable to stay in one of the local hotels so Paddy Hargan suggested that he should take advantage of the offer to stay in the Halls of Residence. The students were on holiday and a number of their rooms had been made available to the old boys.

What Paddy didn't tell Sean was that the rooms, with only one or two exceptions were fully booked .

"How do I know which room has been taken and which hasn't?" said Sean doing his best to speak clearly.

"Quite easy dear boy," said Hargan knowingly, "you try all the doors until you get to one which is not locked and that room will be available. Now be a good fellow and bugger off because we are going to a nightclub and you wouldn't get past the door in your state."

As everyone made their farewells and promises to meet again in the very near future, Pagey walked off into the Halls of Residence.

As he walked down the corridors he noticed paintings of former pupils who had attained high office. There were politicians, churchmen, judges, and important businessmen all looking down upon an intoxicated Page from their hallowed positions on the residency walls. Page busily tried doors as he went, but they all appeared to be locked. Eventually, he came to a room which was open and when he went inside he realized from the assortment of brushes and Hoovers that it was the broom cupboard . A bed was significantly absent and so Page closed the door, but not before tripping over one of the brushes which had been propped up in the room.

Pagey fell over on his way in. Having fought his way out with enough noise to wake the whole school, he desperately walked along four corridors until he got to room 113. It opened.

"Eureka," he cried at the top of his voice. "This will do, even if it is another broom cupboard."

As his own voice echoed in his head he told himself to be quiet, shushing before he entered the room. He was unable to find the light switch but it didn't matter because he could see the outline of a bed in front of him. Pagey then began to undress.

Undressing whilst intoxicated is a very difficult exercise, particularly when trying to remove one's trousers. The effects of alcohol affected his balance and he had great difficulty in being able to remain upright whilst performing this difficult manoeuvre. Pagey managed to remove all but his Chelsea boots and a red bow tie which proved to be most awkward and simply refused to leave his neck.

Page could not bend to get the boots off and in a fit of pique announced for all the world to hear those most poignant words:-

"Oh fuck it."

With that he breathed a large sigh and fell back onto the bed shouting, "Geronimo!"

As he lay back, he realized, horrified, that something was moving.

The something was also horrified that something else was sharing his bed and Pagey discovered that he had unwittingly formed a sleeping partnership with a High Court Judge who, fearing that he had been attacked by a group of IRA sympathizers, shouted "Help!" at the top of his voice before reaching for the electric light switch and his walking stick. He stood with the stick aloft, to find a naked Pagey, in only his Chelsea boots and red bow tie, spluttering profuse apologies for the intrusion.

Any thought that Page had of joining the legal profession were squashed that night and it was to be a few days before I saw him again.

The next morning when I got into the court corridor the usual smoky haze seemed thicker than ever as I made my way to the solicitors' room. Then the smell hit me and I realized that most of the people sitting along the corridor were smoking large cigars.

Before I could get into the room, I was stopped by four clients all speaking at once.

"Who's first?" I said. The biggest of the group, a lad called 'Fingers', was 6' 6" tall and weighed about nineteen stone. It was no surprise to me that he indicated that he was first and the smallest of the group was last. The giant announced that he had a new charge of GBH (grievous bodily harm)and announced that he was definitely not guilty because, to use his own words.

"I only hit him once."

"Yes," said his friend, "but it was with an iron bar."

"It depends upon the nature of his injuries," I told the giant. "If the injuries are serious then obviously that would reflect in the charge."

"What's tha mean, reflects in the charge?"

"Well it means that if he has serious injuries, then taking these into account together with the fact that you had used a weapon, is probably the reason why you have been charged with such a serious offence."

"He deserved a crack," said the giant, "he's an eapa..

"An eapa?" I asked, "What's an eapa?"

"Tha knows," he said, "An eapa - an out-and-out eapa."

I must confess that I had not heard this term before and I asked him to qualify it.

"What's tha mean qualify it?" said the giant.

I breathed a despondent sigh and asked, "What does an eapa mean?"

"Tha knows, eapa shit."

"What?" I asked.

The giant spelt it out slowly

"HE IS A HEAP OF SHIT - AN EAPA, EAPA SHIT, GET IT?"

"Oh I understand," I said to the giant. "An eapa: as in heap of shit?"

"Yes," said the giant, thinking that I was an idiot.

"It was the inflection in your voice that I didn't quite understand."

"What's tha mean inflection in me voice?"

"Never mind," I said, "just give me your charge sheet." As I looked at the charge sheet the giant lit a cigar.

"Does tha want wun?"

"No thanks," I said, "I don't smoke." I looked at the cigar and could see that it was clearly an expensive one. I completed the giant's legal aid application, which he signed with a cross, and he went and sat in the smoke-filled corridor.

I followed him out to shout the name of my next client. "Tom Gifford," I shouted at the top of my voice.

"Argh," came the reply. I went back into the room and sat there waiting for him to appear. I waited ten seconds and then twenty seconds and finally after thirty seconds I wondered what had happened to Mr. Gifford. I got up and went to call his name again.

"Tom Gifford," I shouted.

"Argh," came the reply.

"Where are you?" I shouted.

"He's not here," came the reply.

"Well why did you answer his name?" I asked.

"He's me mate," came the reply. I was confused at that and so I tried someone else.

"James Beresford," I shouted.

"Argh," came the reply. This time I was going to wait to see if he appeared. He did not. "James Beresford," I shouted, "Are you there?"

"No," came the reply.

"Well, why answer his name then?"

"He's my mate as well," came the voice and with that there was also laughter.

I entered into the spirit of the thing and shouted "Well is anybody here?" and with that the entire corridor shouted "Yes".

I then noticed a familiar figure walking towards me through the smoky haze. It was Jack and with him was a small boy who I recognized as Albert. By that time I had christened him "Albert the 'Orrible".

"Morning Steve," said Jack.

"Morning Jack," I replied.

"Morning Steve," said Albert.

"Hello Albert," I said begrudgingly.

Jack asked if I could have a word with him and so I took him into the interview room while Albert waited outside. I noticed that Jack was smoking a large cigar.

"I didn't know that you were in court today," I said to Jack.

"No," said Jack, "I haven't seen you about this one yet."

He handed me his charge sheet which I put into my note book until I had time to consider it.

"I'm not guilty, I haven't done it and I resent it," said Jack. "I'm not having this one, fair's fair, if I've done owt, I'll take it, but I am not having this eapa."

"Eapa?" I queried.

"Yes eapa," said Jack.

"I'll complete your legal aid application and then I will go into Court and see what the evidence is against you, okay?"

"Okay," said Jack and off I went into court.

I had so many things to do that I left Jack's case to one side.

Just then the usher from the other court came in to tell me that they were waiting for me and my case there had been called on.

Now I was in for a grade 4 bollocking. This really dropped me in the 'eapa' for I was needed in two places at once.

As that Bench retired I dashed into the other court and started that case only to find that within ten minutes the magistrates in number one court had re-convened and were demanding my attendance.

As the usher came in to give me the bad news, I noticed that he had a cigar behind his ear.

"You've got to come into Court Number 1, Mr. Smith," said the usher.

"Bloody hell," I said to myself and continued with my case. Fortunately the Bench had to retire to consider it so I ran back into the other court and apologized to them for keeping them waiting.

I understood that the chairman of the magistrates had a council meeting on the hour and so he was not very pleased that he had been kept waiting.

It was just the situation that a juggler has when he has one ball too many. I felt like saying to them, "For God's sake man, how can you possibly expect me to work in two places at once?" But it was pointless as he wasn't interested in my welfare, only his council meeting. As he began to deal with that case the usher from Court Number 2 came in and said that the Bench had come back in and were demanding my attendance immediately. I sat there for a minute and thought if I scream and throw a wobbler it might be the best way out of this particular mess. The other way out would be to induce gastro-enteritis, but I thought better of it and promptly ran into Court Number 2 to receive yet another grade 4 bollocking within five minutes of the last one. As I ran into court, a woman grabbed my arm and thrust a pair of underpants at me saying "Give these to Fred". Fred was one of my clients who was in custody and his wife was using me as the postman to take him his clothes. As I dashed down the corridor I was given a pork pie for another defendant who was in custody. I dashed into the court carrying the pork pie in one hand and a pair of underpants in the other. I put my pen in my top pocket, the pork pie in my trouser pocket and completely forgot about the underpants in my left hand. As I walked into court carrying them, the magistrates looked at me with some disdain and I immediately stuffed them into my other pocket, tendering my apologies.

The magistrate took off his glasses and spoke to me, "You appear to be in a little bit of difficulty Mr. Smith."

"Yes, it's the job Sir," I replied. "It's an eapa."

"I beg your pardon," said the Magistrate.

"I mean I appear to have been required in two places at once Sir," I replied, "and my problems are getting worse."

When the case was finished, I dashed back to the court to take the result and as I went in I saw Albert, sitting on a chair by the door, smoking a cigar. I took it off him and said, "You're far too young to be smoking, young man."

"Giz it back," said Albert.

"Not bloody likely," I said and walked into court. I hadn't realized that the Magistrates were still in attendance so I put the offending cigar into my pocket. It wasn't long before the smoke began to drift out of my pocket and into the open air.

I was presenting a mitigation, oblivious to what was going on until I realized that the magistrates had focused their attention on my left hand jacket pocket.

As I was addressing them, the same lady who had presented me with the underpants, put another pair in front of me on the court Bench. I stopped my address and looked at the magistrates and they looked at me. There was silence.

"Mek sure Arnie gets them," she said. I told her that I would be delighted to pass on the objects and I looked to the Bench.

"And another thing," I said, "he's from a broken home but he's got plenty of underwear." The Bench laughed but refused bail and that was the end of that.

When I left the courtroom, the corridor was even thicker with cigar smoke.

Looking for Jack, I found him in the WRVS tea room and as I crossed the room I saw a young girl sitting on the oak benches. She was fourteen or fifteen and it was obvious that she was playing truant as she had a satchel in one hand but strangely a cigar in the other. I saw Jack out of the corner of my eye deep in conversation with someone I didn't recognize. I shouted him over.

Jack came towards me with a large beaming grin, "Cup of tea Steve?"

"Yes please Jack."

"Chocolate biscuit Steve?"

"Yes please Jack, I think I will."

"Cigar Steve?"

"No thank you Jack," I said. "But I would like to know what is with the cigars, everyone appears to be smoking them."

"Get away," said Jack.

I went to the solicitors' room in the hope of getting out of all the smoke, to find David Walters, another solicitor, busily smoking someone's socks in his pipe.

"Good God, Walters, what's that?" I said.

"It's a Jamaican," said Walters.

"Well let him out, the smell is awful," and with that I fled into the "rat hole", the interview kiosk next to the solicitors' room with the vain hope of getting some fresh air.

The entire building was dilapidated and by the end of the day the court corridors were left filthy with cigarette stubs and empty packets, drinks cans and containers strewn everywhere.

I was reflecting on this when the emphysemic usher called me out again.

"There's a man in the cells wanting to see you Mr. Smith."

"What now?" I asked, almost as if the Usher was to blame.

"Don't know," he replied, "but I have got his charge sheet here."

He passed me the documentation. I read the charge, "That you Jonathan Hawkins on the 7th July did steal one African parrot to the value of £900".

I called to Jack in the tea room and told him that I would see him after I had been to the cells.

When I got downstairs, the jailer asked me if I wanted to see the 'Bird Man of Rotherham'. Before I could answer he asked "Do you think he will get some bird?" I gave him a withering look but he answered his own question. "I shouldn't think so, it's only a poultry offence."

As the cell door opened, Jonathan Hawkins appeared to a call of "Whose a pretty boy then?" from one of the jailers. My esteemed client walked, shamefaced into the interview room. He was a swarthy skinned youth with buck teeth and a cleft pallet which left him with an unfortunate speech impediment which stopped him from pronouncing certain letters. J's became Y's, T's became W's, B's became M's, R's became W's and S's became th's and H's were not in his vocabulary.

He was wearing tracksuit bottoms and a yellow teeshirt with a picture of a bird on it.

"What's your full name, young man?" I said to him.

"Yonathan Orins."

I realised that we were going to have massive difficulties.

"And your address?" I asked.

"Wenty Hoo, Witherthonm Theep Hoom, Wotherthum."

"Come again?" I asked.

"Wenty Hoo, Witherthonm Theep Hoom, Wotherthum," he replied.

"I just missed that, give me it just once more."

"Wenty Hoo, Witherthonm Theep Hoom, Wotherthum," he said again.

"Ah, yes Rotherham," I exclaimed, I had got a word right. "But whereabouts in Rotherham?"

"Wenty Hoo, Witherthonm Theep Hoom, Wotherthum."

"Nearly got it," I said. "Could you just write it down for me on this legal aid application." I thought that this was the best way of dealing with the problem because the lad was clearly embarrassed.

"Ha yes," I said. "22," but then I stopped in horror. I couldn't read his writing either.

"I'll tell you what," I said eagerly, trying to make him feel at ease, "I will ask you a question and you answer yes or no."

"Eh!" came the reply.

"Oh my God," I said to myself. "Of all the cells and custody areas in all the world you had to walk into mine."

"Yes," came the reply.

I did not answer.

Did you pinch the parrot?" I asked.

"Yes er no," came the reply.

"The hard one first," I thought.

"Have you still got the parrot?"

"No," came the answer.

"Where is it now?"

"On," he replied,

"On what?" I asked.

"On," he said again.

He gestured with his hands in a fluttering motion.

"Oh, gone," I said.

"Yes........on."

"Where has it on to, I mean gone to?" I asked, becoming aware that the affliction was spreading.

"Own away," he said sadly.

"Flown away?" I queried.

"Es," he said. "On."

"Where were you when it flew away?"

"Us!"

"Us?"

"Es, us,"

"Would that be bus?

"Es."

"So you were on the bus with the parrot when it flew away?"

"Es."

"Which bus?"

"A wed won."

"Charming," I thought.

"Did the parrot get out of the bus," I asked.

"Es," came the reply.

"Wait a minute," I thought to myself. "I'm getting as bad as him, of course it would have to get out of the bus to fly away."

"Why did you take it Jonathan?"

"Ike arrots."

"You like parrots is that it?"

"Es."

"You didn't keep it long did you?"

"O."

"No?"

I then tried to lighten the proceedings,

"Did you have it sitting on your shoulder on the bus?" I asked.

"Es, ats why on."

"Yes I can imagine."

"Do you know you should not have taken it?"

"Oppose."

"Were you going to keep it?"

"Es."

"Why?"

"Ike arrots."

"It's a shame that, was it a talking parrot?"

"Es," said Jonathan disappointedly.

"I can imagine you would have had some fun with that wouldn't you, teaching it to speak."

Bloody hell I thought to myself, that would have been one confused parrot. Perhaps he was better off taking his chance in the outside world.

"What are you going to plead, Jonathan?" I asked.

"Ilty," came the reply.

"Yes, I think that will be best."

He was frightened that he might have to speak in court, because his speech problem got worse when he was under stress. I realized that this was a case where I would be doing all the talking and, so far as I could tell, Jonathan was happy with that even if I wasn't.

I was exhausted after the interview and was glad to get back upstairs. I couldn't help thinking how on earth he would cope with giving evidence.

When I looked at the prosecution file to see what the case was about, I noticed a short interview which had been recorded contemporaneously by the police. It consisted of four pages, but when I looked at the times at the bottom of the page, it was reported to have taken seven hours!

When I got back to the corridor, it was heaving with cigar smoke and nearly everybody sitting there was smoking. Jack appeared and we went into the rat hole for a discussion. I asked him for his charge sheet so that I could see what he had to face and he reminded me that he had given it to me earlier that morning. I apologized and looked through my note book to find it.

Jack sat there and listened intently as I read out the charge.

"Let's see what we have got this time then Jack," I said.

I read aloud,"That you on the 4th July, did steal four thousand Cuban Havana cigars the property of Ashley Warehouses Limited."

It wasn't until I actually got to the end of the charge that I realized what I had said. I had just been going through the motions, reading it 'parrot fashion' if you will forgive the expression.

I stopped and read it again, this time more loudly than before and I spelled it out slowly and deliberately.

"THAT YOU ON THE 4TH JULY, DID STEAL FOUR THOUSAND CUBAN HAVANA CIGARS, THE PROPERTY OF ASHLEY WAREHOUSES LIMITED."

Jack looked at me completely unperturbed as he drew upon his Cuban Havana cigar.

"Is there any significance between this charge and the fact that everybody on that court corridor is smoking cigars?" I asked firmly.

Jack considered the position carefully as he drew upon his Cuban Havana. He blew out the smoke, creating the impression of a managing director who was about to decide upon a major share deal. Looking at the ceiling and then looking at the floor he drew again on his large cigar. What pearl of wisdom am I going to be greeted with now I thought, as Jack slowly blew the smoke from his mouth. He flicked the ash onto the desk in front of us.

"Tha what?" he asked.

"To put it in English Jack, who has been flogging the cigars on the court corridor?"

"I am buggered if I know," said Jack. He than drew again on the cigar and said profoundly, "You know, I think that he is wrong tha knows."

"Who's wrong? What's wrong? What do you mean who's wrong? What are you talking about Jack?" I asked in a state of confusion.

"Fred," said Jack,

"Fred who?" I asked.

"Tha knows Fred," said Jack.

"No I don't know, I can't understand a word of what you are saying."

"Tha knows, that bloke I was talking to in t' tearoom."

"What bloke in the tea room?"

"Tha knows, him who I was speaking to."

I suddenly remembered Jack huddled in a corner, deep in conversation with a man who I did not recognize.

"Oh yes, I remember him," I said. "What's he wrong about?" I asked thinking that this was the $64,000 question and answer to the cigar query.

"Churchman's Joy," he announced confidently.

I must admit that I was getting extremely frustrated by this time because, whilet I knew and accepted that Jack lived on an entirely different planet, he had completely lost me.

"What are you talking about Jack?" I said.

"Churchman's Joy, it's got no chance at Haydock Park, it's carrying too much weight."

I realized that the discussion with the man was something in the nature of a red hot tip.

"Forgive me Jack, I wasn't talking about Haydock Park or Churchman's Joy or Fred, I was asking you about the cigars."

"Oh them," said Jack, "I found em."

"Found em, I don't think I know what you mean?" I asked.

"Found em!"

"Whereabouts did you find them Jack?" I asked.

"On that lorry," said Jack.

"On that lorry?" I asked.

"Argh, they were delivering weren't they and these boxes were on t' back at lorry so I like found 'em and walked off. It were like an accident tha knows."

I realized that I was getting somewhere.

"You stole them from the back of the lorry," I said. "Is that right?"

"Well I think I fon em."

"Yes but you shouldn't have taken them, Jack, should you?"

"Fair comment that cocker, fair comment, if you put it that way."

After that rather bizarre conversation, it was clear that Jack had to plead guilty to finding the cigars on the back of the lorry, as opposed to them having fallen off.

We decided that Jack would plead guilty to the offence, and I than began to consider whether I could find any mitigation to put before the court.

I managed to borrow the prosecution file so that I could consider the evidence and it was fairly clear that Jack had been seen by two witnesses from the shop, to accidentally, but on purpose, find the cigars on the back of the lorry. They then found their way into the sidecar of Jack's motor bike.

It would have been very helpful if the property had been recovered but unfortunately Jack appeared to have sold most of them to an eager public.

"They're a good smoke," said Jack with the air of an expert, as if he had done nothing wrong.

The usher then came into the rat hole and asked me to go into court for the Bird Man was due to appear.

I decided to tell the court clerk of the defendant's difficulties but unfortunately he would not listen. He had a long list and was determined to finish by 1 p.m. and have his full one-and-a-quarter hours for lunch. After all it was in his contract. I, on the other hand, would spend my lunch hour in the cells watching the poor defendants eat while I took my instructions. I might even find a second or two to have something to eat myself. More haste, less speed, I thought to myself and so I took my place on the solicitors' bench while I contemplated the nightmares that were sure to occur.

"What's the next case?" growled the court clerk.

"Jonathan Hawkins," I replied.

"Is he in custody?"

"Yes."

"What's the charge?" he continued.

"Parrot pinching."

"How long will it last?"

"Forever."

"I beg your pardon?" said the clerk, expecting pleasantries to follow rudeness.

"Not in my contract," I said.

"What are you talking about?" said the clerk.

I didn't have to reply because the Birdman had arrived.

The clerk rustled his papers, looked at his watch and took a deep breath and shouted,

"Are you Jonathan Hawkins?"

"Es" answered the Birdman.

"Well, say so properly," said the clerk sharply.

"What is your address?"

Now we are in for it, I thought.

"Wenty Hoo, Witherthon Theep, Hoom, Wotherhum",

"I beg your pardon" said the clerk.

"Wenty Hoo, Witherthon Theep, Hoom, Wotherhum".

"Come again," said the clerk.

Here we go again I thought, so I interrupted with the full address.

"Thank you," said the clerk looking confused.

The charge was read out and the clerk asked Jonathan for his plea.

Jonathan could not answer at first because of a mixture of nerves and his impediment.

"Well," shouted the clerk, "are you deaf?"

"No Sir," I interrupted. "He has a speech impediment."

"Well why didn't you tell me," said the clerk in a state of embarrassment.

My fist clenched as I felt the urge to remind the clerk that his parents were not married when all of a sudden Jonathan shouted,
"Ilty."

The prosecutor opened his case, and laughter came from the public gallery when they heard the details of the case.

After I had addressed the court, the chairman of the magistrates asked, "Have you anything to say?"

Oh my God I thought, but before Jonathan could speak, the clerk was in like a flash. It was 12.56 pm and he was not for delay.

It is rare to suffer a long retirement so close to lunchtime and indeed at 12.59 pm the Bench returned and fined him £150 and costs.

Most of the lunch break was taken up with Jonathan's paperwork and sorting out how he could pay his fine. I only had time for a cup of tea and a quick telephone call to Wilford back at the office.

At 2.15 pm, the emphysemic usher then went into the corridor to call Jack in. When he walked back into court the usher was coughing loudly. It seemed that the cigar smoke was so bad that it had started off his cough.

I had agreed with Jack that he was to plead guilty to the theft of the cigars because the evidence was overwhelming, but sometimes it is simply not enough to agree with a client that they will plead guilty. Defendants can sometimes simply change their minds almost as if it is an affront to ask them to plead guilty. This was such a case and when Jack was called into court and the charge put to him, he said firmly, "not guilty."

The clerk to the court then asked me if they were my instructions and I told him with a sigh that they certainly were not.

As Jack was a very good client and I didn't want to embarrass him in the courtroom, I thought perhaps just one or two straight left hooks might be sufficient to bring him to his senses, but unfortunately the magistrates would have seen it. I therefore tried to reason with him.

"I thought that you were pleading guilty," I whispered to Jack, trying to be as pleasant as possible through gritted teeth.

"Oh right," said Jack. "I thought that I was pleading not guilty."

"No," I said. "You are pleading guilty because you have done it and you have admitted it."

"Okay," said Jack and I asked the clerk of the court to put the charge again.

"Are you guilty or not guilty?" said the clerk firmly.

"Not guilty," said Jack and with that a sigh of despair went around the room.

As I was about to get up again, he shouted "Guilty" almost as if he had made the biggest concession of his life.

Before I could address the Bench, the chairman said that he would like reports. I couldn't help asking, "Would they be of a psychiatric nature?"

"No," said the chairman of the magistrates. "Full probation reports so that we can look into his background."

The magistrates were sharp enough to see that earlier that year Jack had been sent to prison for driving while disqualified and obviously thought that a probation report might give them a better idea as to how to deal with the case.

"Don't forget to get my bail renewed," said Jack.

"Oh, I never thought about that Jack," I said sarcastically, but again before I could speak the magistrate renewed his bail and Jack left the court shaking his head.

"Your client seems a bit confused Mr. Smith," said the court clerk.

"Not half as much as I am sir," I replied, bowing to the Bench. As I did so the chairman of the magistrates winked at me as if to say "Yes, your job is an eapa isn't it."

When I got outside, Jack was waiting for me with his wife Maj.

"Hello Maj, how are you?"

"I'm all right Mr. Smith," she said puffing on a large cigar. "Will he get nick?" she asked.

"I hope so Maj, I really hope so," and with that they both laughed and left.

Albert was standing at the side of them with the same wide grin festooned upon his face.

"All right Albert?" I said.

"All right Steve," replied Albert. "Have a nice day me old cock."

I grimaced when I heard the little sod make that comment and I tried to smile, resisting the temptation to clout him at the back of the head.

As he turned to walk away, I noticed that he held the remnants of a large cigar in his hand, behind his back. I just shook my head in despair and went back into the solicitors' room.

The WRVS brought me a cup of tea in a cup marked 'coffee' and when I had marked up my files I set off back to the office, taking a deep breath en route to avoid the fumes in the corridor.

Later that afternoon, I put the radio on to hear the latest test score and just managed to catch the racing results before the cricket programme started. I was particularly intrigued with the Haydock Park race which had been run at 2.30 pm. It seems that it had been won by a rank outsider called Churchman's Joy at 30-1

That same night, Wilf and I went out for a Chinese meal on our winnings! We toasted Jack, and his mysterious friend Fred, many times that night.

Chapter Fourteen

WHO WANTS A WILL ANYWAY AND THE RETURN OF SAM

During that meal Wilf and I had decided that the time was right to buy new cars. We had had a very good first year in business and so, the very next day by trading in our old cars as deposits, we bought two brand new Ford Capris with the registration numbers OHE 164X and OHE 165X.

There is something special about the thrill of collecting a new car. There is the smell of the interior and the sparkle of the paint work which you remember forever.

A few days later, we were sorting out our applications for the AA when the telephone rang and David Langley, a client of ours, wanted to speak to Wilf about buying an old folk's home.

David and his wife already owned one such home which was doing very well and they had decided that they would open a second in a different area. David was an electrician cum handyman cum dogsbody and his wife a qualified nurse.

Their homes catered for the elderly who could not look after themselves and who did not have the benefit of relatives to help. Some were perfectly sound in mind but physically deficient and others were physically able but mentally frail.

During the conversation, David said that a number of the residents had expressed the desire to make wills and, in an attempt to help, he said that he would arrange for the Solicitors of their choice to come to the home. As no one was nominated he asked Wilf, but stressed that it was essential for us to visit the home itself, because many of the patients could not travel to our office.

We agreed to help and set a time for the visit.

By this stage my friend Jack Bennett, who was a retired police inspector, had agreed to help in the office, taking statements and preparing cases for me to deal with in court. Jack would see clients and prepare the criminal cases, relying upon his thirty years' experience as a police officer, and ten years experience working in a solicitors' office as a managing clerk.

Jack had retired from his last job due to a heart attack, but when he recovered he needed a part-time job to keep him sane. This

170

arrangement suited us both and Jack agreed to work three days a week soon becoming a great asset.

He was extremely fit for his 70 years, looking particularly distinguished with his white hair and moustache. He had served in the Army in Burma and would often regale us with stories of his service, particularly tales of the Japanese prisoner of war camps.

On the day of the appointment at the old people's home, I collected Wilf and Jack from the office and off we went, to take instructions from twelve residents. By dividing the clients between the three of us we thought that a couple of hours would see the job done. However we were to be proved wrong.

We arrived as lunch was finishing and David and his staff were busy pouring out cups of tea and serving biscuits and scones.

One old gentleman came up to me on our arrival, "I like a bit of scone on a Tuesday," he said with a wink.

"Yes certainly," I said, nodding and smiling in approval, hiding from him the fact that it was Thursday.

When the refreshments were served, David explained to everyone who we were and the reason for our visit and said that we would speak privately to each resident.

We were given a small round of applause and all three of us nodded and smiled in an attempt to make our new clients feel at ease.

David left us and I asked who was first but no one answered. I realized that they were probably a little shy, so I went up to the gentleman nearest to me who was sitting in a large leather armchair.

"Do you know who I am?" I said to the old gentleman, smiling politely.

"No," said the man, "but Matron will tell you if you ask her."

"Yes," I said, "I will see you later if I may, Sir," turning to the next one in the firing line.

Wilf and Jack sat among the various groups and chatted away, introducing themselves. Jack was persuaded to sit in a large chintz armchair and one old lady insisted that he make himself feel at home so he removed his jacket. As he sat there chatting, an auxiliary nurse came into the room to start her first shift. She sat next to Jack and began a conversation.

"You had your bath this morning?" she asked.

"Yes," said Jack not realizing the nurse's error, or indeed the relevance of the question.

"Have you been to the lavatory?" she continued.

"Well I suppose I have, but it is not something that I would like to talk about."

"Don't be shy, I might be giving you a bed bath tomorrow."

"Oh, wait a minute," said Jack, "I think that you have the wrong person, I am not a resident."

"That's what they all say," said the nurse tugging at his arm.

"But he will verify who I am," said Jack, pointing to me.

"I will be with you in a moment Sir," I said to Jack seeing the possibility of a joke. "If you would just like to go with the nurse, I will sort you out in a minute."

"Is this gentleman with you?" asked the nurse.

"I have never seen him before in my life," I said firmly. Wilf had turned the other way because he didn't want the nurse to see him laughing as Jack was escorted to goodness knows where.

My next client was an old gentleman who sat in a wheelchair. He looked very old indeed and had a heavily lined face but a considerable twinkle in his eye.

"Are you a solicitor?" he said staring at me intently.

"Yes I am," I replied.

"I am extremely pleased to meet you," said the old gentleman. "Would you like to sit on this chair at the side of me?"

I thanked him and sat with my notebook and pen at the ready.

He gave his name, date of birth and his age. He was 92.

"You look extremely well for 92, Sir," I said as politely as I could.

"Well thank you young man, I don't do bad really. The only problem I have got is with my legs. I can hear and I can see, but these wretched legs do let me down."

I sympathized with him and it was nice to talk to someone of his age with such mental agility.

"Do you like it here?" I asked.

"Yes I do, I have a lovely room with a pleasant view over the gardens. I have books and the staff are good enough to get me most of the daily papers because I like to keep in tune with what's going on in the world. I am only here because I cannot get about and my family live away, in a flat, so it would be impossible for me to live with them, but they do visit me as often as they can. I am well cared for, and fortunately I am not a burden to anybody."

I was struck by the character of this old man. He was friendly, extremely pleasant and most articulate. We spoke about a will and I took his instructions, which were clear and very concise.

"Who do you like best of all the staff then?" I said to my ageing client, trying to continue conversation.

"They are all extremely good," he said, "but I suppose if I were to choose my favourite, I would say it was Avril."

"Why do you pick Avril?" I said. He thought for a moment.

"Because she's got big tits!!..." said the old man with a grin.

"Next client please," I said.

Another old gentleman came towards me and sat by my side.

"Are you wishing to make a will Sir?" I said.

There was no reply.

"Are you wishing to make a will Sir?" I repeated.

No reply.

"I am a solicitor and I am here to assist people in relation to making a will."

His attention then moved across the room when he stood and shouted "Avril" and then walked off.

I was then approached by an old lady who was extremely smart dressed in a blue Paisley frock. Her hair was snowy white but well kept and she had a bright cheerful face.

"Hello," I said.

"Beg your pardon?" she replied.

"I just said hello, how are you?"

"Beg your pardon?" said the woman.

"My name is Steve Smith and I am here to assist in the making of wills."

"You're Will who?" she said.

"I'm not Will, I'm here to help with a will."

"You've come to help Will?"

"No I'm not here to help Will."

"What's the matter with Will then?"

"No, nothing is a matter with Will, I'm here about a will that people prepare in case they die."

"Has Will died?" she said, looking upset.

"No Will's not died, I am not talking about Will, I am here to ......"

I stopped talking when I noticed a hearing aid peering out of the top pocket of her cardigan. I noticed that there was a slender wire reaching from the hearing aid to her left ear.

"Would you like to turn it on?" I continued, pointing to the machine.

"Turn me on, what do you mean by that?"

"Turn it on," I said, pointing to her pocket.

"Oh, it's a white cardie, I knitted it myself, this is what I have got on."

I was getting desperate by this time and I just said to her, "Excuse me, I'll get help".

With that I went to Wilford who had just finished with one client and said, "Oh, there is a lady over there wearing a white cardigan who would like to see you".

Wilf went straight over to her.

"Hello, I'm Steve Wilford and I am a solicitor, I have come to help with your will."

"Will, I have just been told that he is dead. Well that is what that young man said over there."

"No, I have come to help you to make a will," said Wilford.

"You've come to collect him, are you from the undertakers then?"

"No," said Wilf, "I am a solicitor."

"You're a solicitor?" she said managing to catch that, "My goodness, that was quick if he's just died."

"No," said Wilford. "It's about a will".

"The will?" said the lady, "Has he made a will?"

"No," said Wilford."I've come about making a will".

"Has he left me something?" she said.

"No," said Wilford. "No he's not left anything."

"The mean old bugger," she said, "and I knitted him a jumper last year, I'll have that back for a start."

Many minutes later I heard an exasperated Wilf shout "Jack!!!"

By this time Jack had returned, having convinced the nurse that he was a visitor and not a resident. He was extremely flustered and could not see the joke.

"I am very sorry about that Mr. Bennett" said a very stern looking nurse.

"That's all right, I suppose it was easily done, but I enjoyed the bed bath all the same," Jack said laughing.

I looked at Jack and said, "You've not had a bed bath have you?"

"Oh yes," said Jack, "very nice too I enjoyed it." The nurse blushed and left the room.

My next client was another elderly gentleman, who at ninety six seemed to be the eldest resident . He had all his faculties and told me that he had a long walk every day.

"How do you manage to keep so well?" I asked him.

"Roughage," he said forcefully, "plenty of roughage."

I didn't want to get into that discussion and so I promptly returned to the point of my visit.

I completed his instructions and passed on to the next resident.

She was a lady who was extremely young looking. She was smart, well dressed and extremely mobile.

"Now then my dear," I said, "would you like me to assist you in making a will?"

"Yes please," she said, "and while you are here I would love some advice."

"Certainly madam," I said, "and how long have you been here?"

"Oh, about four years now," she said.

"Well you look extremely well," I said.

"Oh thank you, I am actually," she replied.

I didn't want to discuss ages, but she was clearly in exceptional condition, to say she was a resident. I realized that it is not very polite for a man to ask a lady her age, but I was intrigued, so I plucked up the courage to ask.

"Would you mind if I asked how old you are?"

"Not at all," said the woman, "I am forty seven."

I looked at her and she must have noted my confusion.

"I work here," she said.

"Yes of course," I replied, realizing that I had very nearly put both feet into the middle of it.

"And your name madam?"

"Avril," came the reply.

"Oh, Avril," I said, "I have been talking to one of your friends."

"Who is that?" she asked.

"The old gentleman in the wheelchair."

"Oh Colin," she said, "Yes he's a right handful."

"That's funny," I said, "that's what he says about you."

She told me that he had nine children and I confessed that I was not surprised. Apparently the youngest was only seven years old.

"I have a really difficult time with him when he is in the bath," she said.

"I can imagine," I said, trying not to.

By the time we had finished, the tea gong went and along came a tray with sandwiches and buns. I picked up a tea and a scone and carried it over for Don Juan.

"Here you are Sir," I said.

"Thank you young man, I have seen you talking to Avril. Hasn't she got a big pair of..........."

Before he could end the sentence, I asked him if he wanted any sugar, which altered his train of thought for a moment.

"Yes please," he said, "Two lumps, talking about that have you seen....."

"Milk?" I interrupted.

"Yes please, plenty of that."

With that I left rather quickly.

As we were drinking our tea, a middle-aged man entered and it was announced that the cabaret for the afternoon had arrived. What a life I thought to myself, it probably wouldn't be such a bad thing to get old. The man introduced himself as Ted and his Magic Saw and I was so intrigued that I didn't want to leave until I had seen his act. He took out a cloth case containing a large lumberjack saw about four feet in length. He sat on a chair amidst his eager audience and bent the saw over at the top.

Out of the same case, he took a bow and it was then that I realized he was actually going to play the saw

The first tune was the 'Rose of Tralee' and at the end of it everybody clapped enthusiastically. Trying to finish my cup of tea and to say my goodbyes I was interrupted by Ted and his magic saw introducing his next number 'In a Monastery Garden'.

It was the unexpurgated version lasting seven whole minutes, at the end of which everyone clapped again but a little less enthusiastically this time. As the applause was dying down, I turned to my colleagues but before we could get up, Ted and his Magic Saw introduced his next piece which was the Prelude to Act 3 from La Traviata.

"God almighty," said Wilford, "I can't stand much more of this," but Ted surged on relentlessly.

As Ted was half way through the Czechoslovakian National

Anthem, we sneaked out at the back.

As we jumped into the car, Wilf turned to Jack and asked, "Who is going to volunteer to go back next week and get all the signatures?"

No one replied.

When I got back to the office, Tracy told me that a man called Sam had been in the office, and would call back just before we closed.

"Sam," I said, "it can't be Sam Trueman, he lives in Majorca."

However, at 5.29 pm in walked Sam with a superb tan. He looked fit, very healthy and it was clear that a few months in the warm sunshine had suited him, or at least that is what I thought.

"How are you Sam?"

"I want you to buy my old house back Steve," he told me firmly.

"You've got to be joking," I said, "we have only just managed to sell it, what in God's name is wrong?"

"I want to come home," said Sam almost tearfully, "I cannot stand the temperatures, it's so warm that I can't go out. If I go in the pool, the chlorine in the water upsets my skin, giving me a rash which turns to blisters. I can't stand the food and the people get on my wick. It's too hot to play football and I've got to say I'm lonely."

I sat back in my chair and just stared at him.

"You're a millionaire. You have everything that you want. You have no worries, no stress, no problems whatsoever. All you have to do is just get on and enjoy life."

"I can't do it there," said Sam, "I want to come home."

Sam handed me a bottle of Spanish brandy and said, "You will like this, it's a nice taste and doesn't give you indigestion".

With that Wilf entered the room, having smelt alcohol and was as surprised as me to see our sun-bronzed visitor.

"I'll have a glass of that," said Wilf producing three glasses.

"What about a glass for us?" I said.

"Bollocks," said Wilford and promptly poured the brew.

He sat with us as Sam explained the reason for his visit.

"It was all right at first," said Sam. "It was new, it was exciting and I was really into it if you know what I mean. I wanted for nothing, my meals were always ready on time, I had the choice of food, plenty of wine, plenty of sand, sun, sea and peace and quiet."

"So what went wrong?" I said, failing to understand his problem.

"It was just too much," said Sam, "too much of everything, too easy, too convenient. Oh, I know, everybody dreams of such a life, but the time comes when you have got to start telling yourself the truth and the truth in my case was that I didn't like it. If I could have moved it back to Rotherham and turned out with my pals when it suited me it would have been perfect, but I was away from everything and everybody that I have ever known and it was too much of a culture shock.

"I don't doubt that I have benefited from it in some way, if only that it has showed me where my real life is. I know you will find it hard to understand, but if you had been through it, I think you would feel the same way."

"I certainly wouldn't mind giving it a try Sam," I said.

"Well you say that now, but if you had been there for all this time, having nothing to do but eat and drink fine wines and sit in the lap of luxury, with the hot sun burning down upon you by the side of the pool, you would soon lose interest."

I looked across at Wilford and raised my eyebrows. Wilford was similarly affected, as he plucked his eyebrows from the ceiling.

"What now then Sam?" I asked him.

"I have worked everything out," said Sam, "I have arranged with some Spanish lawyers to give my housekeeper and her husband their bungalow and sufficient land around it so that they can become self-sufficient if they want.

"The villa can be rented and I can have a bit of an income off it and Isi and Toni will have a job, making sure it is looked after.

"Then you can buy my house back. I want you to go to the new owners and tell them that I want it back."

"You're not serious?" I asked.

"I have never been more serious in my life. I want that house back and I don't care how much it costs to get it. I sold it for £30,000 so offer them £35,000 if necessary or even more if you have to. Whatever you do, just get it back for me."

Wilf had decided that Sam was suffering from heat stroke and didn't mean a word of it. But he said, "You are the client Sam. If that is what you want, that is what we will try to do."

That very night, Wilf and I went to Sam's old house, which was now occupied by a young couple with a small baby.

When we asked them if they would sell it, the couple, not surprisingly, didn't want to know. They told us that they had decorated it and settled down quite nicely and didn't want all the inconvenience of a further flit.

We offered them £32,000 which meant £2,000 profit within a matter of a few months, but they were not interested. They softened a little when we mentioned £35,000 and finally a deal was done at £37,500 with the offer of their legal fees and removal expenses thrown in.

There was, however, one slight problem to this arrangement as Sam wanted them out by the end of the month.

The young couple agreed that they would store their furniture at Sam's expense and would move in with the girl's parents until a new home could be found.

As it turned out it wasn't long before they acquired a very pleasant semi-detached bungalow and with the profit made on the house transaction they were able to move quite quickly. They were thrilled and so was Sam, and to us it was another job and another satisfied client.

A month later, Sam called to tell us that he had got his old job back at the foundry.

"I still can't believe he's back home," said Wilf. "You wouldn't have seen me for dust."

Later on that afternoon, Wilford's mother came to visit us and see the office. Having retired and moved to Cornwall, this was the first time that she had been able to make the return journey to the north.

As Wilf was showing her around, he posed the question, "Mother, are you sure I wasn't adopted?"

"I beg your pardon," said Mrs. Wilford.

"Oh nothing," said Wilf, "just thinking aloud, only joking really."

"I don't know what you mean Steven," said Mrs. Wilford.

"It's a long story mother," he said, "I will explain it to you another day" and with that Wilf set off for the pub.

After that, I used to see Sam quite regularly, at the football training sessions. He was training junior football again and enjoying himself enormously. I don't believe he ever returned to Majorca but when I used to visit him, our photograph, taken outside the

Villa, was proudly displayed on his mantlepiece.

Sam had decided to rent out the villa and this proved to be a very good business as there was rarely a week when it was empty. He had gone into partnership with his housekeepers to ensure that they stayed on and did not retire. It is a beautiful place to stay and everyone who does so is amazed to see a beautifully cared for, but extremely stationary Bentley in the garage with only twenty thousand miles on the clock.

Chapter Fifteen

WILF GOES WATER SKIING AND I DISCOVER THE WAY TO WARM UP A WET SUIT

Michael Walker, the manager of Whitegates Estate Agents in Rotherham, was an expert on the subject of flogging houses. However, he was an educated salesman with letters after his name, which he proudly had printed on his business cards.

He shared the same building as us but he had the prestigious ground floor accommodation, and on the first floor there was a dividing door which led to Michael's private offices. Wilf and I used to make a habit of picking the lock and raiding his office for such things as sandwiches, chocolates and booze. This became something of a tradition, and escalated into raids armed with silly string and crazy foam. On such a mission during the summer of 1982 we were shocked to find Michael walking around his office in a rubber suit. As we knew that he had his office walls decorated with photographs removed from certain colour magazines, Wilf spluttered, "He's a kinky git, look at the gear he's got on."

Michael, albeit red faced, went on to explain in great and graphic detail that he had purchased a new wet suit in which to participate in his favourite sport of water skiing. He confessed to us that the letters after his name on his business cards related to water skiing qualifications rather than estate agency exams. We also discovered that he was the chairman of the local water-ski club based at the Treeton Pond, located some three miles from the town centre of Rotherham. The area was quite scenic but I expressed certain qualms about the quality of the water, because it was literally a large pond with no flowing water.

I had heard of some horrific consequences of drinking stagnant water, but Michael assured us that the water was checked regularly and the findings were always made available to the club. He said he would stake his reputation upon the acceptability of the water for sports purposes and so we discussed the prospect of Wilf and I having a day out on the pond.

"Have you got a rubber suit?" said Walker, to a disinterested Wilford.

"Of course" said Wilford, "but I only wear it at weekends when

I am in the park with the dog, I get a big kick out of that."

Walker was speechless.

"Course I haven't got a bloody rubber suit," said Wilford. "Do you think I'm kinked or something?"

"No," said Walker, "I just wondered on the offchance. What about you?" he said turning to me.

"I'm not kinked either," I said, casually, "but the prospect interests me," I said grinning all over my face.

"You've got to be serious," said Walker, "skiing is a very serious business. If you are interested, I will let you have a try, I'll pull you with my speedboat."

"I didn't think you'd be dragging us round with your hands," said Wilford sulkily.

"What about you?" said Walker, noting my distinct lack of enthusiasm.

"Ok, I'll have a go at anything once," I said.

I have to say at this time, I was in my late 30's, still playing football regularly and considered myself to be a dab hand at badminton. The prospect of physical effort did not concern me as much as the toxins and the bacteria that might be in the pond.

"Are we likely to get upset stomachs?" I asked Walker seriously.

"Not unless you drink over a pint of it," he said with the air of an expert.

We decided to have a go and the outing was arranged for the following Friday.

We chose Friday, because if we were to get the dreaded shits then we would require Saturday to get over it and possibly Sunday for hospitalization. We hoped that we would be able to walk and so get to work on the Monday.

Friday arrived, and Wilford appeared in the office in his casual gear looking every inch a tramp. I on the other hand had to dress up because I had cases to deal with in the morning. However, I was finished by 12 noon and on my return found Wilford poring over a beginner's guide to water skiing which Walker had left with him earlier that morning. The first page covered the requirements before embarking upon the sport. 1. "Learn to swim - This sport can be extremely dangerous for the non swimmer!" Before I could read any more, Michael arrived and Wilf started asking questions,

"Will the rubber suit protect me from the cold?"

"Eventually," said Michael, rather knowingly.

"What do you mean, eventually?" asked Wilf.

"Well," said Walker, "when you first get in the water, the suit absorbs a thin layer of it, and because it is obviously cold, it is a bit of a shock to the system. However, within a very short time, the thin layer of water is heated by the body to body temperature and, consequently, you will not feel the cold after the initial shock is over."

"Is there no way we can get warm first?" I asked.

"Well," said Walker, "there is an old dodge."

"What's that?" said Wilf.

"Pee in it," said Walker.

"Beg your pardon?" I asked, believing Walker to have said 'pee in it'.

"Pee in it," said Walker.

"That's what I thought you said," I said.

"Yes, you see, if you urinate in the suit, body temperature being what it is, you will warm up faster."

I looked at Wilford and we were both rather put off by this somewhat unpleasant suggestion, but Michael told us not to be too squeamish because he did it all the time.

"You're joking?" said Wilford.

"No," said Walker, "it's quite common."

"Very common," I ventured, and then a picture came into my mind of a naked Wilford urinating into a rubber suit and so I asked Michael.

"At what stage do you urinate in it? Before you put the suit on or while you are actually wearing it?"

"Either," said Walker, "whichever takes your fancy."

As we were talking, the telephone rang and Tracy reported that a psychiatrist client was trying to make an appointment to see me that afternoon. I told her that I would be out attempting to drown myself, but I would be quite happy to see her the following Monday. I believed Tracy would pass on the correct information to my secretary Sheila, and returned to our plans for the afternoon.

"What about grog?" said Wilford.

"There's plenty in the clubhouse," said Walker, "but there might not be much time for that because it is quite difficult learning to ski and you need all your wits about you. Any more questions?"

"Yes," said Wilf, "just one, what do you do if you need to pay a call of nature."

All three of us replied in unison, "Do it in your suit." We all laughed.

I then received another telephone call to tell me that one of my cases in the Crown Court had been brought into the list at short notice for Monday.

"Bloody marvellous," I said, "that has ruined my weekend, I'll have to run around contacting all the witnesses." I decided that I would try to put it out of my mind and not spoil the afternoon.

I changed into my casual gear in the office and we all called at the sandwich shop before setting off for Treeton Pond.

Leaving the town centre, we drove in the direction of the motor-way and entered an open area of farm land which made me real-ize that even Rotherham has aspects of beauty about it. It was a warm summer's day and the sun was shining quite brightly, mak-ing the area look all that much more picturesque. We turned onto an unmade road, and there in a clearing we saw a stretch of water against a backdrop of grass banks and silver birch trees, waving a welcome in the gentle breeze. Another hundred yards along the track and we saw the clubhouse; an impressive brick building, which Michael explained had been built with money raised by club members after years of fund raising activities. I then realized that this was a lot more than a lark about in the local pond. Having parked the car, we walked to the clubhouse which overlooked the lake. Wilf and I were the only ones without the proper gear, but Michael said that he would let us use the club suits which were usually kept for guests. I was a little concerned at the thought of who may have urinated in my suit before me, but on being assured that they had been rinsed I embarked upon the not so simple task of pulling on a very tight rubber suit.

"Bloody hell, Michael, I'll never get this on," I said straining to pull the leggings above my knees.

"I think you've got the wrong suit on," said Walker, "that's for Wilf." Wilf's suit on the other hand was baggy and clearly three sizes too big. We decided to swap the suits, but not before I had ensured that he had not already urinated into it.

When our dressing was complete, we wobbled off to the water's edge to find a fleet of speedboats of various shapes and sizes awaiting our arrival. Melvyn Blank, who was a serving CID Officer was a member of the club and was keen to watch the grand debut.

"You look a right pair of pillocks in those rubber suits," said Melvyn mischievously.

"That's exactly how we feel," I said, "so less of the encouragement."

"Who's first?" shouted Walker brightly.

Wilf and I pointed at each other and said in unison "He is".

Wilf suggested that we have a small brandy before we embarked upon the vigorous exercise which was to follow.

"Save some for afterwards," said Walker, "it will kill the bacteria."

I asked Walker how fast the boats would travel while I was being dragged behind on the skis.

"Pre-supposing you actually get up on the skis, we should get you up to 30/40 mph."

Undaunted, I questioned him further.

"What's that thing floating in the middle of the pond?" I asked.

"That is the ski jump," said Walker. "The boat passes that at about 35 mph and you position yourself so that your skis touch the bottom of the ramp. You will then be pulled up the ski jump and off at the end and the effect will be to throw you up into the air for about twenty to thirty feet. You then drop into the water again, at speed, to land on the skis. If you wish you can do a somersault during the manoeuvre but this is extremely difficult even for seasoned skiers." I looked across at Wilford and he at me, and I could see Wilford mouthing obscenities.

I looked out onto the pond and saw what looked like half a front door floating past.

"What happens if we hit something like that?"

"Oh there will be a terrible accident and you will be injured, but we always skim the lake to make sure that there are no such obstructions, we will move that."

"What happens if you miss something like that?" said Wilford.

We all joined in, "There will be a terrible accident!"

With that Wilford turned to go, taking his brandy with him, but he was persuaded to stay, providing that I went first. I was given a forty second lesson on how to position myself, lying back in the water with my feet out front and my knees slightly bent. I held onto the towing line and began to say a prayer before being dragged about one hundred and fifty yards around the lake on my stomach.

I was distraught for three reasons:

1. I had failed to get up on the skis properly.

2. I had consumed approximately two pints of Treeton pond water.

3. They had almost drowned me in the pursuit of their own amusement.

"Let's try it again," said Walker firmly.

"Let's not bother," I said forcefully.

"Come on," said Walker, "that was not bad for a first effort."

"You pillock," I replied, as they towed me into the bank.

A deputation was sent to fetch my skis which had left my feet within seconds of hitting the water. They were put back on and once again I was put into the crouching position, when the urge to vomit came upon me. I dealt with that particular call of nature, in readiness for my second drag round the lake. Three or four further attempts followed, before the leader of the group suggested the towing bar.

"What's the towing bar?" I asked Walker.

"Oh, that's for inexperienced skiers who have never been up before. You hold on to a long rail type object which makes it far easier for you to ski."

"Why the bloody hell didn't we try that at first," I said, "instead of consuming nearly ten pints of this lot."

"We thought you'd like the thrill of being able to get up on the skis, unaided."

I wondered if he would like the thrill of being thrown into the pond and held under it, but I thought I would give it one final go.

We were all in position, and two proven skiers presented themselves at each side of me. We could feel the tension on the towing bar, before the boat accelerated away, but this time, my usual performance of being thrown headlong into the drink was avoided and the two burly skiers held me upright.

I have to say that it was a tremendous thrill skiing round the lake at over 30 mph.

When we got back to the mooring, I was exhausted and so were my supporters, who had had to keep my bulk upright during the whole circuit. But it was now Wilford's turn.

186

I noticed that the small bottle of brandy that we had taken with us, for medicinal purposes, was empty.

"Thanks Wilf," I said, pointing to the empty bottle.

"Don't mention it," said Wilford with the nonchalant air of a man whose fear had been dulled by dutch courage.

As Wilf strolled along the mooring, I noted a slight dampness surrounding his footprints, which confirmed to me that he had either been for a short paddle to test the temperature of the water or the layering to his rubber suit was already warm, by other means.

As Wilf strolled in to the water, the initial shock of the change in temperature gripped him around his nether regions. The volume of his swearing clearly indicated that the temperature inside the rubber suit was far greater than that in the pond. When Walker asked him to settle in the water, and stick his feet out, Wilford used a phrase which I recalled from a previous adventure.

"What the fucking hell, have I got into now."

The assembled crew all laughed for it seemed that there is something amusing about seeing one of your friends in gross discomfort. After his first drag round the lake, Wilford was repositioned in the shallow water for another take off. As the engine revved, the tension came on the towing line and Wilf was pulled headlong into the water. He was given further instruction and the exercise was repeated. The dispirited Wilford began to tire, and his habit of 30 cigarettes a day began to tell. On or about the 12th attempt, Wilford managed to stay upright. As he was pulled round the pond, he passed our position and with unbelievable cockiness turned his head, looked back to us and using one hand made a rude gesture. I was unable to see the look of complete horror on his face, as his skis followed the path to the ski jump.

Wilford took off up the ski jump at 35 mph and after performing the most incredible double somersault I have ever seen, he disappeared from sight as he hit the water like a tonne of bricks.

We had all watched the manoeuvre in open mouthed silence.

As the recovery boat brought Wilford back to the bank, he received a standing ovation from all those assembled. We both declined the option for "another go", as we both felt we had drunk enough of Treeton Pond for one day.

We sat and had a drink at the pond side and by 4.45 pm we were all suitably well oiled and none the worse for our experiences. Our speech was well and truly slurred, but it was clearly time to return to the office to pick up our belongings and make our way home. Walker had kindly provided transport for us but it had to leave at 5.00 pm prompt and so there was no time to change.

We were not expecting anyone to be waiting for us at the office other than the odd member of staff who had not skived away early. Wilf went to his room, and in the true traditions of water skiing consumed an enormous brandy while I went to my room to gather such belongings as I required for the weekend.

Sheila, my secretary, came into my room to say that my psychiatrist client had arrived for her 5.30 appointment. I was aghast. I was in an intoxicated condition, wearing a rubber suit with my hair still wet, clotted with the grease, grime and mud of Treeton Pond which I had stirred up while failing miserably to get up on the skis.

Tracy our receptionist, had been given a can of lager by Jack because it was his birthday and as the office had closed at 5.30 pm and because she was waiting for a lift, she thought it an opportune time to drink the lager. The psychiatrist must have been a little concerned on seeing the receptionist reading the paper and consuming alcohol but as she waited Jack walked into the reception, carrying his can of lager.

I called the client through to my office and I felt her eyes fixed firmly on me as I wandered back to the office, shoeless, but with my rubber suit gleaming in the artificial light. As we walked past Sheila's desk, which stood in front of my room, the psychiatrist took a deep breath as she saw Sheila with a can of lager in her hand.

I tried to explain the reason why I was dressed in such a manner which she seemed to accept, but with a marked degree of reluctance.

No sooner had she sat down than Wilford's drunken face appeared at the glass window in the door, then his hand appeared, holding a glass, giving the clearest impression that he was in search of more drink. Before I could indicate to him that I was engaged, he walked in, falling over an electric fire.

He cursed as he stood up, shouting the words, "Swiggo, Swiggo", before noticing the psychiatrist. Wilford was also still in his rubber suit, with the words "Go, Go, Go", on the back. I could not help wishing him gone, gone, gone.

He mumbled, "I'm sorry, I didn't realize that you were engaged," while he removed a bottle of brandy from my glass cabinet. He smiled as he left and turned to my psychiatrist guest to bid her farewell, before falling over the electric fire once again. With that he drew himself up, cursed and left.

"What on earth is going on?" said the psychiatrist, "Why is everyone either drinking or intoxicated?" The only words I could think of to say were,

"Well, it is after 5.30 pm."

"Quite," said the psychiatrist.

As I attempted to put together some sensible sentences, I looked again at the little window in the door. Walker had arrived and he was armed with two tins of plastic string. Before I could reach for my Bible, or jump out of the window, he burst in, firing indiscriminately from the green and pink plastic string cans. Walker had failed, as had Wilf, to notice my guest, and as he turned to leave, he saw her and stopped firing.

More in confusion, than anything else, Walker simply said, "That will teach them, they're always doing it to me". He turned and tripped over the electric fire before leaving the room.

The psychiatrist looked me firmly in the eyes and announced,

"I've come to the conclusion that everyone here is either an alcoholic or completely mad".

I tried to explain to her that she was not expected and occasionally even solicitors have to let their hair down. As I thought I was getting through to her, I looked in horror as I saw another face at the little window in the door. The timing of this visit could not have been worse. It was Page. He entered the room, giving the Nazi salute and marching the goose step. As he entered he broke wind, and shouted, "Vhich vay to zee torture chamber?" With that my psychiatrist beat a hasty retreat, never to be seen again. As she left the room, she tripped over the electric fire.

Chapter Sixteen

I FIND A CHEROKEE INDIAN IN BELFAST

In late 1982, I was to embark upon one of my most interesting cases. It was the sort of case that you would be pleased to do for nothing; and apart from my expenses, I did just that.

Late one afternoon, after going through a long list of appointments, my last client for the day was a Mr. Richard Pavey. I had not met him before, but I had been recommended to him by a client I had acted for some years previously.

Mr. Pavey was a man of average height but striking facial characteristics, with a golden-brown coloured skin. He introduced himself with a marked Welsh accent but I was sure his origins were even further from Rotherham although he was of no group that I could bring to mind. His skin was neither white nor black but rather an unusual hue and I have to confess that I couldn't quite work this chap out. I was perplexed as to where he was from. Mr Pavey explained that he lived in Barnsley but had come to see me about his son, Owen who had been serving with the army in Northern Ireland until his death only a week before. Owen had been in the army for about three years of a nine year engagement. He was stationed in Armagh in County Londonderry. He had been out on patrol with a group of other soldiers, and on his return from the patrol, he was shot by one of the members of his own platoon. Unfortunately the Army had been somewhat tight-lipped about the circumstances pending an inquiry and so Mr Pavey had come to me.

I was astonished by his story but he was quite adamant about the facts of the case. This was indeed a most unusual death and accordingly an inquest was to be held into the matter at the Armagh Courthouse within the month. The purpose of the inquest was to enquire into the death of Owen Pavey and establish, insofar as it was possible, exactly what had taken place. Mr Pavey Senior had some correspondence which he gave me to read. It did not refer to the cause or nature of death but simply invited him to the inquest and offered him transport to the courthouse. He told me that he wanted an independent lawyer to represent him at the inquest so that he could get to the truth of what had occurred.

I knew that this case would not attract legal aid and although I explained that to him, he indicated that he still wished to be represented at the hearing. It was clear that Mr Pavey had little or no funds with which to fight his case as he was not working and relied upon unemployment benefit to survive. However, I believed that this was a case which required representation.

I told him that I would be prepared to conduct the case but it would be necessary for him to pay all travelling and accommodation expenses, and he readily agreed. As it was a case where we would not be given any documentation before the hearing and the evidence would either be given by witnesses or read out from statements at the inquest itself, I pointed out that we would need a 'noter'.

A 'noter' is a person who writes down the evidence as it is given and Mr Pavey said he would also be prepared to meet with the expenses of a 'noter', so I set about taking my instructions from him. I asked him if he thought there was anything sinister about what had happened and he told me that he didn't know but apparently the lad who had fired the gun was his son's best friend.

Understandably, Mr Pavey became rather upset as he related the facts to me and I thought I would help him regain his composure by talking about other things.

I was still intrigued about the appearance of my client and so I asked, "I notice you have a Welsh accent Mr Pavey, is that where you originate from?"

"I lived in South Wales just after the war and I stayed there for many years until I came to live in Yorkshire," he replied.

"So you're a Welshman then?" I asked.

"Well I am now but I don't originate from there."

I was intrigued and pressed the point.

"Where do you come from then?" I continued.

"I'm actually Canadian by birth but I fought with the RAF during the war and when it finished, I settled in Wales."

His mention of the RAF reminded me of the film "Reach for the Sky" which the BBC had re-run the previous weekend in a tribute to the air ace Douglas Bader who had died only a few weeks before.

"Do you find Wales amusing Mr Smith?"

191

His question brought me back to the present as I realized I had connected Douglas Bader with our own Lidster and his septic toe and I must have been day dreaming with an insane grin on my face.

"Sorry Mr Pavey, I was miles away," I said, looking intently at my client.

I still hadn't grasped what was unusual about this man but there was most definitely something different about him so I pursued the point even further by asking him where in Canada he was from. He gave me the area and indeed I think he named the town but it meant nothing to me.

"I thought there was something unusual about you," I said.

"What do you mean by that?" he said with a smile.

"Well you didn't look Welsh," I said, grasping for the means with which to ask the pertinent question.

"Oh I understand what you mean," he said, "I am actually a member of the Cherokee Tribe of American Indians."

That was it! I had indeed seen that look before and the skin colour, then it made sense.

"But Pavey is an unusual name for a Cherokee Indian," I ventured.

"That's my adopted name," he said, "from the people who I lived with in Wales. My real name is Richard Yellowknife."

He had been born in Canada into the Cherokee tribe and he had been brought up on a reservation before joining the forces. When he came to England he met a Welsh girl and after the war they were married and he settled down. It was a most unusual story and in an attempt to take his mind off the case in hand, I persuaded him to tell me stories of his youth and of the tribe itself.

We were getting on very well and I telephoned Tracy to organize some tea. There was no answer however and she then came into the room having been engaged elsewhere. As she brought the tea in, the sound of a trombone came from the top of the landing.

"Have you got a musician on your staff?" Mr Pavey asked.

"Oh yes," I replied, "it's Oscar, he likes a burst now and again."

I could see that Mr Pavey thought it most unusual but we returned to the business in hand and it was soon agreed that I would appear at the inquest and so Mr Pavey, a 'noter' and I would fly to Belfast from Leeds on a date to be arranged.

Having seen him out of the office I told Wilf about our new case. I explained the background and said that I would need someone to attend the hearing with me but he turned me down flat.

"There are two reasons for that," he said. "The first is that one of us has got to be in the office. We can't both be away for two days."

"And the other reason?" I asked.

"You're not getting me anywhere near Armagh, I might not get back."

Wilf was referring to the massive media coverage the troubles in Northern Ireland were receiving, as only days earlier four people, including two policemen had been shot dead in a day of violence.

"Well who I am going to get to go?"

Wilf dodged the question. "Who are you going to persuade to fly to Belfast and then travel to Armagh to the courthouse itself and appear on behalf of a British soldier's family?"

"Well I suppose if you put it that way, I can see the problem."

"Too true," said Wilf. "Do you have to do the case?"

"Well I've promised him now," I said, "and besides it is very interesting."

"It will be very interesting if you get bombed," said Wilford.

"Well you can have all the debts then," I replied and promptly set about thinking who might be prepared to go.

I needed someone with nerves of steel and guts as wide as a bull's neck; a devil may care musketeer with a thirst for adventure.

I have to say that I could not think of anyone who fitted that description.

That evening as I left to collect my car, I walked past Michael Jarvis's office.

"Yes", I thought to myself, "he'll do," and promptly hammered on his door.

"Now then Smithy, what can I do for you?" said Jarvis.

"Well a small gin would not come amiss," I said.

With that, Jarvis produced a little miniature bottle of Martell brandy and said that was the best he could do.

"The only other thing I can offer you is some tea."

"I'll have that then," I said and when it arrived, promptly poured the brandy into it and set about drinking the invigorating brew.

"I will tell you why I have called," I said to Jarvis earnestly. "I have been asked to represent a very nice elderly gentleman whose son has been killed while serving in the army. He has been killed in very bizarre circumstances and I am desperate to help this old fellow get to the truth of his son's death."

"Good on you," said Jarvis. "You'll be interested in that," he added.

"Yes," I continued, "he has asked me to attend the inquest but because I won't be able to see the evidence until the day itself, I need somebody to take notes for me when I have to cross-examine the witnesses. It involves a pleasant flight and one night and a couple of days away. All expenses paid, all meals and all that you can drink, what do you say?"

"Marvellous idea," said Jarvis, "that sounds as though it might be great fun, I'd be delighted to come with you. Where is it?" he asked.

I was dreading that question, but at least I had got his agreement before I had to tell him where we were going.

"Oh it's in Ireland somewhere," I said, rather casually.

"Ireland," said Jarvis, "which Ireland?"

"Northern," I replied earnestly.

By then I detected a rather suspicious tone in Jarvis's voice.

"Whereabouts in Northern Ireland?" he asked.

I took a deep breath and thought he ought to know.

"Armagh," I said, waiting for the explosion.

In the split second that preceded his answer, I imagined all manner of replies, all of them ending in 'off', but to my complete surprise, Jarvis announced, "I would be delighted, I've always wanted to go to Northern Ireland, count me in".

I immediately felt guilty for dragging my friend into such a risky situation.

"How do we get to Armagh?" asked Jarvis.

"I haven't thought about that one yet," I told him, "but we will work something out."

Jarvis burst into laughter. Perhaps this was the musketeer I had been looking for after all.

I then left, agreeing to let him have the date of the trip as soon as possible. Three or fours days later, Mr Pavey rang me and told me that the inquest had been fixed, within a fortnight.

Mr Pavey had told his son's unit commander that he would be

attending the inquest and had been offered accommodation for all three of us. More importantly, a driver was going to be sent to Belfast airport to collect us and deliver us to the Armagh barracks. This was going to save a great deal of time and effort and so Mr Pavey agreed to call in to see me so that we could discuss the final arrangements.

Meanwhile, I had written to the Army, telling them of my interest in the case, and they were most helpful and obliging in their reply. When Mr Pavey came in to see me, he was rather withdrawn. I sensed immediately that there was some difficulty and I asked him what the problem was.

"Well you see, there has been an awful lot of publicity about my son's case, and I rather think I've dropped you in it."

"What do you mean by that?" I asked.

"Well your name's been mentioned in all the newspapers as being my solicitor."

"Well I've seen one of the papers, and I saw my name mentioned but I'm not worried about that. A bit of publicity doesn't trouble me."

"Well it's not that," said Mr Pavey.

"Well what is it?" I asked.

"I've had a letter."

"A letter?"

"Well, I don't quite know how to tell you this," he said.

"No?"

"Well you ought to know, I've had a death threat from the IRA."

All of a sudden I heard alarm bells ringing in both ears.

"What do you mean a death threat?"

"Someone purporting to be the IRA has written to me and threatened me by saying that when we get to Ireland, we will be seen to."

"We will be seen to?" I queried anxiously.

"Yes, seen to," said Mr Pavey.

"Do you mean ......," I began.

"Yes that's exactly what I mean. But I suppose they do it to everybody just to intimidate them."

"Well it's bloody well worked, hasn't it?" I said to him emphatically.

"I wouldn't blame you if you told me that you didn't want to go," said Mr Pavey.

I must admit that the publicity the case had received had interested me and I had discussed it with a number of my friends and colleagues. They were all expecting me to go and I could hardly drop out because of a threat. I convinced myself that the threat was not genuine but just a malicious action intended to cause maximum upset because a soldier was involved. I took a deep breath and told my client that it didn't make any difference to me and that I didn't place much reliance on the letter or indeed its threat.

"Are you sure?" said Mr Pavey.

"Of course I am," I said, lying through my back teeth.

I imagined the headlines if I had taken up his offer to drop out of the case. They would have been really inspiring ... ROTHER-HAM SOLICITOR GETS COLD FEET or ROTHERHAM SOLICITOR BACKS OUT OF COURT CASE or even worse, ROTHERHAM SOLICITOR DONE BY INTIMIDATION.

We were to fly from Leeds airport into Belfast, where we were to wait in the VIP lounge. The Army would come and collect us in one of their armoured personnel carriers and take us to the Armagh barracks where we would be the guests of the Gordon Highlanders.

I decided not to trouble Jarvis with the mention of the threatening letter and, when the day arrived for us to go, I came to Rotherham, collected him and drove to Leeds where we were to meet Mr Pavey.

By this time, I had got to know him rather well and he had asked me to call him Dick. When we got to Leeds on a chilly morning for the 7.30 am flight, we parked the car and met Dick in the airport lounge.

I introduced Dick to Jarvis and they hit it off immediately. When we got onto the plane, Dick treated us to a drink, which I suppose was a little early but it was part of the trip so we each had a large brandy with our coffee. I had brandy because I was nervous, and Jarvis because he liked it.

The flight was fairly short and within an hour we were circling above Belfast. As we were coming in to land, Dick turned to Jarvis and said, "You're both very brave men and I thank you". As he offered his hand to Jarvis and shook it enthusiastically, I took a deep breath and hoped that that would be the end of it, but Dick continued.

"Yes," he said, "very brave men."

"Oh we are used to flying," said Jarvis. "It doesn't bother us at all."

"Oh God!" I thought, knowing that Dick wasn't referring to flying at all.

"No I don't mean flying," said Dick, "I mean coming here to Northern Ireland .... when there's all this trouble..."

"Oh that's all right," said Jarvis. "Lots of people visit Belfast and never see any trouble."

He was saying this only days after the IRA had killed eleven soldiers and four young women in an Irish pub bombing. I was beginning to feel proud of Jarvis but I still rapidly tried to change the direction of the conversation by pointing to a number of fires I could see on the ground below.

"Yes, very brave men," said Dick, "particularly in view of that letter."

I realized that I was done for. Jarvis was on to it like a flash.

"What letter?" he asked, in a disturbed tone.

"The letter from the IRA" said Dick, "about us being blown up when we get off the plane."

Jarvis looked at me and gritting his teeth said, "You didn't tell me anything about a letter."

"I forgot," I said with nothing better to say.

"Bloody marvellous," said Jarvis, "and when did you get this?"

"Oh about a fortnight ago," said Dick. "Didn't trouble old Steve though."

I tried to excuse myself by going to the toilet but was told that as we were about to land I had to stay in my seat.

Jarvis mouthed some words to me which were particularly offensive. I simply whispered back to him, "You know very well that my parents were married" and with that Jarvis sat back in his chair and fastened his seat-belt. I got the distinct impression that he was saying his prayers.

"At least we've got the Army with us when we get there," I said confidently. "I've never been in an armoured personnel carrier before."

"Do they carry coffins?" said Jarvis.

"Now, now Michael," I said, "let's not get carried away."

When we arrived I could not see any armoured cars. Dick assured me that there would be transport available and I was beginning to worry when we were approached by a man in jeans and teeshirt who was distinctive only by his short cropped hair. He had the look of a soldier in civilian clothes.

"Mr Pavey, Mr Smith and colleague," he said referring to a sheet of paper.

"Yes," I said expectantly, looking over his shoulder for the armoured car.

"I'm Lance Corporal Johnson, I'm here to take you to Omar."

"We're not going to Omar," I said, "we're going to Armagh."

"Not according to my orders," he said. "I was told to collect three gentlemen and take them to Omar."

"No, we're definitely going to Armagh," I said.

And then Dick chipped in and said, "I've arranged this with Sergeant McCloud".

"I don't think I can go to Armagh," said the Lance Corporal, "I don't have a weapon. We have to be issued weapons if we are going into that area."

We explained the reason for our visit and the Lance Corporal said that he would have to contact his base. He returned after two or three minutes to tell us that he had to take us to Armagh barracks.

"Where's your armoured car?" asked Jarvis.

"It's over there," said the soldier pointing to an old red Cortina.

My heart sank. Someone, somewhere had made a mistake.

We walked to the Cortina which was parked nearby and I couldn't help noticing that the soldier had kept it within sight for the whole time that he was away from it.

As we set off, I questioned the soldier about the car.

"We thought we were being collected in an armoured staff car," I said.

"I don't know anything about that," said the soldier. "Besides they do tend to stand out a little."

"Do you think we would be better off travelling incognito as it were?"

"Doesn't really matter, British Army cars are a dead give away because they have seat belts in the back."

As I was sitting in the back, I felt decidedly uncomfortable.

As we left the airport, there was a sign that indicated the direction to Armagh and the soldier followed it.

"Have you been to Armagh before?" I asked.

"No, never," said the soldier.

"Bloody marvellous," I thought to myself.

The next half hour was spent asking the soldier a number of questions about the area and about Armagh in particular,

"Armagh's not a very safe place, certainly not for us Brits" he said.

"Bloody marvellous again," I thought to myself.

As we travelled through Belfast I was not impressed with what I saw. In fairness, it was an overcast day which would not endear any town to a visitor.

As we got out of the city centre, we travelled through open countryside. At the side of the road, I saw a dead cow laid on its back. Rigor mortis had set in and its legs were pointed upwards. I commented about it to the soldier.

"Looks as though that's a dead cow," I said looking for an explanation.

"Looks like it," said the soldier, "seems to be dead all right."

Failing to get any explanation, I looked across at Jarvis who looked back at me with a stare that said, "Why have you got me into this?" The journey was uneventful until we took a wrong turning. We got to a rather downbeat area where pedestrians leered into the car as though they knew who we were. When I saw the next sign I felt decidedly uncomfortable. It was almost as if I could sense impending doom. The soldier realized that we were in entirely the wrong area and I noticed a hint of panic in his voice as he expressed his concern. We then approached a round sign which said 'Crossmaglen'.

He performed the quickest three point turn I've ever experienced and we attempted to re-trace our journey. We eventually got across the boundary to Armagh and I breathed a sigh of relief. Lance Corporal Johnson said "I'll ask for directions". I rather hoped that he wouldn't ask one of the locals because I was not sure what we would be met with but within a short time, we came across a group of Royal Ulster Constabulary officers at a checkpoint. They were in the centre of town and were allowing traffic to pass by. Lance Corporal Johnson pulled up beside them and they looked at our car suspiciously. Our driver beckoned an officer to the car and he came towards it with his automatic rifle in hand and on the alert.

"Bloody hell again," I thought, but this time the concern was a little greater. The lance corporal immediately announced who he was and his cockney accent appeared to relax the policeman somewhat. We were given directions and we set off for what we hoped would be Armagh barracks.

As we stopped at traffic lights, I still had the impression that passers-by were staring into the car. It was an unnerving experience which was made worse by the fact that our driver was clearly terrified as well.

We then spotted in the distance, a large building with a castle-like appearance.

"That will be it," said the lance corporal, breathing a sigh of relief.

We drove up to the gates which opened and as we went to the checkpoint we found that we were not in the barracks, but in Armagh prison, the home of the H Block itself. We were allowed to turn our vehicle round and were directed further up the hill where we saw another castle-like building which we were assured was the British Army Barracks at Armagh. As we approached the barracks I noticed soldiers on guard duty outside. I've never been more pleased to see them and we drove into the barracks and after our identities were checked, we were shown into the reception area.

I looked at Jarvis and winked, and he started to laugh.

"Piece of cake," I said to him with a smile.

"Piece of shit," replied Jarvis, and we both laughed.

Within a short time, our host, Sergeant McCloud, came to greet us. We were shown to our quarters and told that lunch would be at 12.00 noon in the Sergeant's Mess.

We enjoyed a superb lunch sitting at the sergeant major's table and at 2.00 pm our car to the courthouse had arrived.

The courthouse was only a matter of minutes away and during the journey we heard the car radio announce a fairly detailed reference to our case, which had clearly caused a great deal of interest in the area.

Reaching the courthouse we saw that the television cameras and a number of photographers were there. On entering the building,

I was approached by a gentleman who looked like a court usher. He had long black robes and introduced himself with a title that I couldn't quite catch. He told me that the coroner wished to see me in his chambers before the case started so Jarvis and I followed him along a warren of corridors until we reached a room marked 'Coroner'. After three short knocks a voice from within shouted "enter" and Jarvis and I were allowed into a rather large room with a huge leather-topped desk in the centre. The walls were adorned with paintings of what appeared to be our host's predecessors and in the corner, hanging on a large oak contraption, was a gown and wig.

The coroner stood, introduced himself and shook hands with us both. He very politely explained the procedure which he wished to have adopted in his court.

At the conclusion of our interview the coroner enquired how long we would be staying in Northern Ireland. We indicated that we would be staying overnight and returning to England the following morning. However he said that there had been a lot of publicity surrounding this case and it would be in our best interests to deal with the matter and then leave as soon as possible. I didn't discuss the point but thanked the coroner for seeing us, left and went into the courtroom.

The courthouse itself was very traditional in style with marble floored corridors leading to oak panelled courtrooms with brass railed docks. The whole place was most impressive. We were to be in Court Number 2 and the smell of brass polish lingered in the cool air.

I introduced myself to the advocate, who was there to give the facts to the coroner and to call the evidence, and he was also kind enough to give me an outline of the case.

The evidence to be called included the soldier who fired the weapon, another soldier who was present when the incident occurred and a pathologist who dealt with the cause of death. There were other statements from witnesses which merely set the scene and as such they were not of a contentious nature and could therefore be agreed without the presentation of oral evidence.

The first witness to give evidence was the soldier who had actually pulled the trigger.

This soldier was Owen Pavey's best friend. They had joined the

Army together and indeed served together both at home and in Northern Ireland. His voice trembled as he took the oath but the coroner re-assured him and asked him to answer the questions as clearly and audibly as he could. He was asked his name, rank and serial number before being asked to recount the events of the day in question.

He explained that they had been on a five-man patrol in Armagh itself. There was a great deal of tension in the city at that time and the squad had been particularly alert to the prospect of trouble. From the way that the soldier gave his evidence, it was obvious that they had been subjected to an incredible amount of stress on the four-hour patrol that day. When they returned to the barracks, they went to the area where weapons were unloaded and discharged. The soldier had held his rifle in a cradle like position waiting his turn. Standing to his right was his friend Owen Pavey and they were just chatting about the events of the patrol, when to use the soldier's own words, "I must have had my finger on the trigger and the gun just went off".

He was asked if he had any intention to shoot his friend and he denied that he had.

He was then asked if there had been any messing about and he denied that as well but in doing so, had great difficulty in retaining his composure.

The advocate left it at that and I was given the option to cross-examine.

It was important for me to show the court that there had been negligence on the part of this soldier, because this would affect Owen Pavey's family's right to compensation.

Under the Crown Proceedings Act a soldier's family were not entitled to compensation for the loss of their loved one while on active duty, although they are usually given some allowances and sometimes a pension.

In certain cases, ex gratia payments are made if the circumstances warrant it and in this case, if we could show that his death was caused by the negligence of another, then the Army might be more disposed to make such a payment. I was left with the unenviable task therefore of cross-examining this man with a view to getting him to accept that he had behaved negligently. This would mean an acceptance that he was responsible for Owen's death. It was not going to be pleasant for the lad and it was certainly not going to be particularly pleasant for me either.

Before I asked my first question, I told the soldier that there would be no suggestion that there had been anything deliberate about his actions. He simply nodded and made no reply. I don't think it was ever in his mind that such a proposition would ever be put.

I asked him one or two general questions about the patrol before turning to the important part of the case, which was when the group re-appeared back at the barracks.

I asked him about the procedure which had to be adopted at the end of a patrol and he told me that he had to go to the bunker, check his weapon and discharge any bullets that there had been in the breech. I then asked him the most simple and telling question,

"Why did you not have your safety catch on your weapon?"

The soldier thought for a second and realizing that there was little point in trying to conceal the truth, simply answered, "I forgot to put it on."

I then asked my penultimate question,

"When your gun went off were you in the process of discharging the gun in accordance with your procedures?" The soldier simply answered, "No".

I then asked my final question, in the certain knowledge of what the answer would be.

"Is it true that if the safety catch had been on at the time the gun went off, this incident would not have occurred?"

Without any equivocation whatsoever, the soldier answered, "Yes that is true, it would not have happened and Owen would not be dead". As he finished his head sank forward as he began to lose his composure. I asked no further questions and sat down.

There was a great silence in the room and it was a second or two before the coroner announced that he had no further questions and the soldier was allowed to leave the witness box. As he did so, he walked past the solicitors' bench where I was sitting and he looked at me for a second. There was a look of relief on his face as he left the room. I looked at Jarvis for a reaction, and he simply shrugged his shoulders. As we waited for the next witness, I sat and thought for a second or two.

It was no clever action or sparkling act of cross-examination as the soldier had no intentions of being dishonest. It was almost as if he was clearing his conscience. From that point of view it was the easiest case I have ever dealt with, but in another way it was perhaps the most difficult.

The next witness was a member of the patrol who confirmed what the first witness had said, although he did his best to assist his friend. He had to concede that if the safety catch had been on then obviously the gun would not have gone off.

Another witness followed in similar vein, before the pathologist gave unchallenged evidence about the cause of death. Fortunately, Owen would not have suffered, as we were told his death would have been instantaneous.

I briefly summed up my case to the coroner, complimenting the soldiers on their honesty and integrity and suggesting that this was one of those awful quirks of fate which had resulted in a dreadful tragedy. I found that throughout my closing address, I was actually mitigating the matter so far as the unfortunate soldier was concerned. All I had to prove was that there was some degree of negligence and indeed this was clearly accepted by the soldier himself and also the other witnesses.

The coroner retired for a short time before returning and announcing "An open verdict".

I looked towards Dick who was sitting behind me but his face did not display any reaction.

As we left the courtroom the advocate for the coroner came up to me, shook my hand and congratulated me saying, "Well done, you should be home and dry now on an ex gratia payment". I thanked him, pointing out that I didn't really do anything other than ask the obvious question.

When we got outside the courtroom the soldier was waiting. As we walked past him he got to his feet and simply said, "Mr Pavey........." He was unable to complete his sentence.

Dick was unable to speak either but I suppose words were not really necessary. The two men shook hands and embraced each other. Jarvis and I left them for a moment to find our driver who was standing by the front entrance with the security staff. He went to collect the car from the security compound at the rear while we waited in the foyer. We were asked not to stand outside but to wait for the arrival of the car when we would be allowed to leave. After two minutes or so, Dick and the soldier came into view. Nothing was said but there was an exchange of glances and with that the soldier was gone. As he left, one of his friends had his arm around him in an attempt to console him.

"Well done," I thought to myself, I had never hated the job as much as I did at that moment.

We got into the car but no one spoke. When we got back to the barracks, we went to our rooms where I sat quietly for half an hour before going down for dinner.

Jarvis and I decided that we wouldn't stay overnight and indeed Sergeant McCloud very kindly offered to provide transport to take us back to the airport so that we could return to England straight away.

While we had an offer of accommodation and a tour of the barracks, Jarvis and I agreed to leave, although Dick decided to stay overnight.

After dinner we set off for Belfast airport. As we were driving through Armagh our driver put on the car radio and when the news came on, it referred to the inquest with a brief summary of the evidence. The news reader reported the "Sensational disclosures uncovered by the deceased's family's solicitor".

The sensational disclosure made no reference to a soldier who had lost his best friend, ruined his own career, and possibly his life, by telling the truth.

As we boarded the plane in Belfast airport, Jarvis and I drank brandy and thought of home but this time our mood was not of merriment. I didn't look back and didn't sing along to "Come on Eileen" playing over the aircraft's radio system.

Three months later Owen Pavey's estate was awarded an ex gratia payment of compensation. I never enquired after Owen's friend as I thought he might prefer it that way.

Chapter Seventeen

SUKI DEVILLE AND THE CASE OF THE
SILVER CHALICE SAUNA

Suki Deville was a high class call girl or so it was said. I still don't fully understand the qualification "High Class". I suppose it must relate to price, but she was certainly a very pretty girl who had just the hint of a prostitute about her. Her real name was Janice South, but I suppose Suki Deville sounded better. She wandered into my office late one autumn afternoon in 1982 as I was about to leave to play a game of football. Bader, Lidster and Clumbem Darker were waiting in reception for me.

"I won't keep you long lads," I said, inviting Miss Deville into my room.

She was tall with jet black hair and the most unusually deep blue eyes I had ever seen. She had a "Colgate" smile which indicated to me that she must have eaten calcium with every meal, drunk gallons of full cream milk and spent the rest of the day brushing her teeth. The thing I noticed most, however, was a small diamond like object fixed into one of her teeth, slightly off centre at the front.

She had a pleasant voice with a hotel receptionist's twang, and the hint of a Scottish accent.

"I have got into trouble with the DSS," she said quietly. "I have been charged with Supplementary Benefits Act offences and they say I signed on and received unemployment benefit while working."

She was so blunt and open about it that I was put off guard. Normally people find it difficult, certainly initially, to talk about their charges, but I realized that this girl was cold and calculating.

She opened a Gucci handbag and passed to me the summonses which had been folded immaculately into a heavily scented envelope, which was simply addressed to "The Solicitor". I looked at the charges which seemed to relate to a period of over eighteen months.

From the information which had been served with the summonses it was clear that the Office of Social Security were saying that Miss Deville had claimed approximately £3,000 to which she was not entitled. It was a serious case, and because of the amount of money involved, my pretty client was staring into the unwelcome arms of Her Majesty's Prison, Risley.

"What do you think I will get?" asked Miss Deville, controlling her concern.

"Are you pleading guilty?" I asked.

"I don't think I have any option, and in any event I have admitted it," she said.

"Well in those circumstances, if you are pleading guilty, we will ask the court to be as lenient as possible. The difficulty is that we are dealing with a large amount of money and the court is bound to take a serious view."

I hoped to give Miss Deville the bad news without creating the impression that I thought she had a hopeless case. Often defendants have no real conception as to just how serious their case is and indeed the police themselves may well have led them into the belief that prison is unlikely. As I and my fellow solicitors are going to be first in the firing line, when the waste material hits the fan, it is better to leave the defendant in no doubt as to what might happen at the end of the day. It is not easy to gauge just when the bad news should be imparted, but in this particular case the defendant was intelligent and I thought it prudent to let her know from the outset that imprisonment was a serious possibility.

After a sharp intake of breath, she asked me how long. I told her;

"Three months out of which you will serve six weeks."

"Is there no prospect of a suspended sentence?" she said.

"There is always the prospect of avoiding imprisonment, but I think that prison is more likely than not."

"When will it happen?" she asked.

"You will appear at court at the end of the month on the date of the summons and plead guilty. It is likely that the court will then adjourn your case so that the probation service can prepare a report about you before the final sentencing takes place. In these circumstances, I think you have eight weeks to organize your affairs."

After giving the bad news, I then set about taking details of the case and the mitigation which we were to put forward. It seemed that Miss Deville had approached the DSS and told them that she was not in gainful employment and accordingly she was allowed an amount of social security benefit.

It had come to the attention of the DSS investigators, that for a substantial period she had been working as a hostess in a sauna/health club in the Nottingham area. It transpired that she was self-employed and paid a "rent" to the owners of the sauna for the use of their facilities. A statement had been taken from the sauna's owners, who had said that for the period covered by the charge she had worked at the sauna paying them a rent of £100 per week. She told me that there were a number of other girls similarly employed.

I was curious to know how she had been found out, but she was unable to help. I said that I would try to discover how the DSS had known about her work if only to satisfy my own curiosity.

As we had covered the main questions of her case and realizing that if I did not get a move on I would be late for the match, I made my apologies and agreed to meet the following week so that I could complete my instructions.

As I showed Miss Deville to the door I found Lidster inspecting his foot for signs of his recurring septic toe problem. Miss Deville viewed the scene, shuddered and headed for the outer door but Lidster just smiled and winked. Miss Deville went on her way and looking out of the window I saw her jump into the passenger seat of a Mercedes sportscar which was driven off at speed. I was joined by Bader and Darker and while I was looking out of the window, I asked Bader if he had ever thought about being a Masseur.

"Tha what?" said Bader.

"Oh never mind, it was just a thought," and with that we set off to the match.

We were beaten comprehensively by a local pub team who according to Bader were fielding three 'ringers', one of whom, the goalkeeper, had played league football on professional terms. We tried everything to get past him, but we all failed miserably, finally losing 4-0.

The following day on my way to the magistrates' court I met the solicitor who prosecuted for the DSS . I mentioned my new client's case and was given something of an insight into the facts. I was interested to know how the DSS became involved, particularly bearing in mind that Miss Deville, as she called herself, had actually been working well out of the area in which she was making her claim.

It seemed that she had been found out quite by chance, as is often the case. Apparently she had been 'clocked' as the criminals call it while working in Nottingham at the sauna. The diamond in the tooth was the give away and she was recognized while signing on in Rotherham. I suppose there are few people with jewellery in that setting, and as she was a particularly pretty girl, she stood out in the crowd. My prosecutor friend was unable to tell me who 'shopped' her and told me that the information came as it normally does from an informant. The informant had a great deal of information and must have had a considerable insight into the workings of the Silver Chalice Sauna.

I found the circumstances very strange and wondered why it was that someone would take the trouble of contacting Rotherham DSS. It was obvious that they knew that she was signing on in Rotherham and lived in the area, but what possible connection would they have with Nottingham?

The next morning I was at court representing a number of ne'er-do-wells including Barry Baldwin from Bolton-On-Dearne. Barry was an ex-serviceman and also a secretary of a local working men's club.

Unfortunately, he had been caught by the police driving over the prescribed limit, but as Barry had lost his papers he couldn't remember exactly what the drink drive reading was. I had taken some details from him, but the idea was to adjourn the case until I had a better picture of the trouble that he was in. All went well with the adjournment until the clerk of the court, who could be best described as a 'pompous shit' produced some papers which showed that Barry had been before the court in the past for driving while over the prescribed limit and had not paid off all the fines. The clerk asked me if I was aware of the fines position and I told him that my crystal ball had been damaged and consequently it was not the sort of thing that I would anticipate. The clerk smiled to himself, thinking that he had got one over on me and promptly called Barry into the witness box to give evidence as to his means. Understandably Barry was nervous, because the clerk had mentioned something about going to prison for being in default.

With the gusto of a man who wanted to be a prosecutor, the clerk set into Barry with relish:-

"I am going to make a note of what you say. I am going to ask you various questions and I would like you to direct your answers to the magistrates sitting behind me. I will then give you the opportunity to make any comments you should wish, either yourself or through your solicitor and the court will then decide whether or not you are so far in default that only a prison sentence is appropriate. If you are, I can tell you that the period that you will be sentenced to will be not less than fourteen days. Do you understand?"

Barry took a deep breath and said "Pardon?"

I will not repeat everything, but the court clerk literally went through the same banter, word for word.

"Do you understand?"

"Pardon?" said a confused Barry, once again.

The court clerk was losing his patience and shouted at the top of his voice "Are you deaf?"

To which Barry replied "Yes".

"Well then I will shout. Do you have a hearing aid?"

Barry replied with further aplomb, "I am sorry about this, I've forgotten my hearing aid".

A number of the solicitors waiting for their cases to be heard were highly amused by these developments and the word went round the waiting room that there was a 'good crack' in Court Number 1.

The solicitors' benches filled up with all the available legal people who were sitting rather like Madame D'farge and the French revolutionaries in front of the guillotine.

The court clerk shouted his message painstakingly and concluded it by saying,

"In so far as you can, keep one eye on the magistrates and one eye on my pen".

"I've only got one eye," said Barry, "Where does tha want me to point it?"

Laughter rang round the room and the clerk realized that he had lost. Barry was ordered to pay his fines at the rate of £5 a week and was allowed to leave the court.

All the solicitors were delighted that he had got one over on this most unpopular of court clerks.

I took Barry into the rat hole interview room to discuss our plan of attack and for the first time I noticed a very thin wire leading from a small object placed inside Barry's right ear.

"You really are deaf," I said to Barry.

"Beg your pardon," he said with a grin "......only when this is not switched on," and his grin turned into laughter.

Barry was a man in his late 60's who had served in the war. He was the archetypal straight backed ex-serviceman who wore the compulsory blazer and regimental badge on the breast pocket. His hair was almost white, but his eyebrows were ginger in colour, giving the clear impression that he had once proudly boasted red hair.

Although he still had his military bearing, he had however lost his battle with his ever increasing waistline which had pushed the level of his trousers well below his abdomen.

His face was weather beaten, but framed by a thin pencil moustache neatly placed underneath a nose which had been flattened by too much attention from other people's fists. He had blue eyes, one of which was bloodshot and the other which was clear and made of glass.

We agreed to meet at court on the adjourned hearing and as Barry turned to leave, I realized that it might be in his interest to produce a copy of his war record. I shouted his name and he turned without difficulty to answer.

"Still switched on is it Barry?" I asked with a smile.

He smiled too but did not answer and I promptly asked him if he would bring his army record to court next time.

"Certainly," said Barry and off he marched. I remember at the time how pleasant I thought it was to deal with such a gentleman.

One day walking through town back to the office I met the investigator on the DSS case against Suki Deville and I took the opportunity to ask him about her. He was a pleasant chap and fairly affable and as she was pleading guilty I saw nothing wrong in speaking to him.

I told him that she was pleading guilty to the matter, but wondered whether he could settle my curiosity by telling me how the DSS became aware that Suki was in "work". He told me that they had received information from an unimpeachable source who knew from first hand knowledge where she was working. I asked if it was an informant and he told me that it was not, but declined to comment further. It seemed that I was never going to get to the truth of the matter. There was no statement in the evidence explaining the position and as she had made a confession I couldn't expect one. Therefore it looked as though I was never going to have my question answered.

Later the following week, Miss Deville came in to see me again. She was early and I caught sight of her alighting from a car outside my office. I could not see the driver of the large Mercedes, but the car was brand spanking new and looked as though it had just been brought out of the showroom.

Once inside my room I became aware that Miss Deville was extremely anxious and before I could say anything she spoke.

"You won't discuss this case with anyone will you?"

"Of course not, I will not compromise you, but I may have to discuss it with people connected with the court proceedings."

She interrupted without warning and said, "I didn't mean that, I meant if someone should telephone and enquire after me, or try to get to know the reason for my visit".

I realized that perhaps the man in the Mercedes did not know the real reason for her calling on me.

I reassured her and began to sort out the question of the costs of her representation. She told me that she did not believe that she would be eligible for legal aid and was ready to pay her costs privately. Being the trusting soul that I am and having every sympathy with her, I asked Miss Deville for my costs "up front" or "on account" as it is better described.

"Let's get that business sorted out straight away," she said and pulled a wad of notes from her handbag.

She was carrying an extremely large sum of money in £20 notes which were encased with a band of paper, fresh from the bank.

She paid the agreed amount and while doing so, I wrote out a receipt.

"I'm not working at the sauna," she said, "I've packed that in."

"How are you living," I said, "if you have no private income?"

"I have some savings and when they run out I will decide what to do."

She was most anxious that the case be delayed. It seemed very important to her and it so happened that I was in a position to help her without compromise, because I had not received any evidence at that stage and I needed time to consider it.

When we attended court I secured an adjournment of four weeks for the evidence to be served and for me to consider it and take instructions.

212

We had one further meeting before the court date was fixed, but her anxiety about the final date of the case and the question of complete secrecy haunted her entire conversation.

I wondered if the absence of previous convictions had something to do with the obvious fear she had of appearing at court, but then it was more the fear of publicity that seemed to be uppermost in her mind.

Her second appearance at court went to plan, and the magistrates ordered a pre-sentence report to be completed by the probation service before making a final decision as to how to deal with her.

She was the focal point of attention waiting outside Court Number 3, as she was not only attractive, but extremely smartly dressed. She stuck out like a sore thumb, at the side of some of the rapscallions who were in a similar plight.

She was not the only DSS fraudster I represented that morning. Another was a young girl called Lavinia Broughton who was from a regular client family of mine and I could not help noticing the stark contrast between hers and Miss Deville's case.

I had not met Lavinia before, but I knew her parents and elder brothers and sisters extremely well. She was by no means nervous as she took large puffs from her Park Drive cigarette while she stood underneath the sign saying "NO SMOKING IN THIS AREA". I introduced myself and took her into the end of the corridor, for there was no rat hole outside Court Number 3. Other Solicitors divided out the distance of the corridor between themselves for the purposes of their conferences with their clients so I took to the top of the stairs, which was just outside the Magistrates' Retiring Room.

The security was non-existent and the possibility of magistrates coming into contact with defendants was almost certain.

How times have changed with the new purpose built courts and tradesman's entrance for the judiciary.

"How many charges have you got Miss Broughton?" I asked.

"Four and twenty five TIC's," came the reply from this most self assured defendant.

I completed the legal aid form which in itself was quite a feat as there was no desk and not even a window ledge to rest upon. I had become quite proficient in the art of writing in that way. I passed the legal aid forms for signature, handing over an old biro which I used for the clients to sign with. I had long since learned not to hand over my best fountain pen as many of the defendants had never had call to use one and invariably they twisted the nib or complained that it wouldn't write.

As she wrote out her name in full, I tried to hurry her along by saying, "Just use your initial for your Christian names".

I thought that 'Lavinia Avril Jeanette Mary Louise Enid Broughton' was a veritable novel but she took no notice, probably because she had got used to the order, as she wrote out the name in full, on three separate places on two forms.

I had the introductory advice green form for her to sign for the initial interview in case legal aid was not granted, but I thought that it was worth the risk and left the green form unsigned in my file. I believed that she would get legal aid which would make the green form redundant, as all the attendances could be claimed under the legal aid certificate or so I hoped.

As she was writing out her name in full yet again, I said, "It is a strange name, that, Lavinia."

She grunted in reply, but I couldn't make out what she said.

"How do your friends refer to you?" I asked.

Anticipating her reply, I ventured to guess the nickname.

"Is it Tina or Tine or Tin or Tie?" I asked.

"No," came the stern reply, "none of those."

"Well what do they call you then?" I said.

"They call me Lav," she said without a hint of embarrassment.

I did not ask her to explain why.

The contrast between her and Suki could not have been wider.

They were complete opposites because on the one hand I had Suki, the dazzling beauty with designer clothes and a brothel for a retreat and on the other poor old Lav, plain and untidy, wearing cheap clothes and designer seconds trainers from the local market, but someone whose morals had been fashioned by prudish parents and an absence of desire from the local males.

It was inexplicable that Miss Deville should look down her nose at such a person when she in fact was the one whose morals were kept in her own filing tray marked "ONLY TO BE USED IN AN EMERGENCY".

Both ladies became the subject of consideration by the probation service and their cases were adjourned for four weeks for this purpose. Miss Deville was first in to see the probation officer, as Lav waited outside.

As Miss Deville left the court, she came face to face with Lav for a split second, probably for the first and only time. I couldn't help but notice the look of disgust on both faces, but I suspect for entirely different reasons. Lav left the court and went to the bus queue outside and Miss Deville walked to a red open-topped sportscar with a personalized number plate and drove off as though she was being pursued by the local VAT inspectors.

Three weeks later I received a telephone call from the probation service to tell me that Miss Deville had failed to attend two appointments. The second letter had been returned marked "GONE AWAY".

The next day, my letter to her confirming the hearing date was also returned with the same message. On the morning of the hearing, Lav turned up resplendent in jeans and a pale blue teeshirt bearing the legend "I SHOT THE SHERIFF". The purple trainers were dazzling in the sunlight which sneaked in through the window at the end of the corridor outside Court Number 3. The court ordered that Lav be placed into the caring hands of the probation service on a twelve months' probation order and a warrant was issued for Miss Deville's arrest.

Approximately one month later, I received an airmail letter from a Mrs. Suki Dorchester-Hall, sent from the Hilton Hotel, New York. It read:

Dear Mr. Smith,

Thank you for your valuable assistance in completing my legal affairs in England.

I am pleased to report that on the 1st September, Guy Dorchester-Hall and I were married here in New York. Guy is now resident here with a full American passport. Fortunately or unfortunately, depending upon which way you look at it, I will be unable to return owing to my commitments here.

In the circumstances, please close my file but keep them with you in the unlikely event of my return.

I would be grateful if you would not disclose my whereabouts to any interested parties.

If my husband and I can place any work with you in England, we will be pleased so to do.

With kindest regards.

SUKI DORCHESTER-HALL

The court hearing had finished, a warrant had been issued for her arrest and everyone's interest was occupied with other matters. The file of Suki Deville began to gather dust.

Six months later, I was making a rare appearance in the Nottingham Magistrates' Court. I was instructed to appear on behalf of a haulage contractor client of mine who had got himself into difficulties with an insecure load on the motorway in the Nottingham area.

Mick was a good driver but like some haulage contractors (but I hasten to add not all) he had lived his working life rather close to the wind and sometimes found himself falling foul of the dreaded Construction and Use Regulations which haunted the very existence of the haulage trade. In normal circumstances, I would instruct agents to appear on my behalf in a 'foreign' town, but this was the fourth time that Mick had appeared in court within the last year and he was extremely worried that the Vehicles Tribunal in Leeds might consider taking his operator's licence away and so he was determined to be represented. I had a very good business relationship with Mick and I like to think he had considerable faith in me. He certainly preferred me to attend rather than some solicitor who he would meet for the first time and who would squeeze his case in among his own, leaving him until the end of the list. It seemed to me to be fair comment and so I agreed that I would make the journey down the M1 to Nottingham.

When I arrived at Court I found that the facts given by the prosecution were entirely different from those supplied to me by my client which meant a further consultation before we went into the courtroom.

"You told me, Mick, that it was a bumper that fell off the back of your lorry on to the motorway," I said.

"Correct," said Mick with an air of confidence.

"But you see Mick, the prosecution tell a different story. They admit that a vehicle bumper was on the motorway but say that it was attached to the wreckage of a Ford Transit van."

"Well it were a bumper weren't it?" said Mick.

216

"Yes but you didn't tell me it was attached to a van," I replied. "Not only that but it blocked two carriageways of the M1."

"Ar, but not for long," said Mick.

"No because the police had it towed off. The first question I wish to ask you is when did you first become aware that the vehicle had fallen from the back of the lorry?"

"When the police pulled me up down the motorway and anyway how do I know it was off my lorry?"

"Because two police officers in the police car say they saw it fall off and had to swerve to avoid it."

"I didn't see that in my mirror," said Mick.

"You haven't got a mirror," I replied. "The police officer said that it was broken."

"Bloody hell, they are doing me for everything, it's harassment," announced an aggrieved Mick.

"Well, that might be the case Mick but they can actually justify the harassment, as you put it, because you did something wrong, your lorry was defective and to make matters worse the prosecutor has shown to me another statement from another road-user who was behind the police car, who also had to swerve and pull in behind the police car on the hard shoulder."

"Oh," said Mick. "I didn't know that they had witnesses."

Mick was distraught at the thought of having to plead guilty to yet another black mark against his name for the traffic commissioners to consider but we had little option in the case but to plead guilty and throw ourselves upon the mercy of the court.

I checked with the court usher as to the order of play and he told me that we were well down the list and he had grave doubts as to whether our case would be on before lunch. A cold shiver went through my system because I had cases in Sheffield starting at 2.15 and if I wasn't there, a grade five bollocking would be the order of the day. I decided to do what I always do in situations like this and that was to creep. I went in to see the clerk of the court and I thought that if I put on an injured expression and told the truth he might have sympathy with me and let me sneak on. Some of the courts are extremely helpful to 'foreign' briefs' and solicitors pride themselves in being courteous to outsiders. However Nottingham does not necessarily fit into that picture because it is a busy court with just one too many cases in the list. The pace is different in a city and so the "aggro" is far more intense and the competition to get on first is much greater.

Fortunately, I recognized my opposite number of the Crown Prosecution Service and putting on my best smile greeted him like a long lost brother.

"Hello Brian," I said shaking his hand furiously, "is there any possibility that you could help me out and get me mentioned first because I have got to be back in Sheffield for an afternoon court and I don't want the old grade five bollocking."

"Hello Trevor," came the reply. "My name, you may recall, is Jerry and the CPS cases are not on first."

"Of course Jerry how are you?" I said correcting myself giving the impression that I was pulling his leg when I got his name wrong,

"What do you mean the CPS cases are not on first?"

"This is a DSS court and they have got a number of cases and unfortunately we are bringing up the rear."

"Flipping heck," I said or words to that effect.

"Looks like a grade five bollocking," said my opposite number with a smile. "Come on I'll buy you a cup of tea."

We went outside to the advocates' room and from there to the WRVS tea room.

"What would you like?" asked Jerry.

"Do you have chocolate?" I asked the attendant.

"Mars or Kit-Kat love," came the reply.

"No drinking chocolate?" I asked.

"Tea or coffee?" came the reply "And we've just one spoon of Bovril left."

"What sort of tea is it?" I asked.

"What do you mean what sort of tea is it? It's tea isn't it, tea ordinary tea."

"How about a drop of Darjeeling or maybe Cantonese blend or even Earl Grey would be nice?" I asked.

The attendant did not reply but promptly put a Co-op tea bag in a white paper cup before adding boiling water and a spoon of milk substitute.

"Sugar or not?" she demanded.

"Not," I replied and was given two packets of sugar one white and one brown.

We walked back to the courtroom and stood outside in the busy corridor. I had taken the liberty of buying Mick a cup of coffee which apparently tasted like Bovril and Jerry updated me on the scandal from Nottingham CPS.

As we spoke, the DSS prosecutor arrived carrying bundles of files and followed by a large number of DSS people.

It appeared that he had one representative for each of his cases. I thought the public purse would have been best served by employing just one. I then saw the clerk of the court and explained my plight. I was advised that the DSS would mention their first four cases and then they would let me squeeze in as a special favour.

I was advised to keep my place and so I sat in court and watched the day's events.

The DSS cases were of people claiming benefit when they shouldn't have. The faces all appeared to be the same, only the names were different. That was until the fourth of the cases came on. I was going to walk out of court to report the position to Mick when I came face to face with the defendant. It was a woman of about thirty with blonde hair. It was not a natural blonde but was well groomed and extremely well cared for. It was one of those instances when you move to the left to move out of the way and so does the other party. You correct that by moving to the right and so do they. The result was that we were actually face to face for a little longer than would normally have been the case. There was a hint of recognition which affected me because her face was vaguely familiar. There was absolutely no doubt about it the girl knew me but I could not place her yet there was something about her.

I sat down in time to hear the clerk go through the motions.

"Is your full name Tracey Deveraux?" The defendant answered with just a hint of a Scottish accent. She gave her address and date of birth and as I watched her I tried to recall where I had seen her before.

There was something familiar about her face but beyond that I could not say where I had seen her before. Her eyes were light brown in colour but her complexion was fresh and had not been concealed with too much make-up. I was convinced that I knew her voice. The charge was that she had claimed something in the region of £2,000 by way of benefit whilst working for a very high class escort agency. While she sat in the dock her eyes caught mine and there was no doubt that she knew me. At the end of the case there was an adjournment for the preparation of probation reports. She was introduced to the probation officer immediately in front of me and as they shook hands she beamed a bright smile. I could not help noticing what appeared to be a diamond like object which had been mounted in one of her front teeth, slightly off centre. It was extremely unusual and I had only ever seen anything like it once before.

The girl left the courtroom without a backward glance and I was left alone with my thoughts. I was so preoccupied that I did not hear the clerk calling on Mick's case or indeed asking me if I was ready.

"Are you all right Mr. Smith?" said the court clerk thoughtfully.

"I beg your pardon?" I said realizing that I was the subject of the question.

"Are you all right?" repeated the clerk. " Can we proceed?"

"Yes of course Sir," I said. "I'm sorry I must have been day-dreaming."

I settled into Mick's case and mitigated as best I could and for-tunately the court was extremely lenient with him. Jerry from the CPS leaned across, congratulated me on the result and explained that the court had dealt with so many DSS cases, they found mine a refreshing change. The timing of the case could not have been better and Mick walked out of court thinking that I was a genius. Outside I tried to explain to him that it was just a piece of luck but he wouldn't accept it saying that it was 'down to me'. I suppose if he had got a bad result that would have been down to me as well so as I was in front I decided to enjoy our success and with that we left the court.

As I reached the multi-storey car park I couldn't help but notice a red Mercedes open-topped sportscar drive off to wolf whistles from a group of labourers who were digging up the road nearby.

"A bit of all right that," said Mick.

"Yes lovely car, I wish I'd got one," I replied.

"No not the car, the bird that was in it," said Mick "Did you clock it? She was a cracker."

"No I didn't see her," I said.

"A shame that," said Mick. "She was a belter, but you will never guess, she had a diamond in one of her teeth, I saw her outside the court when we were waiting to go in."

"Really," I replied, "how unusual".

"Never seen that before," said Mick, "have you, how on earth do they do that?"

"I wonder," I replied and turned to look for my car.

The Suki Deville case would remain a mystery to me but I got an answer to part of the case about three months later.

Having left Sheffield magistrates' court one day, my return journey took me through a rather seedy part of Sheffield where there is a rather doubtful establishment laying claim to be a massage parlour.

The traffic in the road caused me to stop adjacent to these premises and, as I was waiting, the door to the establishment opened and a gentleman with a familiar face and rather wet hair appeared at the door. As I looked across at him, he had no option but to focus directly upon me. He took a deep breath and appeared to be disconcerted, for he clearly recognized me. Although he put a handkerchief to his face as if to blow his nose, it was too late because I had realized that it was none other than my friend the DSS investigator. I gave him the benefit of the doubt, thinking that he could be on 'Observations' although I rather doubted that his DSS expenses claim would make any reference to that visit.

As he hurried down the street with his handkerchief to his face, the traffic started to move and I wondered if there would be any point in touching my car horn and giving him a wave of recognition. As I drew level with him, I got the impression that he was aware of my presence once again and he darted into the first shop he came to which by chance happened to sell ladies' underwear. I would have liked to have seen his face when he realized where he had sought refuge. His apparent guilt gave me the answer I was looking for. He was quite clearly the unimpeachable source in the Suki Deville case but the only question that remains unanswered is whether or not he was acting in the course of his duty. Only a visit to the premises would reveal that answer, so I suppose we will never know.

Chapter Eighteen

GOODBYE MOORGATE STREET, HELLO VICARAGE LANE

As Christmas 1982 aproached, our search for new premises became a priority.

It did not take long to find office space, but in the early 80's the recession had not started and office space which became available was soon snapped up.

Wilford and I found that there were two floors of offices available on Vicarage Lane in Rotherham overlooking All Saints Church and the grassed area which surrounded it. It was in the centre of the town and could not have been better placed. Unfortunately there were no car parking facilities and the offices were two large open floors which would need a considerable amount of work to create individual rooms.

We viewed the offices on a number of occasions obtained quotations for the cost of the work required and finally agreed terms with the landlords.

By the end of November the shop and carpet fitters moved out and we moved in.

On the ground floor we had a reception area which led into a large open area, containing three interview rooms and three typing places. Our secretaries were set up outside our rooms, with me in the first room on the right, and Wilford next door.

Upstairs we had two further rooms, a large room for the typing pool and also some room to spare which we confidently agreed would be used for expansion.

We were extremely proud of what we had achieved and decided that we would move into our new premises just before Christmas.

It was no small task to move ten people, ten sets of equipment and all the furniture that we had accumulated along the way. We also had eighteen months' worth of old files and all our current cases. We engaged the services of a friend and client of mine called Vito Lala who had a removals firm. Vito together with some of his colleagues carried out all the heavy work, while the rest of us pitched in to move our personal effects and some of the office equipment. The move took place over a weekend so as to cause the minimum disruption, but in the event it was an extremely stressful time, particularly when we found that one or two items were too large to be negotiated up the rather small staircase which led to our offices. However with a mixture of expertise, Broomie's hammer and brute force we managed the task by late on Sunday.

By this time the office was in total and complete chaos. I could not find the drawers for my desk, but I did find a framed photograph of Russ Conway propped up against a wall in my new room. Russ Conway, although a very popular television star of the 50's and 60's, had not been popular with me, and so, after making rather abortive enquiries as to its ownership, poor old Russ was left with the rubbish. One of Vito's men, another Italian, said that the picture reminded him of his father and so I presented it to him and offered him another picture which I had found, in the hope that it might look like his mother. It didn't, but he took it nevertheless. I suspect that he is able to show visitors to his home pictures of people that resemble his parents. I discovered that his parents were still living in Venice so it was nice to have something of a memento.

Vito was world tea-drinking champion and every so often there would be a little break for him to indulge in one of his favourite pastimes. The kettle never cooled down while Vito was around.

Wilford on the other hand was world beer-drinking champion and even more impressive than the great Jarvis. He was to lose his title however to 'Ten Belly Norburn', who in turn was beaten by the daddy of them all Webbo*. I once went to watch England play the Aussies at Headingley, only to spend most of the time in the members' bar watching Webbo take the title from Norburn with an astonishing performance of consuming thirty-five pints. As Webbo pointed out, it was during an eighteen hour session, but nevertheless, I have not seen anyone rival the great man.

Wilford was an amateur in comparison, but that day we were introduced to what has now become a well known Italian wine; Lambrusco.

The effects of drinking a litre of that devilish brew can be best described as awful but Vito presented us with a bottle, assuring us that it wasn't particularly strong, but had a very pleasant taste. It is not the sort of drink that will make you drunk, but the after-effects on the digestion are remarkable.

*Nickname of the honourable Gary Webb, local entrepreneur and beer-drinker extraordinaire.

During the search for my desk drawers, I came across a number of boxed items with the name 'Jarvis' written on them. They comprised of a toaster, a box of onions, a large box of horse racing magazines, an inflatable bed which on first sight had all the appearance of a blow-up doll and a pot Buddha which I had presented to Jarvis the Christmas before for services rendered. I put all the items in one corner to be returned, but kept the pot Buddha which adorns my office to this very day.

We had spent a fortune in shop fittings, new carpets and decorations. We had even bought a new telephone system described by British Telecom as 'Tomorrow's telephones today'. The representative told us that "They are so refined they almost answer themselves". I sat in my room as the telephones rang when they were being tested and not once did they answer themselves. Success depended entirely on someone picking up the telephone and saying "Hello". To that extent therefore, British Telecom had lied. On the Saturday evening of our move Wilford and I decided to inspect the 'interesting roof garden' which was mentioned in the estate agents particulars. We made our way onto the roof by a series of metal ladders fixed to the walls. We reached the flat roof which had an incredible view over the town centre of Rotherham. We marvelled at the sight before us and Wilford said, "Yes this is Rotherham". Wilford was a clever man and what's more he was right, it was indeed Rotherham. I gave him A for effort and ten out of ten for citing the bloody obvious; after all it wasn't Dewsbury or Hull; it was certainly Rotherham.

Wilf suggested that we toast our new premises with a glass of Champagne, but unfortunately this was not possible, because we didn't have any Champagne. Two bottles of Mackeson had to suffice. The heavens then opened and rain began to pour onto the roof.

"You know what?" said Wilf thoughtfully.

"What's that Wilf?" I asked, noting his contemplation.

He paused for what seemed an age. He was deep in thought and I expected some pearl of wisdom to be expounded on this most special occasion. I waited until I could bear it no more, when Wilford turned to me with a knowing glance, nodded and said, "It's raining."

"True," I said and we promptly climbed back indoors.

As we left the roof, I tripped over an empty windowbox. We had found the roof garden.

When we got back into the office, a scruffy little urchin walked into reception carrying a large cardboard box. Apparently someone had given him a pound to make a special delivery. We opened the box to find that it contained a ballcock which was rather familiar. We agreed to have the item mounted and displayed upstairs in the gents' toilet. There was a little note from our benefactor which read:-

'I hope this means as much to you as it means to me - Oscar'.

It was a nice thought and as I hung it in the upstairs toilet I could have sworn that I heard the sound of a distant trombone and the clatter of hooves.

At about 9.00 pm we had finished moving in.

One piece of furniture that didn't move with us was the Space Invader game.

John Bradwell had taken it back and indeed by that time we were so busy that we didn't have time to play it. We had a change of premises and also a change of attitude. Owing to the increase in staff, we had increased overheads which meant that we all had to work harder to cover our costs. The afternoon card games and entertaining chit chat had disappeared as the pressure of work began to build up. We had grown in size at quite a remarkable rate and we knew that we could lose the goodwill of our practice as quickly as we had built it up.

However, we still had the benefit of monthly meetings with Michael Jarvis which usually took the form of a five minute meeting dealing with the accounts followed by a four hour session at a pub or restaurant. Various local businessmen joined our list of cronies and the monthly nights out at the dinner club became eagerly awaited events.

The football matches were a standard feature of the week and every Wednesday I would set off to the ground and spend ninety minutes tearing about like an idiot, risking life and limb in the pursuit of sporting excellence.

On the first Monday morning at Vicarage Lane, I was at my desk for 7.30 am. At 8.00 am the signwriter came to print the firm's name on the windows. The large window overlooking the entrance door was to be lettered in gold leaf and it looked magnificent when it was finished.

Just before 9.00 am the rest of the staff started to arrive and with them came our first client into the premises. It was fitting that it was Jack, but unfortunately he had his odious son, Albert, with him.

"It looks very smart in here Steve," said Jack.

"Yes, we're very proud of it Jack."

"It's better than that old office," continued Jack. "That was an out-and-out-eapa.

"True," I said, "but everyone's got to start somewhere."

I looked down at Albert who was staring at me with that same grin on his well-rounded face. I returned the grin.

"How are you Albert?" I asked.

"Where's the fish?" demanded Albert.

"I'm not telling you," I said.

"Don't worry, I'll find them," said Albert.

"Don't worry," I said, "I don't want you running about, because we haven't got everything in place yet."

"Let me have a look at the fish Steve," said Albert, and with that Jack clouted him at the back of the ear.

"Do as you're told Albert."

"Have you ever tried hang-gliding Albert?" I asked.

"Not really," said Albert, "but I've got a kite. Anyway, where's the fish then?" he persisted.

"If you ask me once more about those fish, I'll put you in with them," I said it as if making a joke but I knew I meant every word.

"That's child abuse," said Albert.

With that Jack clouted him at the back of the ear again and said,

"Shut up! You should be used to it." Just at that moment Morris, Jack's eldest son walked into the office.

Jack told me that Morris, his eldest son, had been locked up at Rotherham police station. Apparently he had been interviewed about taking his father's car without consent and also stealing a caravan. It seemed he had borrowed his father's Transit van and had gone out for a ride. When he spotted the caravan he didn't take too much notice of its markings, but with audacious cheek hooked the caravan onto the back of the Transit van and drove off. Unfortunately as he approached the M1, the Transit developed a mechanical fault and he pulled into a lay-by to attempt to rectify

226

the problem. He detached the Transit from the caravan and took what tools he had out of the back. As he was tinkering with the van, a motorist walked up to him carrying a petrol can. He had obviously run out of fuel and he was looking for help,

"Could you run me to the petrol station?"

"No," said Morris, "can't you see I'm busy?"

"I am a Member and as I have broken down you should assist."

"Member of what?" said Morris.

The frustrated motorist pointed to the side of the caravan and the lettering displayed upon it.

"Here's my membership card, I have been in the AA for twenty years."

"Oh," said Morris, shamefaced, "well I'm only helping out because the regular man has got piles."

It was the first thing that came into his head. The customer realized that there was something amiss and stormed off to use his mobile phone.

Morris didn't notice what was going on and while he was tinkering about with the Transit, the police arrived on the scene.

"Hello, hello, hello," said the police officer, "and what have we got here then? Is this your caravan Sir?"

"Yes," said Morris, "I'm looking after it for a friend." Morris was escorted to the police car with a muscular arm on each of his shoulders.

Jack was livid and he couldn't help but castigate his son.

"How could you do such a thing?" he demanded, "And using the Transit into the bargain - why did you do it? Why did you do it?" he repeated time after time.

"The shame, oh the shame that you have brought upon me and my house, how could you do it?"

"How could I do what?" asked the pathetic Morris.

"How could you get caught?" said Jack. "Oh the shame of it, how could you do it?"

I managed to stand in between them and avoid a fight, with the result that both parties apologized for the argument which had taken place. I assured them that no offence was taken and as they walked down the staircase to the entrance door, I could hear the words, "I didn't realize that it was an AA caravan," fading into the distance.

Jack was many things, but at least he was well mannered and, in

227

fairness, he never brought trouble or disorder to the office, apart from Albert of course who was nothing but trouble.

As I turned to leave the waiting room, another youth entered carrying a large cardboard box.

"Excuse me Mr Smith, can I have a word with you please?" said the youth. I was moved by his good manners. He was wearing jeans and a sweat-shirt with a picture of Che Guevara on the front. He explained that he was due to appear in court that morning for offences involving the taking of motor vehicles and asked if I would be prepared to represent him. I told him that I would and if he would make his way to the courthouse, I would meet him there later that morning.

He thanked me and as he was leaving, I ventured the question,

"So you are a supporter of Che Guevara then?"

"Eh?" said the man.

"Che Guevara" I replied, "you're obviously a supporter."

"Oh argh," said the man, "who does he play for?"

"I suppose he plays for Cuba," I said.

"Is he any good?" said the lad.

"Not any more," I replied, "but I suppose you could say that he was once."

"He was a goalie wasn't he?" asked the lad.

"Oh probably," I said, "but before you go what have you got in the box?"

"Peregrine," replied the lad.

"It's not a Peregrine Falcon?" I asked, "It's illegal to have one of those out of the wild."

"No," said the lad, "that's his name Peregrine, after the Falcon."

"Oh," I said, "what is it?"

The lad opened the corner of the box to show me a rather motley looking pigeon.

Rotherham is quite famous for pigeon fanciers and pigeon racing is a local pastime.

"Do you race him?" I said to the lad.

"No," he replied, " I dunt bother," and with that he left whistling as he went on his way. I just shook my head as I walked back into my room to collect my files for the morning court. We certainly saw a wide spectrum of the local population.

I set off for court with a smile on my face which turned to a grimace as it started to rain. "Not good weather for pigeons this," I thought as I scurried along to the courthouse.

The court corridor was packed and the majority of the visitors were inspecting items of bedding and linen which they had obviously just bought. "Oh no," I thought, "Jack's been at it again, whatever is it this time?"

As I walked down the corridor, I saw Jack and his son in the WRVS canteen. Unfortunately, I jumped to the wrong conclusion.

"You have not nicked a load of bedding have you?" I said as soon as I approached him.

"Who me?" said Jack, obviously wounded by my accusation.

"Yes you," I replied, "everybody on that corridor has got bedding."

"Steve, really! Would I?" said Jack.

"Yes you bloody well would, I have warned you about that before."

"I can assure you I'm not even up today, I've just come with him," he said looking at his son.

I appreciated the explanation, although I was not completely satisfied with it but we went to the 'rat hole' for a discussion.

It was obvious that Morris should plead guilty to the charge, having fully admitted it in an interview with the police.

Fortunately, the AA had got their caravan back, so I had some mitigation to give to the court,

"If you need to call me as a character witness," said Jack, "I am agreeable."

"Thank you," I said to Jack, "I will think about that and if I need to call you I will."

With that Jack and his son went back into the court corridor to wait their turn. I on the other hand sat there in disbelief. I couldn't help wondering what view the court might take of Jack as a character witness. I would have got more credibility calling Al Capone.

I managed to call Morris on first and the prosecutor opened his case. As I was about to get up to speak, Jack tapped me on the shoulder and whispered some last minute instructions.

"Don't forget to tell them that I am a member of the RAC," said Jack knowingly, and promptly sat back in his seat. I repeated the words quietly to myself "Don't forget that I am a member of the RAC".

From that day to this, I am still not sure of the relevance of that remark, or why it would be a point in mitigation. The court took a serious view, however, and adjourned the case for reports to enable a probation officer to make a recommendation as to sentence. The chairman of the magistrates said that he was looking at the possibility of community service work. This is where defendants do unpaid work for the community for a number of hours, which varies depending upon the seriousness of the crime.

"Has he any particular skills?" asked the chairman of the magistrates.

I was very tempted to suggest car and caravan theft and burglary, but I didn't think that the magistrates would have appreciated it, so I ventured to say, "No particular skills Sir, but he is a big strong healthy lad and I am sure that the community service organizer will be able to find something for him to do".

I looked across at Morris and wondered what work he could manage. He just looked back at me and smiled and then waved me over.

"I have always wanted to work with computers Mr Smith," said Morris.

"Thank you for that Morris" I said and returned to my seat.

"Was that helpful?" asked the magistrates.

"Not really Sir, he is just confirming that he will be prepared to do any of the work that he is offered," and with that the case was adjourned.

When I got back to the office late in the afternoon, the girls were busy decorating the Christmas tree and soon after my arrival the lights were officially switched on. Apparently, Wilf had eaten two of the chocolate Santa Clauses and a marzipan reindeer. "Typical," I thought and I then found that he had also consumed two of the miniature brandies as well.

As no one had been back to the old offices in Moorgate Street to check for any post, I decided to call round.

I was happy that we had progressed from our little Moorgate Street office, but it was not without regrets.

The brass plate had gone and the building was in darkness. As I opened the door, I found a number of letters on the floor. The majority were circulars which had been hand-delivered and there were a few Christmas cards from well wishers.

I was about to lock the door, when I decided that I would have one last look. Climbing the stairs, I was faced with the infamous latrine, and I could almost hear the voice of Oscar shouting the odds and the name of the winner of the 2.30 at Uttoxeter. In the reception, I thought I heard the girls typing and answering telephones. There was Anne busily typing and answering the phone at the same time, I could almost hear her speaking.

"I'm sorry I am afraid Mr Wilford's not back from lunch yet, we are expecting him at 4.30."

I left the waiting area and went into the interview room. In the fireplace was the gas fire that had never worked, with the gas board condemnation notice still hanging from the grate.

I could see Pagey sitting at my desk answering the phone wearing the plastic breasts shouting, "God bless us all and everyone".

Looking out of the window I could almost see Eric Sharp scurrying forward to the office with his pile of papers and there opposite me in our leather armchair was Lorraine Wilson explaining her fears. Sam was there too with the flight tickets for Majorca. In the spare room was Lidster with his bare foot on the coffee table near my sandwich, "But Bader didn't have any legs," he shouted.

As I emerged on to the landing I could hear Jack Bower and the sound of the trombone; and then there was the real sound of the fluttering of the pigeons in the graveyard in the roof.

I realized I needed the toilet and went into Oscar's old office. There was a pile of racing newspapers stacked up near the door. I closed the door and as I was putting on the light the bulb chinked as its light failed, leaving me entirely in the dark.

I pulled the flush but nothing happened and I turned to open the door. I walked down the stairs and I looked back for the last time. I could see Albert trying to spear my fish with the algae scraper which used to live on the top of the tank. Even the Christmas tree had gone but I found a display Father Christmas in the corner. He did not seem to want to stay on his own, so I put him in my pocket to take home.

The place held so many memories for me most of which were happy ones.

I returned to the new office at a little after 5.30pm to find that everyone had packed up and gone.

The following day would be Christmas Eve and the office would close at lunchtime after which there would be an office party before everyone left for Christmas.

The next morning I had a very light court indeed, with only two cases. One was an adjournment and the other was a prisoner who was fortunate enough to secure his bail for Christmas.

I was back at the office at12.00 noon to sample some of the pork pie and sandwiches which had been laid out for the party. We closed the office and the guests began to arrive.

Bodger was first followed by Tim Johnson from the Building Society and then Mike Walker from Whitegate's Estate Agents, our neighbours. Within a short time the office was packed wth people, when all of a sudden we heard the sound of a bugle being played rather badly in reception. We took a vote as to who it was and the majority of the bets nominated Pagey.

When the reception door burst open, it was the man himself. He was wearing a Father Christmas robe, together with a German general's hat and small dark moustache. He was obviously Adolf Hitler in a Santa Clause costume.

"How do I look?" said the Führer.

"A proper pillock," I answered immediately.

"Thank you," said Pagey, "I thought it would be a success."

Jarvis and Framey, the Mad Scotsman, then appeared and bombarded Wilf and me with plastic string, much to the Führer's amusement.

We were really behaving like juveniles, but it was Christmas and it did not seem to matter. We had prepared a presentation for Jarvis, which began a tradition which continues to this very day. Every Christmas we present him with a pink lavatory brush and being the man he is, he has not thrown one of them away. I gave a speech and Wilford made the presentation managing to remain upright for the whole of the time. The party ended at 2 o'clock and from there we went to the Cross Keys where the landlord had prepared a small buffet for some of his regulars.

Christmas in the Cross Keys was magical and most of our friends were at the party. Wilford entered a drinking competition with the Mad Scotsman, Sixties music was blaring out from the juke box and the atmosphere was wonderful.

Just before 5.00 pm I dragged myself away from the Keys, being attacked as I went along the "valley of a thousand tins of spray string". I shook hands with everybody at least twice and wandered off towards the taxi rank.

I passed the new office and saw that the lights had been left on, so I thought it best to make sure that the premises were secure. I climbed the stairs, which were awash with a sea of plastic string and streamers.

As I opened the reception door, I noticed the Christmas tree lights flashing on and off. Someone had removed the display Father Christmas from the top of the tree and put a Hitler doll there instead. I noticed empty beer cans on the reception counter, and indeed on all the desks as well. The cleaner had been given the night off and my smart new office looked like the aftermath of a brewery trip.

There was a small piece of pork pie left on the buffet, so I picked it up and began to eat it. I sat back in my favourite leather armchair and surveyed the scene. I was struck by sadness, for an empty office at Christmas can be the loneliest place on earth. I turned all the lights off in the office, and picked up some of the debris, including Pagey's bugle, which I attempted to blow. Remarkably I managed two notes, put it down and returned to the reception.

Turning off the Christmas tree lights, I was shaken from my thoughts by the voice of a small boy.

"Ay up Steve," said the voice, "I've been round once or twice but there was no one ere." I unplugged the lights and turned round.

"Albert, what are you doing here?"

"I've come to see you," said Albert.

"But where's your dad?" I asked.

"Oh, I've come on my own, it's my business," said the crafty little entrepreneur who had clearly called to see me about some pressing business venture.

I sat back on a reception chair and announced, "I cannot stop long Albert, I should have been away at 5 o'clock. Is it something that can wait until after Christmas?"

I realized that the little fellow had come a long way to see me, and I also noticed that he was armed with a Christmas card in his hand.

"Is that for me Albert?" I asked.

"No," said Albert, "it's for my mum. Yours is in the post."

"With a cheque no doubt," I said.

"You what?" said Albert, missing the point.

"Oh it's all right Albert, take no notice of me, it's been a long day. Sit yourself down and tell me what I can do for you."

With that Albert sat down and treated me to one of his wide grins that was to haunt my very existence.

I had never really studied Albert closely, but just at that moment, I could not help noticing how much like his father he was; the main distinguishing feature being the grin, omnipresent within this close knit family. He was small for his age, which I suspected was the result of genetics rather than undernourishment. His unkempt hair disguised a cheeky face with a pair of bright gentian blue eyes which shone out of a rather swarthy skin which bore all the hallmarks of the continued absence of soap and water; and the grin, enhanced by the absence of central teeth and a preponderance of gum which accentuated an almost comical appearance. He was actually rather ugly and yet there was something striking about him which to this day I find hard to explain.

Intellectually he was 'Closed until further notice' but he was street wise and as Jack once described him to me. "ee can 'old 'is own in a feight and is niver freetened to get stuck in, mindst thee tha 'ad to feight at ar 'ouse, there were thirteen of us and only wun closet".

As he began to speak I heard the first strains of 'Silent night, holy night' emanating from the tannoy system at the church across the way. The setting could have been perfect. Christmas carols, a lighted Christmas tree, large flakes of snow and Albert!

"You see Steve, it's like this, you'll never believe it."

And do you know, he was right.

To be continued. . . . . . .

234